Walking Europe
From Top to Bottom

The Sierra Club Adventure Travel Guides

Walking Europe From Top to Bottom

*The Sierra Club Travel Guide
to the Grande Randonnée Cinq (GR-5) through Holland,
Belgium, Luxembourg, Switzerland and France*

Susanna Margolis
Ginger Harmon

SIERRA CLUB BOOKS · SAN FRANCISCO

Copyright © 1986 by Susanna Margolis and Ginger Harmon

Library of Congress Cataloging-in-Publication Data

Margolis, Susanna.
    Walking Europe from top to bottom.

    Includes index.
    1. Walking–Grande Randonée Cinq (Trail)–Guide-books.
    2. Grande Randonée Cinq (Trail)–Guide-books.
    3. Europe–Description and travel–1971-   –Guide-books. I. Harmon, Ginger. II. Title.
    GV199.44.E8M37 1986   914   85-18469
    ISBN 0-87156-752-0

Cover design by Bonnie Smetts

Book design by Drake Jordan

Maps by Ginger Harmon and Julie Hichens

Photographs by Ginger Harmon and Susanna Margolis

Printed in the United States of America

10 9 8 7 6 5 4 3 2 1

For Mars and Bill, Jonathan, Sally, Michael, and Katey; and for Grant, Debra, Mark, Kimberley, Cristina, and Timothy

Contents

Foreword

The idea for *Walking Europe From Top to Bottom* was conceived by Ginger Harmon in the summer of 1983 in California.

Research about the route, the terrain, the countries and cultures began at once and proceeded, on foot, throughout the walk during the summer of 1984.

Back in the United States, information, ideas, and draft copy traveled to and fro across the continent throughout the fall and winter.

The bulk of the writing was done by Susanna Margolis in New York in the winter of 1984–85.

Editing and preparation of the final manuscript were done jointly in New York in April, 1985, with the aid of a personal computer.

Acknowledgments

Many people on both sides of the Atlantic helped us turn this project into a trip, the trip into a joyous and fascinating experience, and the experience into a book.

The New York-based national tourist offices of all the countries we passed through gave us valuable information and encouragement. We are especially indebted to Ann Neville, Frederique Raeymaekers, and the entire staff of the Belgian National Tourist Office for so generously expending their own time and resources to provide us with maps; and to Nora Brossard of the French Government Tourist Office for deploying the resources of her office to help us.

Thanks also to the staff members of VVVs and Offices de Tourisme along our route whose names we never learned, but who helped us immeasurably, and thanks to one whose name we cannot forget, Jantien Wondergem of the ANWB office in Bergen-op-Zoom, Netherlands, who answered so many questions so patiently. Our appreciation also to G. B. H. van Woudenberg of the national ANWB office in Den Haag, Netherlands; Jean Friedrich of the Ministry of Tourism in Luxembourg; and Freddy Tuerlinckx, general secretary of the Grote Routepaden in Antwerp, Belgium, for taking the time from busy schedules to answer our queries by mail.

To Bernard Salomon, director of the FFRP-CNSGR, the Fédération Française de Randonnée Pedestre-Comité National des Sentiers de Grande Randonnée, our thanks for his helpful information and his encouragement of our project.

For their help, friendship, and extraordinary generosity, we feel a particular gratitude to the Walstons of Thriplow, England—Oliver and Anne, Rose, Florence, David, and Mosel—and another measure of the same to the staff of the Thriplow Farms office.

Robert Ravaioli, Henri and Monique Deuwel, Deborah Jaffé and Monica Peiser showed us great hospitality from the bottom of Europe to the top.

We are grateful to family and friends for their letters, to David Gillespie for continuing encouragement, to Judith Dunford for holding down the home front, to Robert Harmon for help on too many occasions to number, to Cheri Martin and Fran Bolei for varied administrative tasks, and to Julie Hichens for cartographic assistance.

For checking us on plate tectonics, our thanks to Bill Dickinson, and for checking us on languages foreign to us, our thanks to Georgette Cassen and her mother, Henriette Cassen.

We are indebted to James Cohee, managing editor of Sierra Club Books, for his enthusiasm and support—from the top of this project to the bottom.

In walking 1,500 miles across Europe, we accumulated a great measure of gratitude to the planners, builders, and maintainers of the Grande Randonnée Cinq, and to all the anonymous authors of the GR guidebooks.

Above all, we want to express our thanks to the hundreds of strangers along the way who did us kindnesses and wished us "Bon Courage."

Note on Use of Foreign Languages

The two main languages of the walk across Europe from top to bottom are Dutch/Flemish and French. As he progresses down Europe, the walker will increasingly use and think words in these languages for landmarks, directions, and ways of proceeding along the route.

For that reason, while we translate foreign words initially—and occasionally later on—we have incorporated them into the body of the text as if they were part of the walker's native language, as indeed they will become.

1
Walking Europe From Top to Bottom

It is some 650 miles, as the crow flies, from the Hoek van Holland on the North Sea to Nice on the Mediterranean. On foot, along the trans-European route known as GR5, the distance is nearly 1,500 miles. In the late spring and summer of 1984, two American women walked the GR5. We departed our respective home cities on the two coasts of the United States to rendezvous in London. From there, a train bore us over green countryside to the port of Harwich on England's southeast coast. We boarded a ferry named for the queen of the Netherlands and slept our way across the North Sea. In the morning, we walked down the gangplank, dipped our fingers in the appropriately gray and cold ocean, and started walking. One hundred and seven days later, we walked into Nice, crossed the famous Promenade des Anglais, and stepped into the Mediterranean.

Our path followed almost exactly the route of the GR5—to give it its full name, the Grande Randonnée Cinq. We "edited" the marked route from time to time, detoured from it on occasion, and lost our way—not seriously—with some regularity.

We were outdoors for some six to eight hours every day. We walked at a comfortable pace, stopped when there was something of interest to see, or someone of interest to talk to, or an adventure to pursue, or when we wanted a rest. We carried neither tent nor sleeping bag nor cooking equipment; each day's hike brought us to a place where we could find lodging and meals. Along most of our route, this meant a night in a small, inexpensive hotel where we were able to bathe, change into what we called our evening wear, sit down to be waited on at dinner, sleep in beds, and have breakfast at leisure before starting off again.

For the record, 8 of the 107 days were layover days, although a more appropriate term would be nonhiking days, for we often walked a great deal on those days in the accomplishment of chores or in seeing sights. It's just that we did so without a pack, and without making any progress along our route.

The GR5 took us through five countries—Holland, Belgium, Luxembourg, Switzerland (briefly), and France—and allowed us to set foot into two others—Germany and Italy. We were communicated with in two languages, Dutch (or its Flemish variant) and French; two serious dialects, Luxembourgeois and Alsatian; and numerous local patois. We crossed and/or walked along half a dozen of Europe's great rivers and scores of lesser-known waterways. We rose from sea level to plain to peneplain to rolling hills and traversed three mountain ranges—Vosges, Jura, and Alps. We marched over sandy, saline soil; rich humus; mineral fields; limestone, schist, and granite. Through meadows, fields, pastures, forests, and prairie. On dirt road, country lane, cowpath, Roman road, hiking trail, and, occasionally, a superhighway. Through and around countless towns, villages, hamlets, and into half a dozen sizeable and famous cities.

By our own count, we stayed in over one hundred different hotels, ate or drank in more than three hundred different cafés and restaurants, confronted at least twenty different styles of plumbing fixture. We believe we may be the only Americans to have spent two weeks in Luxembourg as tourists.

It was a particularly wet summer in Europe that year, and we were hit by precipitation in numerous forms, while underfoot we battled the concomitant mud, slick rocks, or slippery trails. We also suffered a heat wave. We fought with mosquitoes in the lowlands and flies at higher altitudes. We were scratched by nettles. Dogs barked at us by day and ate dinner beside us in the evening, in those hotels and restaurants almost all across France where *chiens* are *acceptés*. Muzak piped pirated versions of American rock 'n' roll at us almost every time we ordered a cup of coffee. We each caught a cold; we both had brief and minor foot troubles; one of us was bitten by a dog. We were never in any danger along our route.

Between us, we have hiked in most of the major mountain ranges in the world, through some of its most famous deserts, and along local walking routes and hiking trails in many of the fifty United States, at least ten European countries, the Middle East, and Asia. Our collective traveling or living abroad embraces five of the seven continents. But walking Europe from top to bottom was something else again— the most fantastic of experiences, a walk through history, through a diversity of cultures, through a geology lesson of topographies, through the lives of hundreds of people along the way. Walking Europe from top to bottom was as much living a story as it was taking a hike.

Why walk? For those who don't, there is no convincing answer. As compared to all other forms of locomotion, about the only certain thing you can say of walking is that it is the slowest. You can fly from Holland to Nice in under two hours. A train will get you there in some seventeen hours, including the time spent trundling across Paris to change stations, and you can sleep through half the journey. You can drive virtually the entire distance on superhighways in a day and a half— less, if you keep up with the European drivers. So if what you want to do is *arrive*, walking is not for you.

Nor is it for you if your aim is to "cover a lot of Europe." The 1,500 miles you walk along GR5 represent only a sliver of Europe—a backcountry sliver, at that. It is boondocks and then some—what John McPhee has described in his essay, *North of the C.P. Line*, as williwag, "a place so remote that it can be reached only by first going through a boondock."

Nevertheless, this slow passage down a narrow corridor of Europe gives the walker a quality of contact and, finally, an intimacy with Europe that are simply not possible any other way.

There are moments of sudden revelation, as when you round the bend of a field in Belgium, for example, and confront the silhouette of a medieval village, or when you finally achieve an Alpine pass and look out on a vista stretching for miles in every direction. For the most part, however, awareness does not come in abrupt, isolated instances; rather, it accumulates. The walker doesn't *just* see; the walker *absorbs* sights, sounds, smells, climate, landscape, experience. He gathers his knowledge of Europe through the muscles, through the pores, and, mostly, through the feet.

One step at a time.

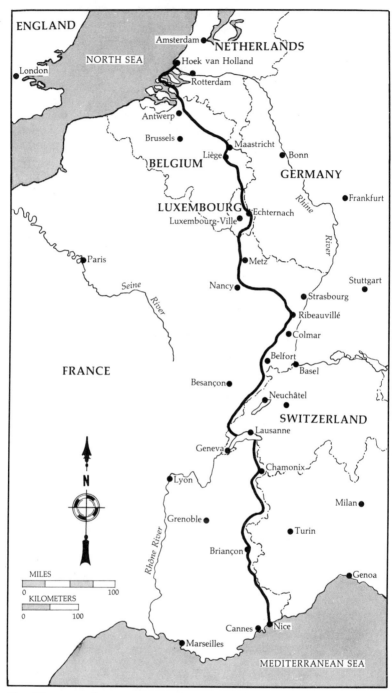

The GR5 top to bottom.

2
Megawalking

The walking route described in this book for the most part follows the Grande Randonnée Cinq, the five-nation, 1,500-mile traverse from the top of Europe to the bottom. No purist worth the name will accept that the Hoek van Holland, the walk's starting point, is the top of Europe, or that Nice, the ultimate destination, is the bottom of Europe. Such individuals must content themselves with the thought that GR5 in any event takes the walker from sea to shining sea, from the gray North Sea that defines septentrional Europe to the azure Mediterranean that is the quintessential symbol of meridional Europe.

This book has been written primarily for people who want to walk Europe from top to bottom all at once. We call them megawalkers.

Not everybody can do this; the megawalk takes *time*. Most Europeans do the GR5 in stages—one piece of it this year, another piece next year, and so on—and this book is also for people who want to walk Europe from top to bottom that way.

It is also for people who want to walk part of the Europe that GR5 traverses. If you want to combine a look at the great cities that are the first-string European tourist attractions with a peek past them to the towns and countryside noted only in the fine print of the guidebooks, if at all, walking is a good way to do it. This book will help.

It is also for people who simply love to walk and who find themselves, or wish to find themselves, in Europe.

There are hikes here for the casual walker who is looking for an easy trek across moderate terrain. There are walks for the seasoned traveler who wants to explore somewhere he has never been before. There are strenuous challenges here for the experienced hiker who loves steep hills and rugged trails.

For the megawalker, there is all of that and more.

Stages and Sections of the Route

As plotted in this book, walking Europe from top to bottom takes 107 days. Ninety-nine of them are spent hiking; the rest are spent seeing sights or taking a rest, or both. Each daily stage is described as a traveler's itinerary—part guide, part information, part story. (For following GR5's twistings and turnings, there are trail markings, route-guides, and maps; see Chapters 3 and 4.)

Each daily stage—*étape* is the almost universally accepted French word—takes the walker to a destination where he can find accommodations for the night. The length of each étape is to some extent dependent on the availability of lodging along the route. Because of this, a few daily stages are as short as four hours, and a few need to be as long as eight hours—even a bit longer. But the great majority average out to about six and a half hours of actual walking time.

Six and a half hours of walking, however, means about an eight-hour day. No one wants to spend every minute of every day just putting one foot in front of the other, so each daily stage of walking allows the walker time to look around, meet people, see sights, visit towns, and lunch in a restaurant or picnic in a pleasant spot. At the end of those outdoor hours, the walker will come to rest in a hotel or hostel or mountain hut where he can stash his pack, clean up, change clothes, relax a while, sit down to a nice dinner, perhaps take a walk through the town, maybe have a chat with some local folks, and eventually sleep in a comfortable bed.

All of the walking is grouped into ten sections, defined by national or regional borders, or, in the Alps, by distinctive topographic and cultural differences. The division into sections also means that the walker

At the end of each day, the walker will come to rest in a hotel where he can relax a while. The Hotel Les Terraces is in St.-Hippolyte, France. Photo by Ginger Harmon.

with limited time at his disposal—even as little as ten days or two weeks—can walk a single section (or more) and feel, justifiably, that he has completed a definitive piece of Europe.

The sections of the walk are:

Netherlands	8 days
Flanders	9 days
Wallonie	9 days
Luxembourg	11 days
Lorraine	12 days
Vosges	13 days
Jura	13 days
North Alps	10 days
Middle Alps	8 days
South Alps	11 days

(Add three layover days at Lake Geneva and in the Alps for a total of 107 days.)

Distance and Time

In hiking, and particularly in mountain hiking, distance is much more meaningfully measured in time than in miles or kilometers. The standard for the walk across Europe is 4 kilometers per hour. That is the standard used in the *topo-guides*, the guidebooks to the Grandes Randonnées (see Chapter 4), and it is the basis for the world-famous Swiss standard, although the Swiss, not surprisingly, make subtle modifications for elevation gain and loss. It is also the pace we found comfortable. As for ups and downs, by the time we reached high mountains, our leg muscles were in such good shape that our uphill times were better than standard, while our downhill times were somewhat less. It all balanced out at the standard 4 kilometers per hour.

The 4-kilometers-per-hour standard means this: if you find that you can walk more than 4 kilometers an hour, you should adjust your estimate of the times we have given accordingly. If you walk less than 4 kilometers an hour, each day's stage is going to take you that much longer than the time we have given.

Measurements throughout this book are metric. To convert kilometers to miles, multiply the number of kilometers by .6 (.621). To convert meters to feet, multiply the number of meters by 3.3. The best thing to do, however, is to begin at once to think in metric terms. Your feet will absorb this knowledge first, and you will soon get a feel for how far a certain number of kilometers is and how high a certain number of meters is.

The same is true of temperature and other measures. Once you have experienced 30 degrees Celsius, you won't have to multiply by 1.8 and add 32 to know that it's hot (86 degrees Fahrenheit). Once you have bought half a kilo of cheese, it won't matter that that's 1.1 pounds (2.2

pounds to the kilogram); you will simply know how many lunches that amount sustains and will act accordingly.

The Itineraries

The description of each day's itinerary tells you where you are going, what you are passing through to get there, and how long the walk is. It does not tell you how to proceed step by step because the trail markings and the topo-guides do that (see Chapters 3 and 4). The itinerary descriptions tell you instead *about* the route and landscape and towns and nations you are walking through, and they will tell you some of the stories of our walk. They will, it is hoped, make you feel at home along the route.

Detours

Where the itineraries depart from GR5, as they frequently do, the impetus behind the departure has been to show the walker something of interest that he might otherwise miss. GR5 is a European trail, built by and for Europeans with the aim of enabling them to get away from it all. Very often, this means that GR5 will avoid—sometimes laboriously—a town or village. It will often eschew the country lane to plunge the walker back into a forest in which he can perhaps have a greater sense of wildness, but from which he can see little, if anything, beyond the trees. Our premise in editing the GR5 route is that Americans in Europe do not want to get away from it all; they want very much to get into it all. They want to visit the small villages of backcountry Europe. (Often, they *need* to visit villages—to buy food, change money, mail letters, and avail themselves of other urban services.) They like to wander backcountry roads and look across open fields to the farms or towns in the distance. They enjoy encounters with the people who live in the areas they are walking through. To Americans, Europe and the life of Europe are foreign and exotic; where a deviation from GR5 would enable the walker to see and experience more of that, we have taken it.

For that same reason, we frequently recommend that the walker simply leave off walking and indulge in the more usual kind of sightseeing. It would be almost criminal to be so near Luxembourg-Ville or Strasbourg or Nancy and not take the time to visit these cities; our itineraries take the time.

Layovers

We have also included layover days in the plan for this walk—for two reasons. One is that anybody who is going to spend a lot of time on the trail is simply going to have to stop every now and again to take care of some chores. Clothing gets dirty and must be washed. Gear wears out and must be replaced. Something gets broken and must be repaired. In general, layover days are combined with sightseeing detours, because detour destinations are usually towns big enough or lively enough to accommodate a variety of needs, including the need for English-language newspapers and books.

The second reason for these layover days is perhaps more important. It is a question of rest. One of the lessons we learned on this trip is that no matter how much you love to walk, and no matter how much fun you are having walking Europe from top to bottom, you will still get tired. Physical weariness is only part of it; physical weariness, in fact, usually goes away with a good night's sleep or even with an energetic next day's walk. The more serious kind of weariness comes from simply doing the same thing every day. The routine of it becomes tiring, day after day after day. It is why they created weekends in the first place. The layover days included in our itineraries are the megawalker's weekends.

Certainly, the walker who feels the physical or psychological need for more than one layover day should take more. We did. At a certain point when we were simply no longer eager to set out on our walk each morning, we just stopped trying. We hitchhiked to the nearest big town, rented a car, and drove around for four days, sightseeing in an area GR5 doesn't go anywhere near. At the end of the four days, we couldn't wait to get back to the GR5 and walking. We set out that next morning like tigers.

One place where the megawalker should consider an extended layover is somewhere on the shores of Lac Léman, Lake Geneva. In distance, this is well beyond the halfway point of the walk across Europe, but the mind somehow sees it as an important crossroads. Northern Europe, the cool, gray Europe of plain and plateau and hill, is behind you. Ahead lies the very serious mountain walking of the Alps, dramatically visible across the lake. It is a good time to regroup, relax, refurbish, and refresh, and the north shore of Lake Geneva is a good place to do it. Here are any number of cities and towns, great and small, where the walker can luxuriate, replenish stores (albeit at typically high prices), call home, change money, and read the *International Herald Tribune* on the day it's published. All these towns and cities are linked by Switzerland's world-famous train and bus links, as well as by the boats that ply the lake itself. Except for Chamonix, nothing even remotely as cosmopolitan will be in the walker's way until the end of the journey at Nice, so calling a halt at Lac Léman is worth serious consideration.

Similarly, we have included two "swing" layover days in the schedule for the Alps. These mountains require twenty-nine days of hard walking, and it's likely that you will want a day off at least twice in those twenty-nine days. Because there are so many pleasant towns and villages on the mountainsides and in the valleys traversed in the Alps crossing, we have not recommended any two stopping places in particular. Be guided by your energy level—or lack of same.

Another Version

It is possible, of course, to walk Europe from top to bottom with no detours, no layover days, no sightseeing. We know someone who did it just that way.

We met two other GR5 end-to-enders the summer we walked GR5—so far as we know, the only other end-to-enders, at least in 1984. One was Owen Jones, a young Briton who was fed up with his job and decided on the spur of the moment to chuck it all for a while and take a nice long walk. Owen moved at a good pace but took his time—that is, he followed variants, made detours, and was not immune to the idea of rest.

The other GR5er was Robert Ravaioli, a Niçois, and there was nothing spur-of-the-moment about his walk across Europe. For ten years, doing the GR5 had been a dream for Robert, and for ten years he planned when and how he would do it. When the time came, he closed his art studio, kissed his wife and two daughters goodbye, hopped a train for Amsterdam, and began walking. It took him seventy-nine days to reach Nice. A young family and a business of which you are the sole proprietor and employee cannot be left for very long. Robert admits that he saw *rien* (nothing) along the route, that if he happened to notice a church that looked interesting or a village that looked welcoming, he simply stared straight ahead and kept walking. Someday, he has said, he would like to go back and *see* all the things he missed along the GR5. But he had a sensational time on his walk and regrets nothing about it. With his gracious permission, we have included his itinerary, the Robert Ravaioli Seventy-nine-day Racing Version of the GR5, for walkers with limited time and unlimited strength. (See Appendix A.)

Costs

Since the exchange rates among international currencies fluctuate—as do prices—it makes little sense to try to put a price tag on the walk across Europe from top to bottom. What *can* be said is that it is a relatively cheap trip, and it is a *very* cheap trip if you watch your pennies, florins, and francs.

The U.S. dollar was particularly strong the year of our walk, and the exchange was particularly favorable to Americans traveling in Europe. Yet even allowing for that financial favor, the per-person per-day cost of walking Europe from top to bottom—three meals, lodging, and incidentals—was considerably less than what the same traveling would have cost by any other means of transportation; it was far less than the per-day cost of a more conventional tour of Europe; it was very much less than the price of a day at a resort.

Both of us who made the walk live in major U.S. metropolitan areas, where the cost of living tends to be relatively high. For us, the cost of walking Europe from top to bottom was, most certainly, less than the cost of staying home.

On Being Made Welcome

We met many other people in addition to the two megawalkers—hikers from various nations, following various routes, out for a week or a month or a day of walking. We met many nonhikers as well—hotel owners and shopkeepers and postal clerks and bank tellers to be sure, but also farmers and townsfolk who gave us directions and people sitting next to us in cafés or restaurants and others who simply walked up to us because they saw our packs and wondered what we were doing.

Ginger's pack was green and bore a white sign with large black lettering which announced "GR5—HOLLAND TO NICE." Susanna's pack was bright red and she had concocted on it, in blue and white tape, an approximation of the U.S. flag; it lacked the requisite numbers of stars and stripes, but its intent was unmistakable.

We had girded ourselves for a certain amount of anti-Americanism. Certainly, we did not expect overt hostility, but we were not unprepared for that occasionally arrogant disdain with which some Europeans view Americans, as if the United States were really an offshoot of Europe and a rather brash, even crude offshoot to boot.

We found none of that. We found nothing like it. We found, everywhere along our route, the exact opposite. Precisely because we were Americans, and women, and not exactly kids, and *walking,* we were everywhere objects of the most affectionate curiosity. Perhaps because Europeans seem to watch religiously the American television shows they claim to disapprove of, many are convinced that Americans do not walk at all. That we should be walking all across Europe, through their country, and at that precise moment through their village seemed to many of these people an event worth noting. We grew rather accustomed to the reaction we caused, developed a set speech in French and English to explain ourselves, and began to take the celebrity in our stride.

Well, not quite in our stride. We never ceased to be pleased by the kindness of people all along our route, and by the pleasure they seemed to take from our being there. There is a fine French word for it: *accueillir*—it means the way you receive or greet someone. We were *bien accueillies* all across Europe, from top to bottom. There are indeed no strangers along the Grande Randonnée.

3
The Grande
Randonnée 5

The Grande Randonnée 5 is one of a network of Grandes Randonnées that crisscross Europe. Grande Randonnée in French is Grote Routepad in Dutch and Flemish—Great Walk or Great Ramble or Grand Wander in English. France alone possesses scores of GRs, as well as connecting spurs of GRs and variants of GRs—everything from a two-day loop walk to the six- to eight-week east-west traverse of the Pyrenees to GR5 itself. Indeed, virtually every bit of France has its GR walking route, and more GRs are being designed and built all the time.

GR5 is also the E-2, Europe-2, because it is one of several long-distance walking routes (six, as of 1984) that link existing national routes.

GR5 Management

Europe's cross-border trails come under the aegis of the European Ramblers' Association (or Fédération Européenne de Tourisme Pedestre), created in 1969 as a kind of common market for hiking, environmental protection, and for promoting greater understanding among nations—or at least among the hikers of different nations. The association is an umbrella for walking, rambling, hiking, and mountaineering organizations in eighteen European countries. For the GR5, the pertinent national organizations in charge are the ANWB in the Netherlands; the Grote Routepaden and Comité National Belge des Sentiers de Grande Randonnée (CNBSGR) in Belgium; the Ministry of Tourism in Luxembourg, working through the youth hostel organization, the Centrale des Auberges de Jeunesse; and in France, the Fédération Française de Randonnée Pedestre-Comité National des Sentiers de Grande Randonnée. This mouthful of an organizational name is abbreviated as FFRP-CNSGR; call it the FFRP.

The story of the FFRP sheds light on how the walking paths within and across European borders have grown and how they are managed.

What is today the FFRP-CNSGR got started just after the war, when the Touring Club Français (TCF) was trying, as was everything else in Europe, to get back on its feet. Within the TCF was a small hiking subcommittee, made up mostly of Alsatians; the TCF's attraction for the hikers was its possession of a mimeograph machine the subcommittee could use to publish trail descriptions. The subcommittee grew and extended the scope of its activities, and in 1947, it separated from the TCF and established itself as an authorizing agency over the trails of France, creating sentiers de petite randonnée (day hikes), sentiers de grande randonnée, and the interconnections that would enable hikers to traverse the whole of France. In addition, inspired mostly by the Alsatians, whose sense of political frontiers was understandably acute, the committee, now the Comité National des Sentiers de Grande Randonnée, began to link its activities with those of walking clubs in other countries and to create trails that would cross national boundaries.

In the meantime, with increased prosperity and leisure all over Europe, the popularity of walking as a pastime grew by leaps and bounds. By 1969, it had become clear that some formal recognition of European walking and walkers was necessary. In France, CNSGR beefed itself up into FFRP, augmenting its original trail marking charter by taking on an umbrella function for numerous related groups; the new organization became part of the Europe-wide Fédération, based in Germany.

Within France, scores of local hiking clubs, camping organizations, and tourism agencies are members of the FFRP. In addition, FFRP serves as the liaison to relevant governmental ministries. It is concerned with environmental protection and with the creation of more and better facilities for walkers, and it has been instrumental in lobbying for legislation that protects flora and fauna as well as trails and the people who walk them.

Like its sister organizations throughout Europe, FFRP is a coordinator; it provides a national perspective on the network of walking routes and monitors the activities of its member organizations. But FFRP has little or no real power. Trail maintenance, for example, is the responsibility of local clubs and of the volunteers they are able to bring out. FFRP can advise the clubs that a trail requires work; FFRP can cajole; it can offer funds—but it cannot impose its management will. Local inertia, interclub rivalry, and politics all get in the way of FFRP's good intentions. One result for the walker is an inconsistency in the system of marking the GRs.

FFRP and its sister organizations must also deal with local governmental authorities and with private owners of land and routes. When, for example, a farmer fences off a field a GR goes through—and he obviously has the right to do so—how shall the trail be rerouted? Will it require permission from another private owner? Can the rerouting somehow cross public land? Will the city fathers of the commune or village be amenable to that? And once a rerouting is decided on, will someone volunteer to mark it? When he does, will he do it right? If he does it wrong, who will see to it that it's fixed? The FFRP has no executive clout in these matters, beyond persuasion. Under the circumstances, FFRP and the other national organizations do an excellent job.

Perhaps the most important work of the FFRP and its sister organizations, at least as far as the GR5 walker is concerned, is the publication of topo-guides. These small paperback guidebooks provide the walker an almost step-by-step description of the GR he is walking as well as sections of detailed topographic maps on which the GR route has been overlaid. The topo-guides give walking times and distances, alert walkers to the presence of provisioning and lodging facilities in an area, and often mention sights of interest. In Holland and the Flanders portion of Belgium, the topo-guides are *topo-gids* and are written in Dutch and Flemish. All the others are written in French. Whatever you call them, and even if you read neither Dutch nor French, they are virtually indispensable when walking the GR5.

The GR5 Route

From the Hoek van Holland, GR5 edges the North Sea coast of southwestern Holland, then treks southeast in a diagonal line across Belgium—first through Flanders, then Wallonie. It goes right down Luxembourg into France, then makes an abrupt left turn to head almost due east across Lorraine to the Vosges Mountains. It heads south along the crest of the Vosges, borders Switzerland as it continues south down the Jura, and comes to rest in the gully of Lake Geneva. Then it winds its way, always up and down but resolutely southward, across great groups of Alps to the Mediterranean at Nice.

Don't think of it as a hiking trail. GR5 is a *route*, combining roads, paths, tracks, and even the main streets of villages and towns. It connects trails that already existed—some of them perhaps since prehistory and the days of the Amber Route, some from the Roman era, many that have been known to generations of shepherds or farmers, others that were the main roads between two points until automobile and highway displaced them. The part of GR5 that crosses the French Alps, for example, has been known as a walking route since the early years of this century, when the Alps started to become a playground, but pieces of it had long been used by sheep and shepherds to reach summer pastures, by craftsmen to get from one village to the next, by armies. Armies also had a great deal to do with the path along the crest of the Vosges, a path that is now a part of GR5. To link the Alps crossing to the Vosges crossing, it was necessary to cross the Jura, along paths and roads and tracks that also, to a great extent, already existed. To connect the Vosges with the highly developed network of trails in Luxembourg, the GR5 builders found paths across Lorraine and built links where necessary. And so on—until a path connected North Sea and Mediterranean, with access, at the northern end, to Britain and Scandinavia and the great walking routes there.

Don't think of GR5 as wilderness travel, either. Perhaps the overwhelming distinction between hiking in the United States and hiking in Europe is that you cannot, in Europe, hoist a pack on your back and disappear for two weeks into an area where you may see no cars, no towns, no roads, no people. On the other hand, you cannot, in the Rockies, climb 4,000 feet straight up to an absolutely isolated meadow and there find a refuge where you can eat a hot meal and drink your fill of wine or beer.

The Europe of GR5 is a land that has been inhabited for centuries. The landfills the Dutch created when they built their dikes have been there for hundreds of years. The highest Alpine meadows have been home to shepherds for thousands of years. It makes for a certain sense of security to know that you are never really *that* far from a road or town or house.

Happily, when you walk GR5, you need not be aware of the density of population or the activities of civilization that may be nearby. There might be a major city or superhighway only a couple of kilometers away, but if it is over that rise or behind that clump of trees, it might as well be hundreds of kilometers away as far as the walker is concerned. The sense of backcountry persists; the feeling of quiet remoteness is almost overwhelming all along the route from the top of Europe to the bottom.

Route Finding

The problem of the GR5 can be summed up in few words: finding your way. It is not a *big* problem, but it is one of which the walker should be aware.

The first part of the problem is what the French call *balisage*—waymarking to the British; trail marking to most Americans. The European federation of all those national walking groups has established an excellent system of GR markings; the problem is that the system is not always adhered to. (Luxembourg and the Vosges use different systems; see those sections.)

The system is a simple one. GR markings are white and red. The basic trail marking, a white horizontal stripe over a red horizontal stripe, means "this is the way; keep going." An X, white over red, means "this is the wrong way; don't come this way." Theoretically, a change in direction is marked, as in much of the United States, by four stripes, white over red over white over red. This alerts you to a turn coming up and may be accompanied by an arrow pointing the way.

Officially, there are two other trailmarking usages. A detour, showing you a spur or variant to some point of interest, is a white stripe

CONTINUE   TURN   TURN   WRONG WAY

GR trail markings. Colors are red and white.

over a red stripe with a white diagonal line cutting them both. A break in balisage, indicating that an unmarked stretch of trail lies ahead, is shown just that way: the white-over-red marking is cut in the middle, and a notation in the space between tells you how many meters or kilometers of no-man's-land you have ahead of you.

In fact, we saw only one detour marker on our entire journey and no balisage-break markers at all. What gave us trouble—what gives every GR5 walker trouble—was the basic balisage that marks the route.

GR5 marker painted on a rock near Col d'Anterne, France. Photo by Ginger Harmon.

Markers can appear anywhere: on rocks, trees, telephone posts, the road beneath your feet, the sides of houses and barns. In some areas, they are indeed excellent: visible when you need them, clear but unobtrusive, with plenty of four-stripe alert signals and plenty of Xs to keep you on the right path. In other areas, there are no four-stripers at all and no Xs—only meager straight-ahead markers, and you have to search to find them. Sometimes, you will pass in the length of a footstep from absolutely great markers to absolutely atrocious markers—or vice versa. You have gone from one club's trail maintenance jurisdiction to another's. On occasion, there is a no-man's-land between club territories, one club having left off marking well away from where the next club began marking. That's when you need to get out topoguide, map, and compass and improvise your own route, or—a tip we learned from the first other GR5 walker we met—hoist your binoculars to see if you can spot the next marker in the distance.

The markers are supposed to be of a standard size so as not to be eyesores. In fact, they range from minute dabs of paint to huge slashes grotesquely disfiguring tree trunks. There are supposed to be standards regulating the frequency with which they appear, given, of course, the availability of objects on which a marker can be painted. In fact, there will be one marker every six feet when your route is perfectly obvious and no markers at all when you have no idea where you're going. Markers are supposed to be regularly maintained by local walking clubs. In fact, the paint is often faded, and the markers are often obscured by plant growth that hasn't been cleared for several seasons. Sometimes, of course, that faint, obscured trail is actually an old GR5 that has since been rerouted and will lead you, if you laboriously search it out, to a high wall along an eight-lane highway.

Which brings us to the second part of the finding-your-way problem: changes in the trail. Americans are no strangers to this fact of life, and of course, when the farmer does fence his field, or when a new highway is constructed, or when someone builds a house on what used to be GR5, rerouting is necessary. When a rerouting is effected, however, the detailed description in the topo-guide—and often the distance and timing it provides—are no longer valid. The absolute rule here is *follow the balisage*. The trail marking is like the traffic cop that takes precedence over all lights and stop signs at the intersection; it beats map or topo-guide. For the walker who has been struggling with the Dutch or French of the topo-guide and is looking for the landmarks it describes, this can be frustrating; it is not nearly as frustrating as getting lost. Again, when in doubt, follow the balisage.

As with all hard-and-fast rules, there may be exceptions to this one. In the summer of 1984, near the Luxembourg-to-Lorraine crossing, new construction and a new highway had simply obliterated sections of GR5. It took all our creativity and a good deal of time to get where we were going. As all topo-guides suggest, we wrote to the appropriate authorities to inform them of the trail lapse and to tell them about the difficulty we had experienced. We later learned that they knew of the problem and were planning to fix it that autumn. By the time we learned this, it *was* that autumn, and we had long since dealt with the problem. Deal with it the walker must. It would be unimaginable for there to be no problems of route or route markings in 1,500 miles of trail passing through five different countries and hundreds of localities within those countries. At first, as foreigners, we were a bit intimidated by the fact that the markings did not always conform to the diagrams of them in the topo-guides. We assumed there was some knack to European trail marking that we Americans simply didn't understand. It wasn't until we met other GR5 walkers and heard their complaints and recitations of the letters they were writing to Paris or Luxembourg or Antwerp that we realized there was no special flaw in our trail sense—*everybody* has problems along GR5. In fact, by the time we reached the Vosges and found some companions to share the trail with, we had achieved the reputation of having "a good nose" for sniffing out the correct route.

You will have *some* trouble, *sometimes*, following the route in *some* sections of Europe. Where you see balisage, follow it. If you lose it, go back to the last place you saw it and try again. Where you don't see balisage, consult your topo-guide description, your topo-guide map, and any other maps and guides you may have with you and improvise a route.

The route problem is but a minor part of the walk across Europe from top to bottom, and it's all part of the adventure.

4
Planning
the Walk

Guides and Maps

The one item that is almost a sine qua non of the walk across Europe from top to bottom is the set of topo-guides to the GR5. The problem is that it is virtually impossible to obtain these in the United States; the walker planning the GR5 megawalk must therefore allow plenty of time to order these from Europe.

These are the topo-guides you will need:

Netherlands:	Noordzee-Riviera Lange-afstand-wandeling van Europoort naar Bergen op Zoom (in Dutch)
Flanders:	Grote Route 5–5A Trajekt der Lage Landen Bergen op Zoom-Grobbendonk-Luik (in Flemish)
Wallonie:	Tronçon Belge
Luxembourg:	514: Luxembourg-Moselle d'Ouren à Ars-sur-Moselle
France:	516: Meurthe-et-Moselle - Moselle d'Ars-sur-Moselle à Abreschviller
France:	502: Vosges, Bas-Rhin, Haut-Rhin, Territoire de Belfort, Doubs d'Abreschviller à Fesches-le-Châtel
France:	503: Gorges, lacs, plateaux du Jura et Tour du pays de Montbéliard de Fesches-le-Châtel à Nyon
France:	504: Haute Savoie du lac Léman au col de la Croix du Bonhomme

France:	527: Parc National de la Vanoise du col de la Croix du Bonhomme à Modane
France:	528: Au pays des hauts alpages de Modane à Larche
France:	507: Alpes-Maritimes de Larche à Nice ou à Menton

Except for the Dutch and Flemish topo-gids for the Netherlands and Flanders, all the topo-guides are in French.

The topo-guides for France are all published by the FFRP. The Netherlands topo-gid is published by Koninklijke Nederlandse Toeristenbond ANWB. The Flanders topo-gid is published by the Grote Routepaden. Both the Tronçon Belge for Wallonie and the Luxembourg topo-guide are published by FFRP.

Theoretically, the walker could write a series of letters to these publishers, which are really the member organizations of the European Ramblers' Association, for information about obtaining the topo-guides: ANWB in Holland, the Grote Routepaden and Comité National Belge des Sentiers de Grande Randonnée in Belgium, the Tourism Ministry in Luxembourg, and the FFRP in France. (See addresses at end of chapter.) But that is a ridiculously duplicative process for getting topo-guides.

A number of bookstores in Britain and the famous Au Vieux Campeur in Paris stock or can order topo-guides, but you cannot always count on these sources having all the guides in stock; ordering delays can add significantly to what is already a time-consuming process.

The best way to get topo-guides ahead of time is to deal with one source, the Grote Routepaden in Antwerp, which stocks all the topo-guides for all of GR5 and whose staff speaks English.

In addition, Grote Routepaden will send the topo-guides you order and bill you at the same time. With most other places, you will have to go through a laborious two-phased process—first inquiring about availability and prices, then sending your payment. See the list at the end of this chapter for the Grote Routepaden address and phone number in Antwerp.

In writing to Grote Routepaden, or any other bookstore or agency, you might also want to inquire about maps—specifically about those that show the GR5 route. These maps are useful for many reasons. First, as adjuncts to the small, highly detailed maps in the topo-guides, they provide the walker a big-picture look at the area he is traversing. Second, they will show efficient "escape routes" to larger towns and cities in case of emergency. Third, they alert you to places nearby that you may always have wanted to see but that are not along GR5 and are therefore not mentioned in the itineraries. Fourth, European maps tend to be very beautiful.

There is an almost overwhelming variety of maps available for the GR5 countries of Europe and a wide choice of scales as well. For the most part, the megawalker will be content with provincial maps of a 1:100,000 or 1:200,000 scale, although in the mountains a more detailed 1:50,000 scale, offering closer scrutiny of topography, may be preferred.

Both topo-guides and maps can be found along the route, and the walker might also want to browse around his hometown bookstore or map store to see what he can find before leaving for Europe. (Beware of carrying too much bulk and weight, however.) But topo-guides are much harder to come by along the route than maps, and the walker who is not armed with these ahead of time may have to detour off the trail to find his next topo-guide.

Language Books

Unless you are fluent in Dutch and/or French, you will need to carry phrase books and/or pocket dictionaries. Do not count on English as a lingua franca of Europe; to some extent, it probably is, at least in the big cities, but GR5 keeps to the backcountry where it simply is not true that everyone speaks English. You will find English speakers, of course, particularly in the Netherlands, but under no circumstances should you rely on this.

General Tourist Information

It can be very useful to query the U.S.-based tourist offices of GR5 countries for general information about your walk and specifically for lists of lodgings and accomodations.

The French government maintains tourist offices in New York, Beverly Hills, San Francisco, Chicago, and Dallas. The Netherlands, Belgium, and Luxembourg all have offices in New York. Switzerland, which GR5 traverses but briefly, maintains tourist offices in New York, Chicago, and San Francisco (see addresses at end of chapter).

Although walking does not get quite the tourism attention that is given to, say, skiing, a phone call to these offices can sometimes elicit useful information and will at the very least produce updated hotel and restaurant lists. Let the staff know the areas through which you'll be passing so they will send you the right lists.

Documentation

You will of course need a valid passport. No visas are needed, and there are no medical requirements.

It is a good idea to join some sort of outdoor, hiking, or mountaineering organization, if you have not already done so. The Sierra Club, the American Youth Hostels Association, the Appalachian Mountain Club, or any other organizations that issue membership cards—particularly if the word *mountain* is in the name—are good bets. Armed with such a membership, you should then apply to the American Alpine Club (see addresses) for what is called a reciprocity sticker, issued by the UIAA (International Union of Alpine Associations). The sticker, for which there is a charge, can be affixed to your club membership card. With it, you can get a reciprocity discount at all refuges run by the Alpine Clubs of the GR5 countries.

A potentially less expensive idea is to join the Club Alpin Français (CAF; see addresses below). Most of the mountain huts along GR5 are in France anyway, and discounts are automatic to CAF members. On occasion it has happened that the presentation of a U.S. mountain club card and a little persuasion have resulted in a discount at refuges run by organizations other than the Alpine Clubs. The U.S. documentation can sometimes open other doors as well. In short, if you are already a member of a U.S. club, apply for the UIAA sticker; if not, it's your choice whether to join a U.S. club or the Club Alpin Français.

If you have a driver's license, bring it with you (carefully encased in plastic). You will not need to apply for the international driver's license for any of the GR5 countries, but the license is handy for identification purposes, and it is essential should you decide to chuck the walking for a while and rent a car.

Students might want to obtain the International Student Identity Card, available from the Council on International Educational Exchange (see addresses).

Getting Mail: The Postes Restantes

A *poste restante* is a general delivery address at which you can call for your mail. In Dutch-speaking countries, you go to the *postkantoor*, and in France you go to *la poste*, the PTT (Postes et Telecommunications). Go up to the window, show your passport, and ask for your poste restante. (Although "poste restante" is a French phrase, the more common usage in France itself is *courrier*.)

In order to have mail to call for, however, you must arrange addresses and approximate times of arrival with your letter writers. The U.S.-based tourist offices of the GR5 countries can give you the addresses for the poste restante locations of your choice. Theoretically, mail will be held for you for thirty days. Since letters from the States take about ten days to reach Europe, you would be wise to advise your correspondents to mail their letters at least two weeks in advance of the date you estimate you'll arrive in a place. If you arrive much earlier than that, of course, you could be out of luck.

Letters should be addressed to: Name,
Poste Restante,
Postal Code (if available)
and Post Office Designation,
Country.

Our postes restantes were:
B-4000 Liège, Belgium
Echternach, Grand Duchy of Luxembourg
68150 Ribeauvillé, France
73150 Val d'Isère, France
1260 Nyon, Switzerland
05100 Briançon, France

For example, a letter sent to you in Ribeauvillé would be addressed:
Your Name
Poste Restante
68150 Ribeauvillé
France

Typically, poste restante is at the central post office, if the town is big enough for more than one post office, so don't panic if they have never heard of you in the first post office you enter.

It is wonderful to get mail along GR5; news from home can be a much-anticipated event, and we found that we read and reread the letters we received for days afterward. But the postes restantes also serve a more practical purpose: if you can arrange ahead of time to have someone send you needed topo-guides, maps, even fresh clothing, you will have that much less to carry. In such cases, make sure your correspondents allow plenty of time for delivery and mark the packages *Hold For Arrival*. Similarly, it's a good idea to mail off no-longer-needed topo-guides, maps, and equipment as you proceed along the route.

One more tip: we routinely wrote ahead to our next poste restante to advise the postal director that mail addressed to us would be arriving, to inform him of our approximate arrival date, and to beg that our mail be held. Several of the postal directors along the way referred to these letters and told us they were a good idea. They seemed to make for a higher level of awareness, in any case. Moreover, you can arrange with your last poste restante to forward mail to your next poste restante; a small charge is usually required for this.

Money

It is possible to live extremely cheaply along GR5. Nevertheless, even living extremely cheaply requires a certain outflow of cash, especially when you are out of reach of your bank for more than three months at a stretch.

The fact is, you are not really out of reach of your bank. No matter how small your hometown and your hometown bank, it very likely is a correspondent of a U.S. money-center bank with overseas branches or overseas banking connections. The megawalker would do well to talk to someone in his local bank about this before leaving for Europe.

In addition, financial services are becoming increasingly global through the use of such credit cards as VISA, MasterCard, American Express,

Diners Club, and others. These are accepted throughout Europe; with them, you may obtain cash—although for a fairly steep interest charge. Carry traveler's checks. It may be possible to purchase these in foreign-currency denominations, but U.S.-dollar traveler's checks are accepted almost everywhere. They are certainly accepted in all towns of any size and in all banks anywhere. Occasionally, a small-town merchant will be unwilling to cash a traveler's check of more than $25.00 (you find this reluctance in the United States as well), but a wad of small-denomination traveler's checks sufficient to last more than three months can give you writer's cramp when it comes to signing them and can constitute quite a bulge in the wallet. In general, the best advice is to cash traveler's checks at a bank and make sure you have plenty of ready cash for purchases. The other reason to cash traveler's checks at a bank, as opposed to in hotels or shops, is that the exchange rate is significantly better.

Credit cards, of course, may also be used for many purchases and for most hotel and restaurant bills as well as for obtaining cash.

Another good credit card to carry is a telephone credit card. It can be used for Europe-to-United States phone calls in the countries along GR5.

Before you leave for Europe, arrange to purchase a small amount of each of the currencies of GR5 countries: Dutch guilders, Belgian francs, French francs, Swiss francs. (Luxembourg accepts Belgian francs.) Stash these, along with some U.S. dollars, in some compartment of your wallet where they will be out of sight but not forgotten. It is always possible that you will find yourself crossing into one of these countries on a weekend or bank holiday, so having some ready cash can be useful for the first few kilometers or hours in the newly entered country.

It never hurts to have some U.S. dollars; even if you don't use them abroad, you'll have bus fare on your arrival back home.

Getting in Shape

While it is true that the walk across Europe from north to south will put you in superb physical shape, it is equally true that you will enjoy the walk much more if you are in good shape to begin with. Contrary to what most people believe, the first bit of flat walking across the Netherlands is extremely hard on the body; it is also the time when your pack will feel heaviest. Planning the walk across Europe should include some conditioning. Moreover, a discussion with your physician about what lies ahead—particularly the Alps—is a good idea.

Enough said.

(The megawalker will note a slightly painful withdrawal at the end of his walk. After a long period of rigorous daily activity, muscles that are suddenly asked to do nothing may seize up. The mind may experience withdrawal symptoms as well.)

There are no particular health hazards along the GR5 route. In any event, all of the countries through which GR5 passes have highly developed systems of medical care. Nevertheless, the walker would do well to carry a small booklet about first aid, at least to heighten awareness of symptoms of such things as heat exhaustion, sunstroke, hypothermia, and altitude sickness.

Rabies (*la rage*, in French) still exists on the continent of Europe. Be aware of it.

The walker should also pay attention to his water sources. If in doubt, add a purification tablet. In general, try to fill water bottles from public fountains, cafés, hotels, or the taps of private homes along the way.

Equipment

Think of equipment in three categories: trail or hiking gear; what we called evening wear—that is, the clothes you wear when you stop hiking; and housekeeping.

Almost everything you carry can go into a sizeable backpack with a padded hip belt. But there are numerous items, particularly those connected with housekeeping, that you may want to keep up front and handy. There are various methods for doing this—some pack belts can be fitted with pockets—but one of the best we found was a squared-off camera bag that could be worn diagonally across the chest, so that it rested at about waist level but out of the way of swinging arms. Ginger carried such a bag, which we called her office, in which she packed camera, film, lens tissue; binoculars; reading glasses and dark glasses; lip balm; pen and notepad; passport; the current topo-guide and a map; nose rag; and her wallet, containing money, traveler's checks, driver's license, credit cards, and calling cards. (These were actually business cards—very handy in Europe where their use is pervasive.) The office, in other words, carried just about everything she needed to reach during a day of walking; she almost never had to go into her pack until the end of the day's hike.

At the end of each day's hike, we changed into our evening wear, a set of clothes carefully wrapped in plastic—as everything should be in Europe—and reserved for bodies that had been showered or at least sponge bathed.

Most of our gear was, of course, trail clothing and hiking equipment. There was only one item on the list that follows that we never used: the silk balaclava, but it was nice to know it was there anyway.

The most important rule about packing in Europe is to be sure everything is watertight. Make sure, before you leave home, that your foul-weather gear works; one good method is to put it on and stand under the shower or under a garden hose. If you get wet in an American bathtub or backyard, you are bound to get good and wet in a European rainstorm. Get new gear.

For top-loading packs, it is a good idea to stuff a large garbage bag inside as a liner; a strong bag (3 mil.) lasts quite a long time, but don't forget to bring an extra anyway.

The best way to pack, both for waterproofing and for convenience, is to put categories of clothing and gear into separate plastic bags. As in the United States, plastic has replaced paper in Europe as the material for shopping bags; these bags usually come in bright colors, so that you can color code your luggage: red bag for laundry, blue for socks, black for sweaters, and so forth.

Finally, in Europe of all places, it is well to keep in mind what Susanna calls her Ultimate Law of Packing:

What you don't need, don't bring.

What you don't bring and do need, you can usually find.

What you don't bring and you do need and you can't find, you can often improvise.

What you don't bring and you do need and you can't find and you can't improvise, do without.

Equipment List

1. Trail Clothing/Hiking Gear

boots (waterproofed and broken in)
knickers or hiking trousers
shorts
tee-shirts or tank tops
long-sleeved shirt
sweater
wool socks
inner socks
underwear
belt
bandana
rain pants, jacket, and hat
parka
gloves
balaclava
long underwear (lightweight)
wool cap

pack with padded hip belt
water bottle(s)
watch
flashlight
matches
compass
whistle
mirror
water purification tablets
pocket knife
repair gear: ½-inch nylon webbing (15 feet), wire (12 inches)

emergency blanket
emergency food
first-aid kit and booklet
lunch and snacks

2. Off-Trail Gear

one evening wear outfit (trousers, nice shirt, sweater, nonhiking socks
and underwear)
running shoes
scarves
swimsuit

3. Housekeeping

toiletries (including soap)
small towel
sewing kit (including sock yarn)
extra shoelaces
extra batteries and bulbs
something to read
hook-on reading light
backup pairs of glasses
address book
notebook and pen
extra film
flash attachment
plastic bags
small folding day pack (good on layover days)
toilet paper

Remember also that, after two or three days on the trail, when your aching shoulders have made it abundantly plain that you brought a lot of superfluous stuff, you can mail it home.

We mailed an electronic typewriter from Bergen-op-Zoom, Holland.

Addresses

GR5 Administration:

European Ramblers' Association
1–5 Wandsworth
London SW8 2LJ
England
(This is not the main headquarters of the association, but it is an English-speaking branch.)

Netherlands:

ANWB afd. RML
Postbus 93200
2509 BA DEN HAAG
Netherlands

Flanders:

Grote Routepaden
Van Stralenstraat 40
2008 Antwerp
Belgium

Wallonie:

Comité National Belge des Sentiers de Grande Randonnée
Boite Postale 10
B-4000 Liège 1
Belgium

Luxembourg:

Centrale des Auberges de Jeunesse Luxembourgeoise
18, Place d'Armes
Luxembourg-Ville
Grand Duché de Luxembourg
Ministère de Tourisme (Tourism Ministry)
77 Rue d'Anvers
Luxembourg-Ville
Grand Duché de Luxembourg

France:

FFRP-CNSGR
8, Avenue Marceau
75008 Paris
France

Club Vosgien
4, Rue de la Douane
67000 Strasbourg
France

Centre Information Montagnes et Sentiers (CIMES)
Maison du Tourisme
14, Rue de la République
F-38027 Grenoble
France

Getting Topo-Guides and Maps:

Grote Routepaden
Van Stralenstraat 40
2008 Antwerp
Belgium
Telephone: (03) 232 72 18

Stanfords
12–14 Long Acre
Covent Garden
London WC2P 9LP
England

Au Vieux Campeur
2, Rue de Latran
F-75005 Paris
France

Getting Credentials:

American Alpine Club
113 East 90th Street
New York, NY 10128

American Youth Hostels
1332 "I" Street, N.W.
Suite 800
Washington, D.C. 20005

Club Alpin Français
7, Rue la Boétie
F-75008 Paris
France

Council on International Educational Exchange
205 East 42nd Street
New York, NY 10017

U.S.-Based Tourist Offices of GR5 Countries:

Netherlands National Tourist Office
576 Fifth Avenue
New York, NY 10036
(212) 223-8141

Netherlands National Tourist Office
605 Market Street
Room 401
San Francisco, CA 94105
(415) 543-6772

Belgium National Tourist Office
745 Fifth Avenue
7th Floor
New York, NY 10151
(212) 758-8130

Luxembourg National Tourist Office
801 Second Avenue
13th Floor
New York, NY 10017
(212) 370-9850

Swiss National Tourist Office
608 Fifth Avenue
New York, NY 10020
(212) 757-5944

Swiss National Tourist Office
104 South Michigan Avenue
Chicago, IL 60603
(312) 641-0050

Swiss National Tourist Office
250 Stockton Street
San Francisco, CA 94108
(415) 362-2260

French Government Tourist Office
610 Fifth Avenue
New York, NY 10020
(212) 757-1125

French Government Tourist Office
9401 Wilshire Boulevard
Beverly Hills, CA 90212
(213) 272-2661

French Government Tourist Office
c/o Air France
One Hallidie Plaza
San Francisco, CA 94108
(415) 986-4161

French Government Tourist Office
645 North Michigan Avenue
Chicago, IL 60611
(312) 337-6301

French Government Tourist Office
2050 Stemmons Freeway
P.O. Box 58610
Dallas, TX 75258
(214) 742-7011

5
Life on
the Trail

Summer brings long days to Europe, especially in the north. The sun may rise at 4:30 or 5:00 and stay fairly high for as many as sixteen hours.

Many of the hotels along the GR5 route don't serve breakfast before 8:00, except by special arrangement, so you often won't hit the trail before 9:00. It is nice to know that by the time you have reached your day's destination, found a hotel, cleaned up, and changed, there will still be plenty of daylight for exploring the town.

In more than a hundred separate hostelries, we hit just two that were grungey enough to be called unpleasant; even those we survived—you can survive almost anything for one night. For the most part, the hotels were clean, comfortable, and fun. We became exceedingly fond of the small, square, nonabsorbent towels; the *minuterie*, the timed light switch in the hallways; the variety of plumbing fixtures with which we had to contend.

The mountain huts of France also have a good deal to recommend them—friendliness, good food and drink, and welcoming atmosphere. But you have to be of a certain constitution or personality to enjoy sleeping perhaps thirty to a room, especially because Europeans appear to oppose the opening of a window at night—even a crack. Again, you can survive almost anything for one night.

Hotels

Lists of hotels are available from tourist offices all along the GR5 route, and it is a good idea to collect these as you go. The lists tell you names, phone numbers, prices, and the amenities available. In most lists, these indications of class are noted in stars, not to be confused with the Michelin stars, which are subjective ratings. The stars of hotel lists are given by the government ministry charged with tourism and are decided by government standards:

★ plain hotel, but comfortable
★★ good average hotel
★★★ very comfortable hotel
★★★★ top-class hotel

In France, two other ratings are used: the nonstarred R.T. signals a hotel so plain it doesn't fall within government standards, while ★ ★ ★ ★ L designates a luxury hotel. We routinely stayed at one- and two-star hotels and found them more than adequate. The bath and toilet are often down the hall, of course, and the minuterie in the hallway can turn a nocturnal visit into a race against time as you sprint down the corridor with, you hope, your way lighted for you at least as far as the next minuterie switch.

People who like to read in bed are advised to bring a battery-run light that can be affixed to the book itself. Lighting in many of the small hotels of Europe tends to be a single 60-watt bulb twelve feet away on the ceiling, and no amount of furniture moving makes reading in bed possible.

The hospital corner is virtually unknown in the Europe of the GR5. This means that if you pull down the covers to get into bed, all of the bedding simply comes apart and you will have to remake the bed entirely—at least, if you're that kind of person. Susanna, who is very much that kind of person, devised an ingenious method for bed entering: sit on the pillow, then slither your feet under the still-taut blanket and inch your way down carefully. This often results in the feeling of being swaddled or straitjacketed, so you may need to toss and turn a bit before getting comfortable.

Because hotels can charge more for a room if there is a shower in it, some hotels have taken to installing ready-made shower stalls in some rooms—often right smack in the middle of the room. This is an amusing solution, but worthwhile.

Showers, baths, and sinks with two faucets generally have hot and cold in the reverse of the American system—but not always. Usually, the red faucet is hot, and the blue is cold—but not always. It is a good idea to test the waters before scalding or freezing yourself.

The small hotels of Europe are very much built and run for travelers, and they provide virtually all of the conveniences you require. They have bar and dining room, can sell you stamps or mail your letters for you, and offer a homelike atmosphere the megawalker will come to cherish.

Gîtes

A gîte is a resting place or lodging, and France is covered by a network of gîtes d'étape, gîtes ruraux, gîtes-chambres d'hôte, and more. Gîtes are usually homes or former homes—farmhouses in the countryside—that provide a range of accommodation, from primitive, hostellike lodging and no meals to very comfortable, well-furnished châteaux where the traveler can dine en famille. Official gîtes are marked by round green signs which describe what kind of gîte it is, but there are also bed-and-breakfast-type private gîtes along the way.

The Huts: Mountain Refuges

The mountain huts (*refuges*, in French) along GR5 also vary greatly in level of comfort and in quality. Some offer small rooms, even private rooms, in addition to *dortoir* sleeping—a dormitory, usually with upper and lower sleeping-bunk shelves on which mattresses are lined up side by side. Some offer full-scale meals while others require that you arrange for food ahead of time or cook your own. Some are clean and charming; others are not clean and lack the more obvious charms. All will look good to you at the end of a hard day of mountain walking.

The disparity of offerings among the huts makes it essential for the walker to carry food at all times when in high-mountain country. The walker can also check with tourist bureaus in mountain towns to ascertain whether or not food is offered and/or to make arrangements for meals.

On arrival in a hut, the protocol is as follows: Leave your clodhopper boots at the door (there is usually a place reserved for this) and change into either your own running shoes or slippers that the hut may provide. Check yourself in for the night with the *gardien* or *gardienne*—the person in charge—and leave some sign of yourself on your chosen mattress: your pack, your sleeping gear, something.

It is an absolute violation of hut protocol to move anyone's stuff off a mattress, although this happened to Susanna one night in a very crowded hut in the Alps. She promptly put her stuff right back on her chosen mattress and dumped the intruding gear on the floor. It worked.

Even for the nonfastidious, it is a good idea to put a bandana or jacket on the pillow before you rest your precious head on the same spot that has held some fifty years' worth of other precious heads. In the morning, it is *de rigeur* to fold the blanket(s) you have used and replace same at the foot of the mattress.

Your own toilet paper can be useful at several of the huts.

Amis de la Nature

The refuges of the Amis de la Nature are both gîtelike and hutlike but different enough from both to deserve their own explanation.

The Amis de la Nature—Friends of Nature—is an organization that sprang from the European labor movement. It was created in Vienna in 1895 to provide workers the opportunity to commune with nature. The organization spread throughout Europe and into the United States.

The Amis run trips and excursions, give courses in mountaineering, administer vacation camps for children, adults, and families. The megawalker will frequently see Amis de la Nature gîtes, refuges, or hostels—whatever you like to call them—particularly in Belgium and in the Vosges. They are run by *bénévoles*, volunteer workers, and are always worth a stop for refreshment and a chat at the least. As accommodations go, the Amis de la Nature lodgings tend to be simple but of high quality.

Hostels

Hostels are everywhere in Europe, although, strangely, most of those along the GR5 are somewhat off the trail. The walker who plans to stay in hostels should be armed with an American Youth Hostels Association (AYH) membership, the required sheet sack (required even more in European hostels), and the *International Youth Hostel Handbook for Europe and the Mediterranean*, published by AYH and available from that organization.

Hostels in Europe, particularly in the urban areas, are often very large, well equipped, clean, pleasant, and heavily frequented.

Camping

This book is written primarily for people who do not want to camp out, but a word about camping and European campgrounds is in order.

What the French call *le camping sauvage*—wild camping—is practised pervasively in Europe, although it is officially forbidden to camp in national parks and theoretically forbidden almost everywhere else. European campgrounds are equipped with a wide range of facilities and regulations. Many are caravan (trailer) campgrounds with fixed caravans; in these, the walker may sometimes be able to negotiate a single night's rental of a caravan.

Walkers who want to practice le camping sauvage or bed down in legal camp-sites should of course bring the appropriate equipment.

Eating

Eating is one of the great adventures and one of the extraordinary pleasures of walking Europe from top to bottom. The experienced American hiker/backpacker will delight at being able to climb 4,000 feet straight up to find himself in a hut where he can be served a four-course dinner, complete with wine. The walker in the Vosges will form his impressions as much from lunches at *fermes-auberges* (farm inns) and dinners in wine towns as from his step-by-step progression up and down hills. The beer lover will learn to keep a sharp eye for the huge and colorful pennants that announce cafés in Holland and Belgium.

Saltwater fish at either end of the trip, freshwater fish all along the journey, asparagus in season, the melon sent up from the Mediterranean, berries—and tarts made from berries, veal in every form, mushrooms, Belgian chocolate, and above all, the lunches you can build from fresh bread, an incredible variety of cheeses, sausages, patés, and a tube of Dijon mustard that fits easily into a pack: these are among the great joys of the walk across Europe.

Getting Along Along the Route
Planning the Day

It is a good idea to familiarize yourself somewhat with the next day's itinerary *the night before*—at least so you know whether or not you should plan to picnic or lunch in a restaurant. (However, it cannot be repeated too often that the GR5 walker should *always* carry food.)

Communicating

Armed with phrase book and pocket dictionary, the walker is equipped with the basic resources for getting by. One of the happy facts of megawalking, however, is that the prolonged familiarity with the languages of the journey—Dutch (or Flemish) and French—will eventually produce an ability that goes beyond merely getting by.

Certain words, phrases, and usages are particularly germane to walking GR5. Two megawalker's lexicons, Dutch (Flemish) and French, are appended for reference (Appendices B and C).

Encounters with people along the route are among the best experiences of walking Europe from top to bottom. Even if your attempts to communicate in the language of the natives are halting and labored, the effect is worth it. You are in their country, after all.

Getting Information en Route

In the towns and cities along the GR5, the walker will find a wide range of tourist information facilities—from the tiny, easily missed storefront with its mimeographed information sheet to lavish centers with multilingual staffs and a virtual supermarket of slick brochures.

Anywhere in Europe, these offices may be denoted by a sign marked with a curving, lowercase *i*. In Holland and Flanders, they may alternately be marked VVV, for Vereniging voor Vreemdelingen Verkeer (roughly: Association for Foreign Travelers). In France, look for Syndicat d'Initiative, Bureau de Tourisme, or Office de Tourisme; if you are inquiring in person, just ask for the *tourisme*.

These offices typically provide information only about the province or region or area in which they are located. They are specifically local offices, not national, and can thus offer the walker guidance to nearby accommodations, eateries, and events. Many also stock local maps and walking-route maps, and in some, the staff members are unusually informative.

Tipping

Service charges are usually included on the bill at restaurants and hotels. Check this, however. If service is not included, the usual 10 to 15 percent should be left. Even when service is included, it is customary to leave some loose change.

Phoning

Do not phone directly from your hotel room without first ascertaining what charge the hotel makes for this service; some surcharges on calls to the United States can go as high as 500 percent. Use your credit card, or call collect, or use the assisted facilities in post offices (you give the number to a clerk who assigns you a booth); or best of all, get lots of coins and call from a public phone booth on the street. Even in the boondocks, a great many of these are equipped for direct dialing to the United States, with instructions in English tacked to the wall of the booth.

Photography

Bring as much film with you as you can, remembering, however, that it will feel heavier on your back than you think, and travel with it in lead-lined bags, at least through airports. When you must buy film in Europe, be aware that the price of films marked with a *P* includes the cost of the processing, which means European processing. We routinely mailed film back to the United States once we had a few exposed rolls in hand; this avoids the dangers of heat and other potential hazards of holding onto film, especially in a backpack that is traveling 1,500 miles. On layover days in larger towns, it may be possible to find one-day processing for color print film.

A filter is a good idea; there can often be a good deal of haze in European air.

Conservation Consciousness

There is a growing awareness throughout Europe of the fragility of the environment in general and of particular ecosystems. National parks, regional parks, nature preserves, and the so-called tranquility zones are all part of the attempt to preserve unique environments and to spread and enhance conservation consciousness.

In the defined areas of parks and preserves, rules are posted listing do's and don'ts for the walker: don't bring your dog along, don't pick flowers, do stay on the trails. Unfortunately, the rules are not always followed.

American walkers, however, have a responsibility to follow the rules even if Europeans do not; we are, after all, guests here. Similarly, in villages, towns, and along sections of the GR5 that pass among private lands—places where regulations are not posted—Americans have a particular responsibility to act as if they were posted. Stay on the marked route wherever possible, and, as the saying goes in the United States, leave nothing but footprints; take nothing but photographs.

As foreigners in Europe, we Americans have some duty to be cleaner than clean when it comes to the environment. Where conservation behavior is concerned, we should be, like Caesar's wife, above suspicion.

Manners and Customs

The French *always* shake hands—a single, short shake. A handshake anywhere, if it is your own custom, is never out of place.

Towns in Europe have what are called half-days, days on which every store in the town closes early. Saturday is often a half-day *in addition*.

Lines in Europe are like lines in the United States. In small-town shops and markets, they tend to move slowly as people exchange news and gossip. Be patient.

If you call a taxi, especially in the small towns, and if it must come from a larger town to fetch you, you will probably be charged for the trip out to get you as well as for the trip to your destination.

Tickets—for *téléphériques*, ferries, concerts, and so forth—are usually flimsy pieces of paper that can easily get lost or ripped in a backpack. Exercise appropriate caution.

All gates along GR5 should be closed after you, unless they were open when you arrived. In short, leave all gates as you found them.

European first floors are American second floors. What Americans call a first floor Europeans call a ground floor.

The Europeans use a twenty-four-hour clock; 2:00 P.M. is 14:00, and so on. Many digital watches are equipped to handle either the twelve-hour or twenty-four hour clock; if you have one, you might consider setting yours to European time.

European dates go day/month/year; 3/6/86 is not March 6, it's June 3.

Laundromats exist in Europe, but mostly in the larger towns and cities. Launderettes—laundry shops—are more frequent. If you go to one, be sure to tell them that you want your clothes dried after they're washed. Otherwise, you could end up with a sopping mass of clean clothes.

Why any of these customs should be as they are is what makes them customs. Consider how ours must look to them.

Laws of Megawalking

In our journey across Europe, we had the opportunity to formulate numerous laws and principles that can serve as invaluable guidelines to walkers of the GR5—at least by alerting them to unavoidable occurrences whose consequences are, for the most part, completely frustrating. These laws are described throughout the book, and a complete canon is reproduced in Appendix D.

Walking Europe From Top to Bottom

Section	Kilometers	Total Kilometers	Total Miles
Netherlands	157	157	97
Flanders	232	389	242
Wallonie	180	569	353
Luxembourg	211	780	484
Lorraine	250	1030	640
Vosges	287	1317	818
Jura	326	1643	1020
North Alps	214	1857	1153
Middle Alps	216	2073	1287
South Alps	290	2363	1467

6
The Netherlands: Getting Started Flat Out

The Dutch look out on the world through the spotlessly clean single-pane picture windows of their trim houses. When they are not looking out the windows, they are washing them. We actually saw a woman vigorously scrubbing an upper-storey window during a heavy rain. When the Dutch do leave the neat, comfortable interiors of their win-dowed homes, they become active sports and outdoor enthusiasts. They bicycle and skate, they boat and go sailboarding, they play team sports, and they are great hikers. By far the predominant nationality among the hikers we were to meet in the Vosges, the Jura, and the high Alps was Dutch—Netherlanders delighting in the steep ups and downs they cannot find at home.

The Dutch deserve the reputation for unfailing politeness so often ascribed to the English across the shared North Sea. Some people attrib-ute the persistence of good manners to the density of the population—one of the highest in the world. Civility, it is suggested, is a necessity when people live so close together. Dutch politeness, however, goes beyond genteel courtesy, and the Dutch completely lack the ethnocen-tricity that typically afflicts the insular British. That may be due to their language. As one Dutchman we met put it, "No one is about to labor to learn Dutch, so we must learn to speak other peoples' languages in-stead." Or it may be due to the spotlessly clean windows. In any event, this is an outward-looking, extremely tolerant people—gentle and gen-erous with foreign visitors.

The name Holland really refers only to two western provinces, North and South Holland, although the appellation is used routinely, even by the Dutch. The country is appropriately called the Netherlands—a low, low land. It is only in the south and east of the country that you find hills; in the narrow tail of the country that dips down between Belgium and Germany, the nation's high point of 321 meters, is achieved at Vaalserberg. The GR5 walker, however, treks land that never rises above 5 meters in altitude.

The country is also waterlogged. It is a delta, formed of the sediment left by waterways draining north from the continent to the sea. Medieval travelers are said to have complained that they couldn't tell where the water ended and the land began, or vice versa. If you look at a map from that era, the Dutch lowlands appear to be a cluster of floating chunks of earth, suspended, barely linked. There is more land now than there was then, and the land hangs together with more stability—all the result of the clichéd struggle against the sea, which has been going on in the Netherlands since about 500 B.C.

It was then that the Frisians, in the northernmost part of the country, began to construct hillocks—*terpen*—to hold back the wind-whipped tide. For the next fifteen centuries or so, farms and even churches were built atop these hillocks, the remains of which may still be seen in the vicinity of Leeuwarden (well away from the GR5 route).

The first dikes were built around the year 1200. They made it possible to dry portions of land to create an early form of polder, an arable field reclaimed from water. Much of this initial work was wiped out in the thirteenth century, when thirty-five huge floods submerged the coastal plain, creating such new bodies of water as the Lauwerszee and the Zuiderzee (today re-formed by man into the freshwater IJsselmeer).

Then came the windmill. In fact, a sort of windmill, called the pivot mill, is attested as early as 1274, but it wasn't until around 1350 that the first one was used to drain the marshes and dry lakes. Less than a century later, in 1421, the disastrous flood of Saint Elizabeth's Day engulfed the southwestern region of Zeeland, with a loss of ten thousand people and the destruction of sixty-five villages. This flood led to a spurt of growth in the use of windmills, and over the next several centuries, the creation of polders became a highly refined engineering art.

A polder, a plot of land reclaimed from the sea or from a lake or marsh, is surrounded by dikes, and its water level is controlled, typically by a pump—windmills in the old days, then steam pumps, now diesel or electric pumps. Many of the polders along GR5 have been built up above sea level; at low tide, sluices are opened to allow excess water egress to canals that feed into the sea. Other polders are crisscrossed by a network of narrow collecting canals and edged by larger canals along their dikes. Pumps move the excess water into the collecting canals and then into the larger peripheral canal. Sometimes a chain of pumps is needed to ensure the right water level.

The seventeenth century saw a burst of polder building and the refinement of the engineering skills needed to plan and build the dikes of Holland. It was in 1667, in fact, that the idea was first put forth to close off the Zuiderzee—an idea implemented some 250 years later.

In succeeding centuries, more and more land was reclaimed, land held by a network of dikes. The wide nothingness in which Holland floated on those medieval maps was filled in by solid, if soggy, earth, and the irregular outline of the country's North Sea coast became an almost continuous wall of dikes. The draining of the Haarlemmeer in 1853 created 162 square kilometers of new land. The Zuiderzee Plan, begun in 1920 with a dike, created the freshwater IJsselmeer and 2,050 square kilometers of new land in five great polders. The Delta Plan, put into effect in 1957, created a succession of barriers to block the sea from the estuaries of the Rhine and Meuse Rivers; the GR5 walker gains intimate knowledge of the Delta Plan as he treks across the Plan's barriers and dikes—bottom-of-the-feet evidence that the Dutch struggle against the sea is no cliché after all.

The Dutch are a homogeneous people, primarily of ancient Germanic origin with a little Celtic mixed in. A small group of South Moluccans, a larger group of Surinamese, and a still larger influx of foreign workers—mostly from Mediterranean countries—together make up a little over one-tenth of the population. The most distinctive indigenous subgroup are the Frisians in the north; they cling to old customs, and their language, Frisian, is taught alongside Dutch in their schools.

The ancient Frisians, along with the Batavi tribe, occupied what is now the Netherlands in pre-Roman times; the Romans came as far north as the Rhine and stayed till about 300 A.D. Then it was the turn of the Franks, who absorbed the Batavi and subjugated the Frisians while integrating the Netherlands into a wider empire under Charlemagne. At his death, the Netherlands was subjected to routine Viking invasions and pillagings until, by the tenth century, governance of the area was in the hands of a number of feudal states, officially vassals of the Holy Roman Empire but effectively semiautonomous—the bishopric of Utrecht, the duchy of Brabant, the powerful counties of Holland.

Consolidation—through arms, marriage, and outright purchase—began under the dukes of Burgundy in the fourteenth century. Burgundy's possessions passed then to Austrian Habsburg control and, eventually, to the Spanish branch of the Habsburg dynasty.

Philip II of Spain, inheriting the Netherlands in 1555, encountered strong anti-Spanish and anti-Catholic opposition from the Dutch nobility and from the Calvinists in the northern provinces of the country. Opposition grew into the Dutch Revolt of 1568, led by William I, Prince of Orange, resulting in the Eighty Years' War. The 1648 Peace of Westphalia recognized the independence of the seven northern provinces as the Republic of the United Netherlands. The predominantly Catholic southern provinces remained loyal to Spain as the Spanish Netherlands—later, after the War of the Spanish Succession, as the Austrian Netherlands.

Every American schoolchild knows about the trade and shipping that made the seventeenth century the golden age of the Netherlands Republic, the era of the Dutch East India Company and the Dutch West India Company and Henry Hudson sailing up the exquisite New World river that bears his name. At the mouth of the river was the island of Manhattan, which another Dutchman, Peter Minuit, bought from the Indians for goods valued at twenty-four dollars. The Dutch built a fort there and called it New Amsterdam. By 1644, the governor could report that some eighteen languages were spoken in the settlement, and a Jesuit priest described this melting pot as having the "arrogance of Babel," a judgment many still hold more than three centuries later.

When the Netherlands finally lost control of the seas to England, a period of decline set in. The Republic was dissolved in 1795 when the French took over; in 1810, the northern provinces were incorporated into the French Empire. Napoleon's eventual defeat brought about a short-lived reunification of north and south as the Kingdom of the Netherlands, but the south withdrew in 1830 as the Kingdom of Belgium.

What was left of the Kingdom of the Netherlands entered the twentieth century in severe economic difficulties, made more pronounced by World War I and the Depression of the 1930s. Germany overran neutral Holland in 1940; the occupation claimed 240,000 Dutch citizens, many of them Jews, and left the country in ruins.

In conjunction with the other Benelux countries, and exhibiting the diligence and industry for which they have long been known, the Dutch fought their way back to prosperity, transforming themselves from a colonial power into a leading member of the European community. The transformation was presided over by the greatly loved Queen Juliana (the constitutional monarch reigns but does not rule), who abdicated in 1980 in favor of her daughter, Queen Beatrix.

Despite inflation and unemployment, similar to that suffered by virtually all industrialized nations in the 1970s and 1980s, Holland maintains a high standard of living (and an advanced welfare system), a diversified economic base, a favorable balance of trade. Life expectancy is high, and the nation claims a 100 percent literacy rate for its adult population. It also continues to uphold its well-known traditions of enlightenment and tolerance.

Three of Europe's major waterways—the Maas (in French, the Meuse), Rhine, and Scheldt rivers—enter the North Sea through a common delta in the southwest of the Netherlands. The Maas has come 896 kilometers (560 miles) from eastern France; the Rhine, rising in eastern Switzerland, has flowed some 1,300 kilometers (820 miles); the Scheldt has completed a 430-kilometer (270-mile) journey north from France. The walk across Europe from top to bottom begins by traversing this delta, "jumping" the waters of these rivers and making a path across the islands and transformed quasi-islands they flow through.

Shortly after crossing the Netherlands' eastern frontier, the Rhine splits into three distributaries: the IJssel, the Lower Rhine, and the Waal. The IJssel continues north, but the Lower Rhine becomes the Lek and flows into the North Sea as the Nieuwe Waterweg; GR5 crosses the Nieuwe Waterweg on Day 1 of its passage down Europe.

The Waal also feeds the Lek, but its main body continues more duly westward to fall into the Haringvliet, into which the Maas, under a variety of names, also falls. GR5 goes across the Haringvlietdam, thus passing over the mingled waters of the two rivers.

The canalized Scheldt mixes its waters into the Westerschelde and Oosterschelde; GR5 goes atop dikes along the latter and crosses, by ferry, a waterway that connects it to Grevelingen.

During the night of January 31 to February 1, 1953, the Delta was hit by a savage northwesterly storm. The wind whipped up the sea's waves and brought them crashing in among the narrow waterways and up over the land. Dikes were damaged at 600 places and breached at 89 places; 72,000 people were evacuated. The death toll was as overwhelming as the tide: 1,853 people lost their lives. In addition, 200,000 hectares of land were under water, 47,000 homes were destroyed, and 34,000 cattle died.

The disaster accelerated plans for the implementation of the proposed Delta Plan, begun in 1957 and completed in the mid eighties. The Plan called for construction on a massive scale: primary dams facing the sea; secondary, backup dams closing the estuaries; sluices; locks; storm-surge barriers; highways, bike paths, and bridges. The sea wall created by this complex abridges the coastline by some 700 kilometers, creating freshwater reservoirs, combating salinity in the water, and establishing new areas for recreation. GR5 passes over two of the primary dams of the Delta Plan, the Haringvlietdam and the Brouwersdam. On the Haringvlietdam is the Delta Expo—an exhibition devoted to the Delta Plan, and a must-see stop for the GR5 walker.

Grote Routepad 5 (GR5's Dutch/Flemish name) passes through three provinces of the Netherlands—South Holland, Zeeland, and North Brabant. Most of the walk is through Zeeland, a set of natural or man-made islands and peninsulas separated by the fingers of estuaries and canals, and crisscrossed by dams, bridges, and ferries. The clayey soil GR5 traverses is worked agriculturally as pastureland and for some crops, especially potatoes. There is also industry here, although, except for striking views of the refineries at Europoort, the walker sees little of it. Zeeland is also known for goldsmithing.

Holland as a whole boasts 4,339 kilometers of navigable waterways—3,487 of them canals—and the GR5 walker is never far from some body of water or other. There are four primary implications of this fact: fish, water birds, boats, and water sports.

Commercial fishing in Holland has declined since the 1930s, but the sports angler is very much in evidence, and both markets and menus feature eel, cod, sole, mackerel, and of course, herring, as well as oysters and mussels.

Gulls, herons, egrets, terns, bank swallows, oyster magpies, swans, and a great variety of ducks populate the canals, ponds, and marshes among which GR5 wends its way. Along the shoreline of Holland (as well as in the interior), certain areas have been designated *Natuurreservaaten*, nature preserves, where birds, including many rare species, are protected.

The number of boats along the waterways of Holland is legion, and their variety is stunning. Perhaps the most distinctive—and the most wonderful—are the long canal boats, long as a city block to a New Yorker's eye, and virtually all hold. A tiny house-cabin sits astern or on top of the low-slung hold cover, though many of these boats have been converted into full-scale houseboats, their holds turned into living quarters.

Also dotting the waterways are the extravagantly colored sails of sailboards and we saw land sailboarding as well, on skateboards. The Dutch have an ingenious way of hitching their sailboard carriers to their bicycles; they pedal down the many bike paths of Holland, trailing their long sailboards, heading for a windy body of water.

There are two bikes for every three people in the Netherlands, and there are about 10,000 kilometers of bike routes. The bicycle is, of course, as Dutch a symbol as wooden shoes, Hans Brinker's silver skates, or the boy with his finger in the dike (the latter two, by the way, are inventions of an American's imagination), and Netherlanders of every age, size, and shape ride everything from no-gear clunkers to fifteen-speed racers—alone, in small groups, and as members of clubs sporting the latest in cycling gear.

The GR5 walker may come to envy the natives on their cycles, gliding along smoothly and seemingly effortlessly, because the walking in Holland is possibly the most difficult along the entire GR5 route. "How can that be?" people ask. "Isn't Holland tabletop flat and almost entirely paved?" The answer is yes, and that is precisely the problem.

Walking long stretches of relentlessly flat trail is extremely tiring—and hard on the body. It is physically tiring—you use the same set of muscles all the time. It is mentally tiring—you can see straight on to where you are going; there are no surprises up ahead. The pavement underfoot—and much of the GR5 in Holland is bike path, a smooth stone or asphalt surface—adds to the problem; it is not a surface that gives at all underfoot as you plod onward at a steady pace. The constant pounding to your feet, shins, and knees is further exacerbated by the heavy backpack, although of course it feels heavier now than it will after a few weeks of walking.

There are ways of dealing with the problem of walking in the Netherlands. First of all, as you walk, change things—and keep changing things. Quicken your pace, then slow it down. Lengthen, then shorten, your stride. Shift your pack higher up on your back for a while; then let it sit lower.

Stop frequently, especially at first. The straight, smooth path ahead of you is no incentive to stopping, so you may need to make a concerted effort to do so. Whenever possible, rest your legs in an elevated position—you can always use your pack for a foot rest—and do some stretches and flexes that use your muscles in a new way. Keep your eyes peeled for the fluttering flags that mark cafés and stop for some good Dutch coffee or, even better, Dutch beer—or Genever, if you dare. We devised the Megawalker's Absolute Law of Travel here in Holland, a guiding principle that served us well on coastal plain and Alpine slopes, from the gray North Sea to the azure Mediterranean—to wit: "The unentered café is not worth the ground it stands on."

The hardship of walking in the Netherlands might lead one to recommend biking the GR5 here instead of doing it on foot, except that there are parts of the GR5 route that are accessible *only* by walking, and certainly the experience of walking provides a unique feel for the central facts of the Dutch landscape—as well as a clear look inside Dutch homes through all those sparkling picture windows (sometimes you must peer past elaborately designed stitched screens).

The experience of walking in the Netherlands provides the inescapable feeling that you are in country that, except for the works of man, would be virtually underwater much of the time; fully one-third of Holland is below sea level at high tide.

There are constant reminders of this. Along GR5 are polders and canals, dikes and windmills dating, in great measure, from the fourteenth to the eighteenth centuries, while the huge, modern breakwaters of the Delta Plan, recalling one of the worst natural disasters in recent history, give dramatic evidence of the tenuous protection these manmade works provide. Like people living below a dormant volcano, the Dutch insist on staying home, even if home is ringed around by danger.

They have their reasons. The landscape looks, unabashedly, like all those paintings by Cuyp, van Ruysdael, Hobbema, Van Goyen. The dune grasses and tall poplars that line the road (and serve as windbreaks) may date from just a few years ago—only 8 percent of the Netherlands is wooded, and that is planted—but you have seen them in paintings from the seventeenth century, and the picture they frame is familiar.

Americans will rightfully feel a sense of familiarity about many things Dutch. In the eastern United States, in particular, many place names, especially along the Hudson Valley, are of Dutch origin, and fractured Dutch is still in evidence in some of the most resonant names in New York City—Brooklyn, the Bronx, Harlem. The distinctive gingerbread embellishment of the wooden houses along the Hudson is matched by the curlicue look of the wood trimming on the brick houses of Zeeland, and sometimes by elaborate flourishes in the brickwork itself.

Americans owe a good measure of gratitude to the Dutch nation and people, who have figured prominently at important moments in our history. It was the Netherlands, after all, that gave a brief haven to the Pilgrim Fathers after they fled England and before they embarked for Plymouth. John Adams was the first American ambassador to the Netherlands where, in 1782, he negotiated a loan that made an important difference to the young American nation. The local Frisian government, in fact, was in favor of formal recognition of the new country and persuaded the central Netherlands government to grant it—the first sovereign state to do so.

The number of Americans of Dutch origin is enormous, and many among them became prominent and powerful. Martin Van Buren's family came from the town of Buren, in Gelderland, well off the GR5 route. But on Day 7 of the walk across the Netherlands, the GR5 walker passes near the village of Oud-Vossemeer, original home of the Vanrosevelt family—known as Roosevelt in the United States.

The GR5 route from Hoek van Holland to Bergen-op-Zoom is 157 kilometers long. It divagates. At the very outset, the walker veers east in order to find a crossing over the Nieuwe Waterweg that will enable him to return west. GR5 then continues to dip southwest before zigzagging mostly east and then mostly southeast to Bergen-op-Zoom and on to the border. It isn't exactly a straightforward beginning on the route toward Nice.

It takes eight days.

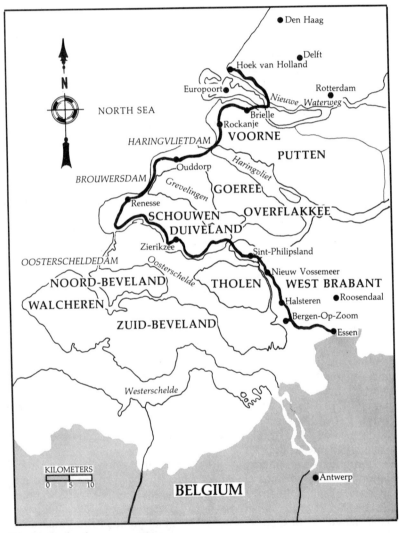

The Netherlands

The Netherlands

Day 1	Hoek van Holland to Brielle	22 km	5-½ hr
Day 2	Brielle to Rockanje	19 km	4-¾ hr
Day 3	Rockanje to Ouddorp	19 km	4-¾ hr
Day 4	Ouddorp to Renesse	17 km	4-¼ hr
Day 5	Renesse to Zierikzee	28 km	7 hr
Day 6	Zierikzee to Sint-Philipsland	21 km	5-¼ hr
Day 7	Sint—Philipsland to Bergen-op-Zoom	31 km	7-¾ hr
Day 8	Bergen-op-Zoom (layover)		

Day 1: Hoek van Holland to Brielle (ca. 22 km, 5-½ hr)

Hoek van Holland, the corner of Holland. Whether you arrive by train from almost anywhere on the continent (via connections) or by boat from England, the starting point for the walk down Europe is the same: the train station, which doubles as the ferry port, and which is equipped with a currency exchange and a cafeteria-style restaurant.

Emerging from the station, turn left on the platform to egress. Past the edge of the platform, you get a good view of the lively port, bustling with water traffic headed for Rotterdam or the open sea; beyond, across the Nieuwe Waterweg, you can see some of the installations of Europoort.

The street called Harwichweg is at a right angle to the port; turn right on it. Stay on Harwichweg—past an intersection that points toward the center of town, through a residential area—until you arrive at Rijpstraat. Turn right—this is all still residential—and proceed to the camping area.

GR5 begins here. The sign reads "ANWB Wandelroute, GR5, Hoek van Holland–Bergen op Zoom." Bergen-op-Zoom, now the last major stopping point on the GR5 in Holland, used to be the start of the trail to Nice. But in 1983, on the occasion of its one hundredth anniversary, the ANWB (Netherlands Tourist Authority) decided to fill in the missing link and make GR5 truly a trail from sea to sea.

From the GR5 sign, the walk down Europe seems to begin in a town park. Bike paths also wend their way among trees and lawns, and a bridle path is covered with soft wood chips. Fittingly, the route starts as a flat path, lined by Queen Anne's lace, following a narrow canal.

Throughout this first day, the walker confronts many of the facts of life of megawalking the GR5. For the next 107 days, he will be looking at and for red and white stripes. Right from the outset, the walker will learn to hunt for them almost anywhere and in any form—head-on, sideways, on signpost poles, sides of structures, underfoot, on tree trunks, behind him. Right from the outset, the walker will find that the trail marking doesn't always work as it should.

He will also learn, starting today, that GR5 alternates between town and country, suburb and field, highway and country road and dirt path. After the first stretch through the city park of Hoek van Holland, GR5 emerges onto a road, crosses it, then enters a narrow lane. Suddenly, you are in countryside. Hares race through the fields. Farm buildings and sheds stand on the horizon. For us, the entry into this rural area coincided with the departure of the sun. The day grew gray, chill, foggy. The landscape softened, became mistily eerie, a Dutch painting. Then just as suddenly, we emerged from this painting onto a sleek new highway.

GR5 crosses the Oranjekanaal and stretches along Oranjedijk. Here you meet another fact of life of GR5—gates. From here to Nice, you will be opening, and making certain that you completely close, a variety of gates and stiles as you travel a GR5 right-of-way through somebody or other's private property. The reason for this first gate will be clear if you see the numerous benign cows we saw when we passed through. Lambs, goats, and rabbits also abound in this clearly agricultural stretch of walking, while along the canal you can spot grebes, ducks, and swans. The day we were there, we saw a nesting swan, with the father swimming protectively nearby—a rare sight.

Civilization looms again at the outskirts of Maasluis. GR5 gains a high dike and proceeds between two great thoroughfares—railroad track to the left, the traffic-filled Nieuwe Waterweg to the right—before arriving in the square of the town. A canal makes an artery through the

Brielle, The Netherlands. Photo by Ginger Harmon.

middle of the square and is lined on both sides with warehouses whose gabled roofs and high, peaked loading entrances come right out of the seventeenth century. Also of note is the town's *grote kerk*, or cathedral. Maasluis is a good place to pause for refreshment. Situated between the Nieuwe Waterweg and the Nieuwe Maas, it is a lively port; from here, the walker takes the ferry over to Rozenburg.

Rozenburg, laid out neatly on a narrow spit of land, offers a windmill near its church. GR5 does not actually pass the mill, so if you want to see your first Dutch windmill, you must make a slight detour. GR5, meanwhile, crosses the Calandkanaal on a high bridge, then crosses another bridge, dips down to the canal, and heads on toward Brielle.

The outskirts of Brielle are a network of canals lined by pleasure boats tethered in front of mobile homes and cottages for vacationers at the Brielse Meer. The town itself has played an important role in Netherlands history, for here the Martyrs of Gorkum were executed in 1572, their deaths a signal for the uprising against the Spanish occupation. Brielle maintains numerous vestiges of its past—in particular, the fortifications, the old houses lining the canal, and the fifteenth century Saint Catherine's church, still unfinished. It is an enchanting place, a quaint, quintessentially Dutch village—a good stopping point for the first stage of the walk across Europe.

Day 2: Brielle to Rockanje (ca. 19 km, 4-¾ hr)

GR5 turns west at the start of this day's walk, curling around the North Sea coast of Voorne island. The area is a seaside resort; in addition to all the water sports available on the sea and inland lakes, there is a major nature preserve here—some 2,000 acres of dunes with flora and fauna unique in Europe.

Despite the hearty breakfast routinely served in Dutch hotels (not just bread, rolls, butter, jam and coffee, but boiled eggs, slices of meat, and cheese as well) the walker would do well to buy some provisions before leaving Brielle. It is certainly possible to leave GR5 and detour into Oostvoorne for lunch, but carrying a picnic gives you a choice at midday, and food you don't eat today may be needed the next day or the next. It is time in any event to begin to get into the habit of keeping food in the pack.

It is only some 7 kilometers to Oostvoorne, following between the Oosterlandse Rak canal, dotted with pleasure boats tied up along the shore, and the flat, flat farm and grazing land of the Polder Klein Oosterlund. At a major intersection—four narrow lanes converging— make a sharp right toward Kruiningergors, a recreation area filled with some 14,000 bungalows—prefabricated for the most part, quite compact, and very close together. The site is right on the Brielse Meer, a large lake, and provides weekend and vacation homes for Rotterdamers, who find it as easy to commute to Europoort from here as from Rotterdam itself.

We learned this from the proprietor of a café we stopped in for a midmorning break. The café was perhaps more properly a nightclub, but the owner graciously opened it for us. Though it is not true that "everyone in Holland speaks English," this gentleman certainly did, having lived in Detroit for some time and having worked in a rodeo near Kansas City for a while. What is pretty certain is that those Hollanders who speak English speak it extremely well—if occasionally, as in this case, with a decided Western twang peppered with Motown street talk.

Just at the end of the lines of bungalows and caravans, GR5 suddenly gains a large rotary intersection of a major highway. It is here that a spur trail from Europoort joins GR5, coming in from the right. Veer left toward Oostvoorne, following a long, straight, promenadelike walk, called, in fact, Boulevard. It offers distant views of some of the industrial structures of Europoort—huge oil tanks and tall container cranes, standing like awkward giant birds on the far shore of the Oostvoornse Meer beyond the Hartelkanaal.

Leaving Boulevard, the route begins to wander out along the dunes; now is the time, if you have decided to lunch indoors, to turn left into Oostvoorne. It is a pleasant town, with restored remains of a castle dating back to the year 1100, but offering as well such up-to-date facilities as banks, a post office, a VVV office (for obtaining hotel lists, if needed), and a slew of *frituurs*.

A *frituur* is an extremely useful Dutch snack shop featuring the sweetly flavored fried foods the Dutch favor—with more than a touch of former colonial cuisines mixed in. So, for example, a deep-fried meatloaf and onion combination will be garnished with a peanut sauce. A so-called hamburger might actually be veal sausage and will invariably be topped with sweet mayonaise. And always accompanying these snacks will be what seems virtually the Dutch national dish—French fried potatoes, very good, and eaten in heaps at meals or by pedestrians on the street.

From Oostvoorne, GR5 tracks along the Duinen van Voorne, the famous dunes with their unique ecology. The uniqueness derives from the fact that no drinking water is pumped from here; the soil thus retains its natural moisture, and vegetation and animals can be found here that are nowhere else in Holland. GR5 also passes two lush dune lakes, Tenellaplas and Breede Water, then stretches through an area filled with greenhouses—the Dutch call this "glass farming," a more lyrical term.

Rockanje is the other resort town of the area, with plenty of accomodations, restaurants, and shops. The town hall exhibits remains from the Iron Age and the Roman era. The oldest building still extant is the Dutch Reformed church in the town's center, built around 1550. The nine polders of Rockanje were reclaimed between 1300 and 1500; the walker should take note that he is standing—and walking—on pretty recent turf.

Day 3: Rockanje to Ouddorp
(ca. 19 km, 4-¾ hr)

This stage brings the GR5 walker across the great Haringvlietdam into Zeeland province and tracks the wide nature preserve known as De Kwade Hoek. No walker should miss the Delta Expo, at the far end of the Haringvlietdam.

The way out of Rockanje begins along a pleasant, wooded path; keep an eagle eye for the quick right turn off the route, at a white house with the word "t'Zandeke" painted on it. The right turn leads to the beach, where GR5 turns left along the sand to the dam; ahead, the walker can make out the seventeen sluice gates of this massive complex.

It is a long, unrelenting walk of nearly 5 kilometers across the dam, but the Delta Expo building at the opposite end offers a coffee shop for refreshment. Here also are exhibits, models, and maps that give a striking picture of the complex system of water management at work in the Netherlands. The history of the Delta Plan is told in slide shows and in a stirring movie about the disastrous flood of 1953. There is an English version of the movie, and Expo personnel will likely be agreeable to showing it for the English-speaking walker, but the movie is so dramatic in its documentary simplicity that even seeing it in Dutch, as we did, makes an impression.

The Haringvlietdam and the entire Delta Plan are about a good deal more than safety, though keeping the sea at bay is the major consideration. Water management, the salinity of the water being managed, and shipping are also of vital concern. The flow regulation scheme for the battery of Haringvliet sluices—seventeen of them, each 56 meters across—is determined by such factors as the supply-and-demand laws for fresh water (for domestic, industrial, and agricultural use); the movement of water in polders and recreational areas; wastewater discharges; the removal of water from inland polders; and the prevention of seawater incursion.

The Delta Plan is intrinsically linked to all the other water management works of Holland. Since water will find its level, what gets stopped from egress here must eventually egress somewhere else. Here, simply, is how the Haringvlietdam plays its part:

The Haringvliet is fed by the final waters of the Rhine and Meuse. Originally, the Rhine is supplied by the meltwaters of glaciers in Switzerland and Austria. This in itself is a fluctuating variable, but the Rhine is also fed along the way by adjoining waters in the various countries it flows through. The water level in the Meuse, meanwhile, depends on rainfall in France, Belgium, Luxembourg, and the Netherlands.

The level of flow of these waters determines whether the Haringvliet sluices will be open or closed, and by how much. If the flow is high, the sluices are opened; often the polder pumps must work all out to prevent flooding. When the flow is low, the Haringvliet closes. The water is directed into the Nieuwe Waterweg and beyond, although if too much water is discharged north, it could cause strong currents and could threaten floods. At an average water level, the sluice openings must be maintained at just the right calibration to ensure that enough water goes to the Nieuwe Waterweg and keeps out the salt.

About as remarkable as the dam itself is the story of its sixteen-year construction—a story that Delta Expo unfolds in its exhibits. An artificial island was built in the middle of the estuary, and in the final phase, a cable railway was constructed to drop concrete blocks in place. It is possible to take a guided tour into one of the engine rooms of the Haringvlietdam and get an insider's look at the largest hydraulic engineering work in this part of Holland.

From Delta Expo, GR5 moves along roads to Havenhoofd, at the edge of De Kwade Hoek. The day we were there, we had hoped for a lunch stop at Havenhoofd and had brought no provisions. But Havenhoofd is simply a cluster of houses, with no restaurant or frituur in sight. It looked like a long way to the next meal when we heard what sounded like a Good Humor wagon bell, coming from a slow-moving truck. The truck turned out to be, providentially, a kind of circuit market, stocked with produce, a great variety of canned goods, beer, soda, and wine. Thus provisioned, we were able to enjoy a lavish picnic on the dunes, and although we were to see these traveling groceries on more than one occasion throughout Europe, they are not to be counted on.

De Kwade Hoek is a long stretch of dune. GR5 goes along it on the Oostdijk, which leads into Ouddorp. (A shorter variant of the trail goes across the dunes. Where it heads back up to the road, turn left into town.) Ouddorp is a pretty place that fans out from a main square in which sits an off-center tower. In the square and along some of the streets are elegant, antique structures. The town has a number of pensions for lodging, and a good array of eateries and taverns.

The war came here. A monument to the fallen of 1940–1945 lists the names of the local people who died then; two died in Ouddorp, the others in places as distant as Oswiecim—Auschwitz.

Day 4: Ouddorp to Renesse (ca. 17 km, 4-¼ hr)

A day of dunes and one long, long dam as GR5 edges the grey North Sea, then crosses to the island of Schouwen and begins to cut southward.

Head out of Ouddorp and up the dunes. At last you are really along the open sea. The beach along it is wide and low, with curling surf. The dunes are another nature preserve, so GR5 keeps to their land side, between sand and polder. A tall lighthouse tower signals your route and breaks the flatness of the landscape.

Grasses and shrubs hold the dunes and afford some privacy to the beach bungalows tucked just over their crest. On the polder side of the route, woods obscure the parking lots for seaside visitors. The plantings are home to many birds; on a fine day, the walker will hear their songs—although they sing in Dutch, of course. The dunes swing around and end at the Brouwersdam.

Built between 1963 and 1972, the Brouwersdam has no sluices. Rather, with its backup, the Grevelingendam, Brouwersdam has turned the Grevelingen estuary into a saltwater lake and serves as a causeway linking the islands of Goeree and Schouwen. The GR5 walker will come to know the Brouwersdam well because he will spend what may seem like years walking across it.

On the day we were there, a cheery sunny Sunday, this walk provided an eyeful. On seaside, lakeside, and all along the wide roadway, Netherlanders were taking their ease. Fishermen after eel, surfboarders, sailboarders, land sailboarders, cyclists, strollers, sitters on the beach, drivers of motorcycles and fast cars lined the waterfront and the raised dike that divides the waters. There were birds aplenty as well: seagulls swooping overhead and black-capped terns pointing their bills to the water. It was very lively, and at intervals we came upon the odd refreshment van—instant outdoor cafés from which to watch the world go by.

When the dam finally does end, GR5 makes a sharp right along a highway, again between dramatic dunes on one side and green polder on the other, to Renesse, a seaside resort known for its good sand beach and its popularity with Germans. The castle of Moermond is just 1 kilometer out of town—if you feel like walking some more. Constructed of brick, the castle dates from the sixteenth and seventeenth centuries and encloses a fourteenth-century portal.

Day 5: Renesse to Zierikzee (ca. 28 km, 7 hr)

A long day, in which the GR5 walker cuts across the Schouwen-Duiveland, then turns eastward along dikes to reach Zierikzee, one of the most enchanting towns in the Netherlands, if not in all of Europe.

From Renesse to Haamstede, the route follows brick-topped lane and narrow paved road. GR5 avoids the center of the village, but Haamstede can provide the walker a second cup of morning coffee—or a first, if you got a really early start, which is recommended—and is an important decision point for the day's walk.

A look at the maps shows that GR5 now makes a wide half circle around Haamstede to come down to the Oosterschelde; it then backtracks along the dike to Burghsluis. It is a walk that edges the town, then goes alongside a thoroughfare until it tops the dike. From here the walker has a view of the Oosterscheldedam, the final link in the Delta Plan. In fact, by the time construction on the Oosterscheldedam got under way, conservation groups had begun agitating against some aspects of the Plan. The outcry was so great that the plan was modified. Oosterscheldedam is therefore not a complete barrier, but allows tidal flow and creates environmental havens for much of the sea and plant life displaced by the Delta Plan.

A second look at the map, however, shows that the walker can improvise a route from Haamstede to the Oosterschelde, reaching the water further to the east—at Burghsluis perhaps, where the Rijkswatersraat (government water management authority) has its Oosterschelde offices; or at Kundekerke, further along the coast; or even at Schelphoek. Slicing this looping meander of the GR5 would lop off a good bit of distance and save some time. In addition, it is no real loss in terms of trail surface; GR5's official route is mostly on road also.

In any event, the highway walking ends in the nature preserve called De Schelphoek. From here, the trail goes up onto the dike—passing through a series of badly marked fences—and through waving grass along its slopes.

GR5 follows the dike almost the full 7 kilometers into Zierikzee. It is a dramatic and beautiful walk along the gray waters of the estuary, lapping regularly up the slope of the dike. (Here is the perfect place to take the picture of yourself with a finger in the dike.) The high grass changes to a pavement, sometimes of concrete blocks, sometimes of pebbles and tar. Surf fishermen cast for sole off this dike, while on the land side, sheep and lambs graze on grass that is strikingly green beside the dark, shadowy water. Soon the walker notices that, for the first time along GR5, there is no sound or sight of cars, nor even any bicycles—only the foot traffic of fishermen, some strollers, and the megawalker himself.

Though the earth is very flat here, the slope of the dike obscures the view inland; you can really only see out to the water, except for an occasional glimpse of a tower ahead. Until suddenly, the trail pops up over the dike and there is Zierikzee, a town that seems to have stopped changing in the sixteenth century, spread before you.

Head for it, and spend what time you can seeing its sights. Zierikzee has existed for more than eleven centuries; at the height of its power, in the fifteenth century, it was a strongly fortified town surrounded by a moat and enclosed by walls whose gates were closed to foreigners. The tower visible from the dike is the Sint-Lievensmonstertoren, the bell tower of the Gothic cathedral built in 1454 and destroyed in 1832. Another spire adorns the beautiful *stadhuis*, the town hall; on Thursday, market day in Zierikzee, a carillon rings from the tower. Walk through the former gates of the town—Noordhavenpoort, Zuidhavenpoort, and Nobelpoort—and admire the façades of the houses, especially along Havenplein.

Day 6: Zierikzee to Sint-Philipsland (ca. 21 km, 5-¼ hr)

GR5 edges the southeast coast of Schouwen-Duiveland (the Duiveland section), then ferries across to the small created island called Sint-Philipsland, and again edges the sea to the town of the same name.

Out of Zierikzee and across polder back to dike, GR5 cuts upland again to reach Oosterland. The roads that cross the surrounding polders are lined with graceful poplars, and the agricultural fields are divided by them. The trees, planted very close together, form a flexible barrier against the winds that would otherwise shoot across this flatness, bearing off whatever was in their way.

From Oosterland, GR5 again wanders among polders, then gains the dike and proceeds inside it to Zijpe, a few buildings that serve the ferry crossing. Happily, one of the buildings is a restaurant, in case the walker has to wait for the ferry, which plies back and forth across the narrow Mastgat.

From the ferry landing on Sint-Philipsland island, the walker follows the roadway, turning sharply right to gain the dike and follow it all the way into town.

"Town" may be an optimistic word; Sint-Philipsland is really a small village, just inside the very low dike, which has a windmill perched on it.

It was a cold, dank evening when we were there, with thick fog rolling in from the water. We settled happily into the cozy bar-restaurant of the hotel, putting ourselves in the hands of the cheerful proprietors, who served us a hearty Dutch dinner. It was a particularly welcome dinner; in Oosterland, Zijpe, and all along the day's route, all shops and eateries had been closed, and our nutrition for the day had consisted of a few crackers and some breakfast rolls we had squirreled away for just such an eventuality. A few cheerful men were ranged at the bar, and one kept feeding coins to the jukebox. It was a tranquil ending to what had been, for us, a long day of harsh weather.

Suddenly, bedlam. In came a large group of people, some forty strong—men, women, and children—hailing one another, laughing, ordering beer and Genever. Each person was equipped with a box looking something like a geiger counter, with a handle, paper tape and needle, and a clock on the side. Meanwhile, half a dozen men broke from the crowd, settled themselves at a round table in the center, and waited for the others to report.

It was a group of colombophiles, owners of homing pigeons trained for racing. This is a sport notable for the extreme lack of effort required by participating humans, apart from raising and lowering glasses. The pigeons, however, had earlier been trucked to starting points and then released. Upon a bird's arrival at the homing point, a marked rubber ring was removed from its leg and dropped into the clock-box to record the time. The Sint-Philipsland hotel was the center for reporting the results, and the working group at the round table was the squad of judges, calculating handicaps and recording the final scores before too much beer had been consumed.

The sport of pigeon racing is particularly popular in nearby Belgium, where an estimated 123,000 colombophiles stage some 25,000 races annually. Betting on the sport is said to be pervasive and often for high stakes. In the bar in Sint-Philipsland, it certainly looked to us like a congenial way to spend time, though perhaps the pigeons would not agree.

Day 7: Sint-Philipsland to Bergen-op-Zoom (ca. 31 km, 7¾-hr)

In fact, the walker can make this a 22-kilometer day as far as Oude Molen/Halsteren, where lodging is available, and continue on to Bergen-op-Zoom the next day, still arriving in good time to both enjoy and make use of the city. It is also possible to edit the 9 kilometers from Halsteren to Bergen; a look at the GR5 route on the map shows that it is a circuitous way of avoiding the heart of surburban life, and a variety of other routes is certainly available. Bergen itself is a good place for provisioning, chores, and a pleasant rest, so however you get there, you should look forward to making it a longer-than-usual stop.

And however you get to Bergen, there is the feeling—if not the fact—that you are moving away from the North Sea; the next ocean you see will be the Mediterranean, a long way away.

GR5 proceeds along the dike out of Sint-Philipsland, then skirts the highway for a while until it crosses the Eendracht. This narrow body of water forms part of the Scheldt-Rhine Canal, cutting through southward to Antwerp and beyond.

The landscape now turns decidedly agricultural, as the walker enters the western part of the province of Noord Brabant. Past the village of Nieuw Vossemeer (Oud-Vossemeer, in the distance, is the original homestead of the Roosevelt clan), walking the slightly elevated dike between polders, gazing at poplars and windmills against the horizon, possibly too late for tulips but not for lilacs, the walker comes to Kladde, a minute village that beckons with its café (closed, of course, the day we passed by).

From here, GR5 winds confusingly; it seems as if the trail builders' purpose is to loop around the increasingly evident suburbs of Bergen-op-Zoom. At Oude-Molen, the walker crosses the road that leads directly into the center of Bergen; Halsteren lies along here, with the possibility of lodging right on the highway. GR5, however, continues to zig and zag to avoid the encroaching urban sprawl, passing through a *recreatieterrein*, a pleasant park with soft paths through woods.

The urban reality cannot be avoided, however. GR5 passes over major highways and enters a complex of apartment houses and shops before arriving at the Bergen-op-Zoom railroad station. From here, it is an easy walk to the *grote markt*, the beautiful main square of Bergen-op-Zoom.

Day 8: Bergen-op-Zoom (layover day)

Bergen-op-Zoom is a city with its own anthem, an exhortation to solidarity dating from the Spanish siege in 1588, which the city successfully withstood. It had been, since 1287, the seat of a powerful seigniory and later the seat of an important annual market fair. In 1533, Bergen became a marquisate, and the marquis's court, the *markiezenhof*, remains one of the town's most splendid sights. A fortified city through most of its history, Bergen lost its ramparts in 1867, but the boulevards that loop around the center trace their path.

After a week along the dunes and dikes and villages of the North Sea coast, Bergen-op-Zoom seems a metropolis. In fact, it is a small port, linked to the eastern Scheldt by canal. Today, it is best known for the show it puts on at Carnival time, and for the asparagus and anchovies cultivated in its vicinity.

But there is plenty to see here, starting with the grote markt itself, ringed by restaurants with sidewalk cafés tailor-made for the foot weary. The stadhuis, markiezenhof—which houses a cultural center, Sint-Gertrudiskerk (Saint Gertrud's church), and the gatehouse prison are other major attractions. All are within a short walk of grote markt. The VVV is just off the grote markt, and the walker will be happy to find GR5 topo-gids here as well as information about Bergen itself.

Bergen seems a metropolis for other reasons as well. The museum in the markiezenhof devotes some galleries to exhibitions, and there may be a concert on. Americans will feel at home walking through ethnic neighborhoods—a number of workers from Mediterranean countries have settled here—and enjoying the hugely popular restaurants some of the Italian immigrants have opened in Bergen.

It's a good place for chores. In Bergen's shops, you can replenish supplies, and at its modern post office, you can mail home those items you thought you might like to have with you but that clearly have been unnecessarily weighty in the backpack. Phone calls are easy to arrange from here, and if your hotel room has a radio, you can pick up the BBC World Service and get some news.

If your room does not have a radio, you can get news anyway. Bergen stocks American and British newspapers and magazines.

Moreover, Bergen-op-Zoom is something of a tourist center, offering water-bus tours along the Scheldt to Antwerp and Zierikzee. Numerous cafés and clubs (including some jazz clubs) cater to the tourist trade, providing, especially on weekends or in the season, a nightlife that will seem positively glamorous after Brielle, Rockanje, Renesse, and the like.

7
Belgium: One Nation, Two Identities

For the walker, the border between Holland and Belgium is unmarked and unapparent, yet there are differences between these two low countries. For one thing, Belgium is smaller, although the Grote Routepad 5 traverses much more of Belgium than of Holland. The topography is subtly different; geology and climate have divided Belgium and the Netherlands since Pleistocene times. The Quarternary era was the last time Belgium was covered by the sea; it has since always formed part of the Continent. The Netherlands, on the other hand, might be underwater even now were it not for the works of man. This fact, and corresponding differences in climate, have created a distinct morphology in Belgium, and this in turn has influenced the patterns of human occupation here.

Up to a certain point, however, the political history of Belgium is not unlike that of the Netherlands. The Belgians as well as the Dutch have been ruled in turn by Rome, the Frankish kingdom, the Holy Roman Empire, Lotharingia, a set of fragmented feudal principalities, the Burgundians, the Spanish Habsburgs, the Austrian Habsburgs, and the French. Belgium has been an independent nation only since 1830 and it has been a tenuous independence at that: German troops occupied the country in both world wars of this century. Flanders fields in World War I and the Ardennes in World War II are well-known battlefields; the damage to Belgium on both occasions was considerable. Belgium's empire, which flourished in the nineteenth century, lost its last great glory, the Congo, in 1960. Perhaps because of this recent history, Belgium has played an active role in the European unity movement and has profited from the recovery that the movement has helped to bring about.

Although its coal industry has declined since the end of the war, Belgium remains a highly industrialized nation at the heart of industrial western Europe. While its soil is relatively poor, an industrious agricultural community regularly realizes a high yield. Most of the country's gross national product comes from commerce, trade, and tourism.

The Kingdom of Belgium (Koninkrijk Belgie in Flemish and Royaume de Belgique in French, to accommodate the country's two major languages) is the nation in the middle. It is a natural intersection between East and West, northern and southern Europe. People and ideas have crossed back and forth here since prehistory, and the nation remains an exemplar of the synthesis of Europe. It is a nation of two cultures (and a third recognized minority), a fact that has produced both an enrichment of the national heritage and a certain amount of social and political tension.

Memories of war abound in Belgium. Spa, "pearl of the Ardennes," thanks its heroes of two world wars. Photo by Ginger Harmon.

A linguistic line—and to a certain extent, a cultural demarcation— runs across Belgium from west to east. To the north, more or less, is Flanders, inhabited by the Flemish speaking Flemings, a Teutonic people, mostly Catholic. To the south of the line is Wallonie, inhabited by the French-speaking Walloons, a Celtic-Latin people, nominally Catholic but known above all for being anticlerical. The identities of both populations date from at least the third century. The bickering, tension, and occasionally strong separatist sentiments that divide the two peoples have gone on almost since then and became particularly noticeable when the two cultures were fused into the single nation of Belgium in the nineteenth century.

The differences between Flemings and Walloons, and the desire of each to preserve its separate identity, have been a major fact of Belgian political life in the twentieth century—with occasional overtones of violence. Wallonie is larger in area than Flanders, but the francophone population is less numerous—some four and a half million to five and a half million Flemings. In addition to having a higher birth rate, Flanders typically enjoyed a faster process of industrial development than did Wallonie. The skeptical Walloons have traditionally voted Socialist, while the Flemish majority has tended to favor the Christian Socialist Party. Tensions flared in the sixties, with a strike—occasionally violent—around Liège in 1960-1961, and again in 1966-1968, with linguistic clashes at the University of Louvain. Both episodes provoked government crises.

Through a succession of legislative initiatives over the years, the Belgian parliament (Belgium is a constitutional monarchy) federalized the nation according to linguistic borders. There are four federal entities: Flanders, Wallonie, the German-speaking cantons in the southeastern corner of Belgium, and the capital city of Brussels, which is officially bilingual in Flemish and French. GR5 does not pass through Brussels, but it traverses all of the three other linguistic areas.

For us, the walk across Europe hit a certain stride in Belgium, as we overcame weather, language barriers, and the problem of losing our way. It was here that we formulated several of the important guidelines for the trip. Foremost among these was the First Law of the Trail, to wit: "If you haven't seen a trail marker for 200 meters, even 100 meters, then no matter how pleasant the path under your feet, no matter how sure you are that you are going in the right direction, no matter that this is absolutely the only possible way the trail *could* be routed, go back." Retreat to the last marker, look around again, check the topo-guide, check the map, try another way until you *do* see a marker. The time you spend at this will be far less than the time you spend coming back or rerouting yourself after having gone kilometers out of your way. Only once in our entire 2,400-kilometer walk across Europe did we really get lost, and it was in Belgium, when we disregarded the First Law of the Trail.

It was also in Belgium that we first came upon the sacrosanctity of lunch, a fact of life that is even more pronounced in France and ridiculously pronounced in southern France. However, our experience of it in Belgium gave rise to the Primary Principle of the Sacrosanctity of Lunch: "The walker starved for lunch will, at midday, enter a town lacking cafés or restaurants at the precise hour that the food shop is closing." We were also able to formulate the corollary to this Principle, the Immutable Law of the Half-Day Closing: "Any town's scheduled half-day will occur on the day the walker arrives in that town." In Belgium, when you need something, get it as soon as you can—and always carry something to eat.

Belgium's cuisine is world renowned, although along the GR5, eating tends to be simple. As befits a cool, wet climate, there is an emphasis on rich and savory food, and sweets tend to be very sweet. Belgian chocolate, served everywhere and virtually always—including every time you order a cup of coffee—is extraordinary. Since chocolate is a particularly apt trail food, eat it with impunity.

Belgium is a beer lover's paradise. Beer is the national beverage, and Belgians have routinely held the European record for per capita consumption of suds. On one occasion, when the title was lost to Poland, a nationwide effort was launched to regain it, fueling a rare unity between Flemings and French-speaking Walloons, and by the following year, Belgium's undisputed first-place status was restored. The country boasts nearly 200 breweries and scores of local and regional nonlabel beers. Blonde, dark, sweet, bitter, fresh, aged, light or full-bodied: one of us tried hard to taste all the beers of Belgium; it was not possible, but the effort was delightful. Be sure to try Trappiste, brewed in Cistercian abbeys and a great advertisement for the contemplative life of the monastic order.

The itinerary for the walk across Belgium takes just over eighteen days—including a layover day in Liège. It is a walk of some 412 kilometers (256 miles) across five provinces: Antwerp, Brabant, Limburg, Liège, and Luxembourg. The direction is south/southeast, a direction which, in a sense, simply opposes the route of the Maas (Meuse, in Wallonie). On its arrival in Belgium from its source in the hills of eastern France, the Maas makes a wide meander north and west to empty into the Haringvliet in Holland. GR5 vaguely follows its bank, but goes against its flow.

Belgium is a country of lowlands and low plateaus, yet three topographic regions can be distinguished, and the walk across Belgium touches all three. On entering the country, you are in Low Belgium, where the route crosses a portion of the Kempen, the Campine Plain, a vast area once composed of heath and fen that tilts gently eastwards toward the sea. Between the Kempen's sandy hills and the city of Liège is Middle Belgium. Cross the Maas valley and enter the rolling hills and the forests of the Ardennes in High Belgium. Once a mountain range, the Ardennes is now a series of low, rounded plateaus and deep valleys. It is a heavily wooded region, and thick with history.

Generalities about national character are at best odious, at worst pernicious. Nevertheless, our impression of the Belgian people is at such variance with the silly stereotype of a dour, gloomy, cold-shouldering people that it bears some mention. It is the climate of Belgium that can be dour, gloomy, and cold; despite it, the people of Belgium are singularly cheerful, welcoming to strangers, cooperative, and affectionate. We did find that it was necessary for us to break the ice first—crack the first smile or utter the first hello—but once that was done, the response could not have been warmer.

In the areas we walked, Americans are infrequent tourists, and American walkers are a real oddity. Most people at first thought we were Dutch; when they heard us speak English, they assumed we were British. They were unfailingly polite to us on both counts. But when we announced that we were Americans, politeness gave way to something much deeper. We had the impression that for Belgians of a certain age, the part played by American soldiers in Belgium's World War II experience remains a vivid memory. From these people came an outpouring of what can only be called gratitude, which we, as surrogates for the soldiers who did the real work, felt almost embarrassed to receive.

8
Inland
to Flanders

In Flanders fields the poppies blow
Between the crosses, row on row
—John McCrae, 1915

So they do—not just in graveyards, but everywhere: in meadows, along the edges of fields, beside canals—brilliant red blossoms on graceful stems, fluttering in the wind. A single poppy flower seems a fragile thing, if gloriously beautiful; a field of poppies in the distance is a solid sea of scarlet.

Back when Veteran's Day was still called Armistice Day, World War I veterans, dressed in their doughboy uniforms and sporting American Legion hats, stood on the street corners of U.S. towns and sold red poppies made of crepe paper. Some of the veterans were mutilated— peg-legged or one-armed mostly—and the poppies they handed out recalled the particular horrors of the battles in Flanders fields.

Flanders fields saw action again in World War II, and in the fortieth summer after D-Day, the summer of our walk, there was abundant evidence of this. We repeatedly saw posters announcing the expected return of U.S. Army units that had liberated the towns along the route. At a crossroads near the village of Wiemesmeer, we missed the returning airmen by only one day; an unusual Saturday mass was being celebrated to give thanks for their imminent arrival.

Strolling across the now peaceful fields of Flanders, the GR5 walker will come to appreciate the poppies, despite their inescapable association with war, for their bursting brilliance against a backdrop of otherwise muted colors. Flanders is earth-toned all right: dark green in the lush fields and woods, brown in the mottled flanks of cows—the walker will see and be seen by more cows than people in crossing Flanders— gray in the achromatic Flemish villages and often dreary Flemish weather.

The summer of 1984 was an unusually wet summer all across the continent of Europe, but the Flemings took it in their stride. Each day, we asked any number of people when the sun would come out. The response was a cheerful shrug or the assurance that our walking, taking us south, would bring us to the region of sunshine. Our favorite answer came from the elderly woman who ran the dank café we happened on in the town of Westmalle.

The day was overcast and drizzly, and the café was unlit. Peering within, however, we saw a number of desultory drinkers, so we entered and asked, in French, for sandwiches and beer. Our presence caused even the somewhat grizzled barflies to look up warily, and when we explained who we were and what we were doing (Americans! Women! Walking!), the place burst into cheerfulness.

Madame remarked that it was not *beau temps* for a vacation—not good weather—and we agreed.

"When will the sun come?" Susanna then asked.

Madame's face lit up at once in a beaming smile. "Jamais!" she replied with obvious pride. "Jamais le soleil en Belgique! Jamais!" (There is never sun in Belgium! Never!)

Flanders—Vlaanderen—as defined by the law establishing linguistic frontiers for Belgium, consists of the provinces of East Flanders, West Flanders, Antwerp, Limburg, and the northern half of Brabant—excluding Brussels. But at its most extensive, during the Middle Ages, the historic county of Flanders stretched beyond its present-day territory to include parts of what are today France and the Netherlands. It was, in that era, the center of economic activity and political development in the Low Countries—so much so that, until this century, the name Flanders was routinely synonymous with Low Countries.

The county of Flanders was established in the ninth century as a fief under the French crown; it remained a French possession until the early sixteenth century. The independent-minded and powerful counts who ruled here soon came into conflict with the growing economic might of the guilds that controlled the profitable woolen textile industry. In the fourteenth century, the conflict grew into rebellion. The counts promptly turned to their liege lord, the King of France, for support, while the burghers of Ghent and Bruges allied themselves with the English. The turmoil produced the first democratic governments in northern Europe—a short-lived experience which ended in the fourteenth century when Flanders came under Burgundian rule and lost its independence altogether.

The harsh rule of the Hapsburgs, who inherited Flanders from Burgundy in 1482, led to economic and cultural decline and, in the sixteenth century, to general revolt throughout the Low Countries. "Pacified" by the Spanish, Flanders was separated from the northern provinces and suffered further decline. The region turned into a battlefield, seeing repeated warfare between the Spanish Habsburgs and the French. In fact, France succeeded in seizing many areas of southern Flanders— the region of modern France known as Nord-Pas de Calais, with Lille at its center, is French Flanders, with windmills to prove it.

By the eighteenth century, Flanders had taken on the predominantly agricultural aura it presents to the GR5 walker today. What was left of it became, in 1815, a part of the kingdom of the Netherlands and was incorporated into the new kingdom of Belgium in 1830. In the twentieth century, Flanders again turned into a battlefield.

Today's Flanders is bordered to the west, north, and east by the North Sea and Holland, and by Wallonie and France to the south. It is Flemish-speaking; one well-traveled English-speaking Fleming we met told us that Flemish is to Dutch as American English is to British English—perhaps too simplistic but a good working formula.

Theoretically, all Flemings also learn French in school and have a working knowledge of this language spoken by the other half of their nation. But along the GR5 route, the theory seems more honored in the breach than in fact. The Dutch mastered in Holland will still be useful in Flanders. By way of compensation, the walker may find that his rusty high-school French is at least as good as and occasionally better than the French of many Flemings speaking *their* high school French.

GR5 bypasses the bristling port city of Antwerp (fifth largest in the world and a thriving commercial and industrial center) as well as the noted tourist attractions of western Flanders—the elegant Gothic cities of Bruges and Ghent, the galleries and cathedrals that house the masterworks of the likes of Rubens, Van Eyck, Brueghel, and Bosch.

Instead, it takes the walker gradually southward and eastward across the Flemish plain—touching the provinces of Antwerp, Brabant, and Limburg—toward the hills of the Ardennes in Wallonie. In a loose sense, the route parallels the Albertkanaal (Albert Canal), built between 1930 and 1939. This canal links Liège on the Maas (Meuse, in Liège) to Antwerp on the North Sea; it thus connects the inland cities of the Benelux countries and France to the ports of the north. The walk along the route of the canal through Flanders is a walk of some 232 kilometers (145 miles) in nine days through gently rolling pasturelands and fields separated by thick hedgerows and pockets of deep, dark woods—Hansel-and-Gretel woods, Ginger called them.

This walk into agricultural Flanders takes the walker distinctly inland and presents an appearance entirely different from the tortured coast of Holland, with its dikes and dams and polders. Here instead are green fields that seem to flow outward in vast stretches. No more smell of the salt sea, but rather the rich odors of dark soil, new-mown grass, manure. The terns and gulls are gone from overhead; instead, you hear the songs of meadow birds or watch a cattle egret scoring a free ride on the back of a cow. You have gone from dramatically coastal to placidly pastoral, and you have left behind the sense of that constant struggle to preserve or reclaim land. Land is here in abundance, rich lush earth in your vision and underfoot: you walk now on soft paths—sand and pine needles and mud—and happily leave behind the pavement of Holland's bike routes.

The latter part of the walk, in the province of Limburg between the Demer and Maas rivers, takes the walker across the Kempen. Known in ancient times as Taxandria, this vast, sand-and-pebble plain slants slightly seaward. Grass heaths, sand dunes, strands of pines, fields of Scotch broom, and sudden spurts of ponds adorn this landscape. In the past, its seeming uselessness made it a favorite area for both monasteries and military maneuvers. Then, in the late nineteenth century, coal was discovered in the Kempen and a mining industry was developed, aided by the construction of the Albert Canal. The industry has fallen on hard times, however, and now the Kempen is a region known for its nature reserves, land that the industry's very decline saved from reclamation. In these reserves, sand dunes and marshland and their accompanying bird- and wildlife are sacred.

But this is by no means a wilderness walk. Though GR5 assiduously tries to avoid towns, cities, highways, and industry, you are never really far from them. Many of the pastures and fields have been created anew; most woods have been planted; and always somewhere on the horizon is the silhouette of a village church spire. The countryside has few wild things—you will see flowers, birds, squirrels, even deer, but in no great abudance. This is domesticated terrain—bucolic, not wild.

Each day in the walk across Flanders, the walker passes through two or three of the curiously quiet brick villages of the region, with their turreted churches and pointed town hall roofs. GR5 frequently bypasses these villages and sticks to woods and fields, but to the walker from overseas, the villages of Flanders offer both provisions and interest, and we have altered the route a bit to take advantage of them.

The route must be changed for another reason as well: the paucity of lodging across Flanders. On more than one occasion, it is necessary to detour from the route of the GR5 in order to find accommodation

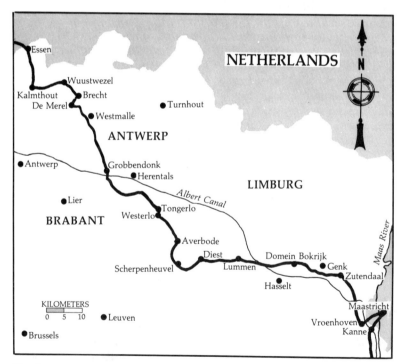

Flanders

for the night; usually, it will be possible to make this detour in a taxi or a bus, or by hitching a ride—both to the hotel in the evening and back to the trailhead the next morning.

In Flanders, we learned the lesson of phoning ahead for a hotel reservation once you know where you'll be that night—and we learned how easy it is to do. Even if you have not armed yourself with a hotel listing from the VVV, it is a simple matter to ask your previous night's hotel staff to find you a place and to phone for a reservation at the next stopping point; you pay the cost of the call. The only time, throughout our entire walk across Europe, that we arrived at a destination and found no room at the inn was in Flanders. It was on a Saturday night, and it taught us well always to reserve ahead for weekends—a practice we followed religiously for the rest of our trip. In the summertime, in Europe, you can be sure you're not the only person on vacation—especially on a weekend and even in backcountry boondocks.

Flanders

Day 1	Continuing from Bergen-op-Zoom (Holland) to Essen	16 km	4 hr
	Essen to Kalmthout	13 km	3-¼ hr
		29 km	7-¼ hr
Day 2	Kalmthout to Brecht	20 km	5 hr
	Detour to De Merel	4 km	1 hr
		24 km	6 hr
Day 3	De Merel to Brug 11	2 km	½ hr
	Brug 11 to Grobbendonk	30 km	7-½ hr
		32 km	8 hr
Day 4	Grobbendonk to Tongerlo	25 km	6-¼ hr
Day 5	Tongerlo to Westerlo	2 km	½ hr
	Westerlo to Scherpenheuvel	19 km	4-¾ hr
		21 km	5-¼ hr
Day 6	Scherpenheuvel to Lummen	25 km	6-¼ hr
Day 7	Lummen to Domein Bokrijk	24 km	6 hr
Day 8	Domein Bokrijk to Zutendaal	22 km	5-½ hr
Day 9	Zutendaal to Vroenhoven	28 km	7 hr
	Vroenhoven to Maastricht	2 km	½ hr
		30 km	7-½ hr
		232 km	58 hr

Day 1: Bergen-op-Zoom (Holland) to Kalmthout (ca. 29 km, 7-¼ hr)

The route out of Bergen-op-Zoom begins from the youth hostel, Jeugdherberg "Klavervelden," on Boslustweg. In front of it stands the wooden pole that was the start of GR5 before the 1983 extension to the Hoek van Holland. A sign on the pole points back to the North Sea and forward to the Riviera but also indicates Essen, the first GR5 destination in Belgium.

From the sign, GR5 proceeds on sandy trails, zigzagging eastward and south. It soon comes to Wouwse Plantage, a name we loved, and a place, it turned out, where we were able to enjoy a final Dutch beer on Dutch soil.

The Dutch-Belgian frontier at the Essen crossing is unmarked. There is no roadblock or checkpoint or customs station in or near the town, although we were told that random sorties by customs officials attempt to halt or at least stem what is said to be a lively drug traffic between Antwerp and Amsterdam.

Before the crossing, however, GR5 simply goes along the border. If there are two of you, you can walk side by side, as we did, each in a different nation. If you are alone, you can straddle the frontier, with one foot in Holland and the other in Belgium. Moreover, the border path is a dirt lane; after the unrelenting paved paths of the Netherlands, entering Flanders on an earth track seems a promising omen.

Yet despite the invisibility of the border, Essen somehow—perhaps simply by the power of suggestion—*seems* different. A neat, trim exurb of Antwerp with a lazy railroad depot, it is not a remarkable town, but its architecture seems at once darker and slightly more inclined to the Gothic than anything the walker has thus far seen in Holland's countryside.

It was our plan to lunch there, so we called out to the first person we saw, appealing first and in vain in French, then in phrase-book Dutch, for directions to a café. We followed his directions as we understood them until we came to the first place that fit the description. It turned out to be the refreshment bar of a rather fashionable and clearly private tennis club—we thought people had looked at us strangely as we marched confidently past the tennis courts, but no one said a word except in welcome. Dusty from our walk, dirty with sweat, and hardly chic in our clodhopping shoes and backpacks, we stood out conspicuously in this hotbed of comfortable, middle-class fitness: well turned-out women in designer tennis outfits, men sporting shirts with logos on the pockets and wearing aviator glasses, children with the latest athletic equipment. All were very friendly, as were the proprietors, who rustled up hefty sandwiches and cold drinks. Several people spoke English quite well and, between matches, a lively discussion ensued about the best place for us to spend the night—Kalmthout, everyone agreed.

Immediately after we left the tennis club, we passed the commercial café, open to the public, to which we had undoubtedly been directed in the first place.

The homes of Essen looked like the sort of place our tennis friends would live in—comfortable, suburban, well tended. Once past the town limits, however, the GR5 walker once again strolls sandy lanes and enters an area of weekend homes hidden in the trees—getaway bungalows for escapees from the urban sprawl of Antwerp.

Real country begins soon enough, as exurb gives way to open fields and open fields lead to the heaths and pine forests of the Staatsreservaat der Kalmthout Heide. *Heide* means "heath," and *Kalmthout* means "calm place," and the Kalmthout Heide is aptly named. Yield here to the temptation to drop your pack, pull out your binoculars, recline on a dune, and watch some birds—or to take off your boots and wiggle your toes in the sand.

At the end of the Heide, GR5 does not follow the obvious road out, but continues on into a parklike arboretum to emerge on the road called Putsesteenweg, just at the bar-café known as Heihoeve.

The beers of Belgium have been mentioned in these pages before, and the Heihoeve is as good a place as you can find to inaugurate your Belgian beer drinking—if you haven't already. Sixty-three varieties of beer are served here. Behind the bar are glasses of every shape and size, each with a different brewer's crest. The bartender somehow fills the right glasses with the right beer every time, a skill that can only be maintained because the bartender is not actually drinking the beer. Susanna ordered Trappiste—thick, dark, moody, and potent—while Ginger, who claims not to like beer, became a convert to Duvel, one of the nation's most famous brews.

Our hotel was only a couple of kilometers beyond Heihoeve. In preparation for coming hardship, we had chosen to stay in a charming country inn where waiters in black-tie served us a four-course meal in the highest tradition of Belgium's haute cuisine. To be sure, the food in Holland had been tasty and well prepared, but what a joy, after a long day's walk, to sit down to a meal prepared with garlic, spices, and herbs, and to end with fresh strawberries and aged cognac.

Day 2: Kalmthout to De Merel (ca. 24 km, 6 hr)

Today's stage is problematic because of the paucity of lodging on this section of GR5. As a result, it will be necessary, at day's end, to detour to find a night's sleep; even then, the pickings are slim. Moreover, there is only one town along the way where the walker can count on lunch and/or provisions—Wuustwezel—which fortunately comes along more or less at lunchtime.

So much for dinner and lunch; breakfast, this first morning in Belgium, is also a new experience. Gone are the cold cuts, the wurst and salami of Dutch mornings, though you may still get a boiled egg and perhaps some cheese. Gone too are the cold slices of bread, replaced by hard rolls. Ginger's theory, first propounded in Belgium and demonstrated along the way, is that the further south you go in Europe, the less hearty the breakfasts—but, fortunately, the stronger the coffee.

Good strong Belgian coffee, accompanied by Belgian chocolate, was a help on our first Belgian morning. Though we were tending southward, Europe was not getting any dryer. The sky threatened with our first cup of coffee, and the drizzle began with our second.

The way out of Kalmthout is through suburbs and along streets busy with cars and trucks. The walker will note signs on the fronts of many homes that warn graphically of attack dogs within, so it will come as no surprise to see a number of establishments given over to dog training. We passed one place where an animal was being put through his paces, directed by a trainer and paired with a hapless human dressed in fortified clothing who had the role of victim.

Then, quite suddenly, GR5 turns onto a dirt lane, and the Flanders of travel posters appears: cows grazing in green fields dotted with farm buildings along the horizon. The route enters a cathedral-like grove of giant elms and beeches before again tracking dirt lanes that edge more wide fields.

In Wuustwezel, we came in out of the rain to a café where a TV was on. It was the day of the Brussels marathon, and the picture was of sopping wet runners on slick streets kicking muddy puddle water up into the camera lens. The rain was evidently nationwide.

The 9.5 kilometers from Wuustwezel to Brecht is quintessential Flanders. Even in a downpour, swaddled in Gore-tex and knee deep in mud, we would remember this as a near-perfect walk. The route is a winding one, bringing the walker hither then thither to skirt fields or dart in and out of small woods. Cows seemed not to mind the rain, the mud, or us—a few steers looked up as we intruded on their turf, but Ginger reminded them of their fate, and they turned away at once.

GR5 skirts Brecht, but the walker should head for the center of town. Here are cafés and restaurants where you can get directions to the vacation center, De Merel, 4 kilometers away.

A sports weekend was just winding up the night we stayed there, a wet and soggy night. The weekend had been the occasion of numerous sports competitions among athletic clubs made up of most, if not all, of the policemen and firemen of Antwerp province. The wet lawn of the center was littered with athletes; the entrance to the hotel was choked with them. There was evidence everywhere of track meets, soccer, tennis, basketball, and—amazingly—baseball!

No one paid us much attention, but someone found us rooms. Athletes ran along the corridors, and the loudspeaker made incomprehensible (to us) announcements, which were invariably followed by loud cheers. Music and dancing followed the awards ceremony and continued late into the night. Susanna swore the next morning that the last sound she heard before finally falling asleep was the voice of Frank Sinatra singing "New York, New York."

Day 3: De Merel to Grobbendonk (ca. 32 km, 8 hr)

Flanders fields, edged by poppies. Cows graze. The earth is green and lumpy. Stands of tall trees break the landscape. The buildings are red brick, with sloping slate roofs. In the distance, at almost all times, you see the spire of a church, always a dark pointed silhouette, or the turrets of the stadhuis—the town hall. This is the walk to Grobbendonk.

Walker and cyclist near Zoerselhof, Belgium. Photo by Susanna Margolis.

From De Merel, walk southeast till you come to the Kempens Kanaal. Follow north along the bank to the bridge, Brug 11 Het Kempens Kanaal. You can see GR5 on the other side as you walk the tree-lined bank, but you must cross Brug 11 to reach it.

A paved road winds away from the canal, but GR5 takes to dirt lanes. Westmalle is officially bypassed, but if you need provisions or a bank, as we did, it is easy to plot a detour to the town along back roads. It was in Westmalle, in a dim café, that we were cheerfully given the cheerless news that there is never sunshine in Belgium. We had also hoped to mail postcards in Westmalle, but the post office was closed—lunchtime—and we had no stamps. Fortunately, the postman was lunching right there at the bar with us, although he too was unsure of the postage required for air mail to the United States. Suggestions were put forth by some of the other drinkers, and a vote was taken. Ten francs won the election.

GR5 crosses the Antwerp-Turnhout highway before continuing among fields. If you want a sit-down lunch in an interesting place, head for the Hotel-Restaurant Zoerselhof. You will need to detour: just after the turnoff for the youth hostel, at Schriekbos, continue straight where the GR5 turns right. This brings you along a route of impressive homes, many of them new but trying hard to look rustic to blend in with the cow pastures they have displaced. The Hotel-Restaurant Zoerselhof is a grand but fading country estate surrounded by a splendid formal garden. It is lost in its modern suburb, out of place and out of time. This—and the garden—are its charm. If you take this detour, it is possible to map your own route back to meet GR5 at highway 579.

Cross the highway and head for the woods and if you are fortunate, you may well meet August Lambert, who presides over the Grote Routepad from his house along the route. Lambert takes great interest in the walkers of GR5, and indeed, the Lambert family has a very good reason for such interest. This is the story of the Grand Romance of the Grand Route:

In the early eighties, soon after the GR5 markers were established along the Lamberts' front lawn, a young Dutchman, hiking the route, knocked on Lambert's door and asked for a glass of water. Unfailingly hospitable, Lambert invited the young man in. (We were invited in as well, for coffee, biscuits, and the story.) Lambert plied the Dutchman with information about the area—including advice about a nearby campground, to which, in fact, he then drove the weary hiker. As he dropped him there for the night, Lambert told him, "If there's anything you need, just knock on our door."

Half an hour later, there was a knock on the Lambert door, but it was someone else from the campground reporting that the young Dutchman had managed to spill boiling water down his leg and was now in the hospital. Lambert, the young man's only acquaintance in the area, hurried over and brought the Dutchman home to recover in the comfort of the Lambert house, there to be nursed by Lambert's pretty daughter, Els, herself an avid hiker.

And so, of course, the young Dutchman and the pretty Flemish girl fell in love. They were married in June, 1984. The cover of their wedding invitation was a drawing of two hikers meeting at a crossroads under a legend proclaiming, "He came along this road, she came along that road. Now their roads converge." Their honeymoon was a walking tour.

A walk of 8 kilometers remains for this stage, beneath a lovely canopied woods speckled with light and shadow. Near Grobbendonk, the GR5 turns to meet the GR5A, the variant coming from Ostend. A short detour from the trail is necessary to reach the center of Grobbendonk, where a variety of lodgings is available.

Day 4: Grobbendonk to Tongerlo
(ca. 25 km, 6-¼ hr)

This is essentially a farmland walk again, except for the first few kilometers, when GR5 curves around the city of Herentals and skirts the industrial and coal mining areas of the Kempen.

From Grobbendonk to the little station of Bouwel, the route follows a busy highway that crosses the Albert Canal. The barges plying the huge canal are several hundred feet long. These are often family-run businesses; in the stern are the living quarters complete with lace curtains, laundry drying on lines, and, on the roof, the family car.

Across the canal, GR5 follows dirt lanes through dairylands separated by hedgerows and parklike woods. The day we walked through, we flushed a pheasant in the woods and, checking where he had come from, found violet rhododendrons nearly hidden at the base of moss-covered trees.

Nooderwijk is a drab enough town, though the café on its edge was a welcome sight to us. Susanna was falling victim to one of the Laws of Inevitable Occurrences: "Sooner or later, your feet will hurt." In this case, it was one foot, the left, and specifically the arch, where something, as she described it, kept "punching up like a fist with every step."

The Belgian beer at the café proved an excellent antidote to foot-soreness and an aid to genial conversation. Again, the patrons could not quite believe that two American women were actually walking through Nooderwijk and that they were on their way to Nice. We had the impression that we were providing a topic of café conversation for days and even months to come—an impression that would persist across Europe. However, amid the general conviviality, Ginger fell victim to another of the Laws of Inevitable Occurrences: "Sooner or later, you will lose something."

In this case, it was her camera bag, stuffed with camera, cassette recorder, and other essentials. We discovered this 10 kilometers later in the hotel in Tongerlo, where we learned a good general rule of travel in Europe: You can order a taxi almost anywhere, but take note that you may have to pay for the distance it must travel to pick you up.

Actually, it was the hotel proprietress who called the taxi, which had to come from Herentals, some 20 kilometers distant. The taxi was a Mercedes, so we rode in style back to Nooderwijk, where we found a cheery reception and the camera bag.

Tongerlo is a pretty town; its center is just a kilometer from GR5. Right on the route, before detouring into town, is the imposing Norbertine Abbey, begun in 1130 and surrounded still by high walls and the remains of a moat. Inside the Abbey is a particularly valuable copy of Leonardo da Vinci's *Last Supper*; it is believed to be the work of Leonardo's pupil, Andrea del Solario. The Abbey library also includes a complete *Acta Sanctorum*, one volume of which was published in the Abbey.

If you are too late for the Abbey on arrival in Tongerlo, you might visit it the next morning before leaving.

Day 5: Tongerlo to Scherpenheuvel (ca. 21 km, 5-¼ hr)

Along these 21 kilometers are many places where you might wish to linger. It would be wise to phone ahead for a hotel reservation at one of the numerous hostelries of Scherpenheuvel; for a small charge— usually just the cost of the phone call—the staff of your previous night's hotel will do this for you.

You might, for example, wish to linger in Westerlo, which GR5 avoids just as it avoided Tongerlo. Eschewing GR5, proceed along the road, following signs and/or a map to get to Westerlo. It is a pretty town, filled with shops, and, on the day we were there, market day was in full swing in the airy grote markt. It was even a sunny day, so after all those kilometers through muddy agricultural turf, it was a delight to see some of the land's produce looking robust and colorful in the sunlight: tomatoes, lettuce, carrots, radishes.

The market stalls here are a moveable feast; they open out from the backs or sides of trucks that travel easily from town to town to catch the different market days. Some were hung with sausages and meats. Some were fitted out with spits on which chickens were roasting, others with refrigerator cases lined with fish, including the much-favored North Sea eel. Then clothing stalls, costume jewelry, tools, kitchenware. Hawkers gathered onlookers and demonstrated their products; on the day we were there, both the ultimate bicycle repair tool and the ultimate furniture polish were being demonstrated to the milling crowds.

Leaving Westerlo, the GR5 is easily found. It follows a majestic tree-lined lane past a stunning castle, the Kasteel de Merode, elusive behind iron gates and high flowering shrubs. It then proceeds along soft, sandy soil made even softer by pine needles as the trail enters planted forests— the furniture business of the area makes profitable use of these woods. The trail is an equestrian path as well; the day we passed through, a handsome teen-aged horseman on a lively jumper showed off for our benefit against the backdrop of the Abbey of Averbode, which dominates the woods.

Founded in 1134, the Norbertine Abbey of Averbode is considered one of Europe's most important monasteries; it is a popular destination for pilgrims and is used regularly as a retreat. A fourteenth-century gate house opens into an enclosed courtyard, across which pass monks and nuns in full habit—a scene unchanged since the twelfth century. The imposing white stone church, however, is baroque, with a beautiful lofty ceiling and a sacristy below. In the Abbot's house is an embossed plaque by Pieter Paul Reubens, though we were not invited in for a look.

The village of Averbode consists primarily of cafés and restaurants that serve visiting pilgrims; it is a good place for a lunch stop.

GR5 now moves toward the town of Zichem. Just outside of town (a very short detour leftward along the highway from the trail) is a fascinating little museum that was the birthplace of Ernest Claes, a popular and prolific Flemish author. It is said that every Fleming has read Claes's *De Witte Van Zichem*, (translated into English in 1970 under the title *Whitey*). The museum, however, has been set up to show what a typical nineteenth-century farmstead home would look like, and it is filled with artifacts from the period as well as Claes memorabilia.

Between Zichem and Scherpenheuvel, on a rain-soaked day, we found ourselves bemoaning the relentless flatness of the walking and the colorless, almost dismal towns of Flanders. As if on cue, the landscape began to roll and weave. We headed actually uphill and looked down, with surprise, on the charming town of Scherpenheuvel, with bright flowers in every window, warm and cheery cafés, and the kind of picturesque architecture that is every American's idea of the quaintness of Europe.

In the center of town is the baroque seventeenth-century Basilica of Our Lady, with a high, graceful cupola dotted with gold stars that stand, as if impaled, on short metal bars. Scherpenheuvel is one of Flanders' most famous and important pilgrimage sites. What appears to be the town's main industry is the sale of religious objects, displayed, Coney Island style, in stalls around the Basilica and in shops throughout town.

Day 6: Scherpenheuvel to Lummen (ca. 25 km, 6-¼ hr)

GR5 goes some 25 kilometers from Scherpenheuvel to Lummen, but the walker will probably go at least another 5 kilometers seeing the sights of the charming city of Diest. Plan to spend some time there and stay for lunch. Again, it might be wise to call ahead to Lummen for a hotel reservation with the warning that you may arrive late.

Diest, on the Demer River, is a treasury of Belgian monuments to the past. New construction has been kept away from these monuments, so that Diest presents a virtually intact, unspoiled picture of a bygone Flanders.

The town lies some 10 kilometers from Scherpenheuvel. Where GR5 meets GR512, just 2 kilometers beyond Scherpenheuvel, the walker must take care to bear left on GR5. Eight kilometers later, GR5 actually circumambulates Diest. The American walker, however, should detour into the town itself. This one is not to be missed.

Head for the lively grote markt and find the VVV just off the square. Tourist information, in English, is available here, and you can ask to leave your packs as well—but be sure to inquire about lunch-closing hours, so that you don't return to fetch your pack only to find the VVV closed.

Ancient Diest is still within the walls and ramparts that have protected it since the town was the fief of the House of Orange. The founder of the Orange-Nassau dynasty, represented today by the royal family of the Netherlands, was William of Orange, also known as William the Silent (1533–1584). He inherited his princely title from his cousin, René of Chalon, who was born in Diest, and William's son, Philip-William, is buried in the church of Saint Sulpice here. The center of the town is the grote markt, surrounded by elegant buildings of the sixteenth to eighteenth centuries. A number of these have been put to good use as sidewalk cafés that dispense Diest's famous beers—Gildbier and Diesterse—or as pleasant coffee houses serving pastries, crêpes, and the famous Belgian waffles known as *gaufres*.

The focal point of the square is the imposing church of Saint Sulpice and the handsome town hall right next to it. Saint Sulpice, of red sandstone and in Gothic style, dates from the fourteenth century. Inside are an unusual sculpted wood pulpit and sixteenth-century stained glass windows. The church is also known for its carillon.

The flag-bedecked town hall beside the church dates from only the eighteenth century, but its restored Gothic crypt houses a museum with excellent collections of medieval art, seventeenth-century silver chalices and necklaces, and three sets of impressive armor.

Many of the streets leading from the grote markt are worth a wander—both for their charm and because it is possible to find English newspapers here—but take the Koning Albestraat to the *béguinage* of Diest.

The *béguinages* of Belgium (*begijnhof* in Flemish) took definitive form in the thirteenth century as enclosed, self-contained, conventlike villages where widows and unmarried women could lead a religious life in a lay sisterhood as secular nuns—*béguines*. (The name has no relation to Cole Porter or ballroom dancing; it derives possibly from a Middle Dutch word for beggar and/or from Saint Begge, the Mother Superior of a convent in Andenne, near Namur, who died in the seventh century.) In a béguinage, the women wore habits, performed religious offices, and swore obedience to the Superior, but they took no vows of poverty, and many were women of wealth. During the day, they were free to attend to their own pursuits, but in the evening they returned to the béguinage, the gates of which were then locked.

The city-within-a-city that is the thirteenth-century béguinage of Diest has been lovingly preserved, both as a museum of the past and as a vital center for art and restoration. It is, in sense, the gentrified center of Diest.

The entrance is through a striking baroque portal, dating from 1671. Just inside is Saint Catherine's church. The restored homes along the picturesque streets of the béguinage date from the sixteenth to the eighteenth centuries. One is a museum, a restored béguine's residence that opens onto a communal courtyard divided into small gardens. The guided tour offered to this residence is well worth taking. Other homes in the béguinage have been made into art galleries, a lace-making school, antique shops, craft centers, and at least one elegant restaurant.

Wander out of the béguinage via Schaffensestraat, then turn right to loop back to the grote markt along Leopoldvest—you will have seen Diest.

Take care leaving the town to rejoin GR5. There is a chance for confusion with GR561, so be sure you are heading for Schaffen on GR5, which stays mostly in fields and woods, avoiding suburbs, villages, and highways until it reaches the small town of Lummen.

Day 7: Lummen to Domein Bokrijk (ca. 24 km, 6 hr)

At Diest, GR5 entered the province of Limburg; for the megawalker, this is the final province in Flanders. As recently as half a century ago, Limburg was largely sandy moors with family farms scattered few and

Cows grazing on a foggy morning near Lummen, Belgium. Photo by Ginger Harmon.

far between. It was the poorest province in Belgium. But with the discovery of rich deposits of coal, mining and related industries brought a new prosperity to Limburg. Prosperity, in turn, brought population growth, expanded urban centers, and extensive reclamation of farmlands. In the 1970s and 1980s, lower profits pretty much put an end to the coal industry in Limburg; only the damage to the area remains.

But it is not all damage. Happily, several significant nature reserves were carved out of the region before it was too late; they afford the opportunity to see the Kempen countryside much as it was a century ago, and GR5 traverses some of this preserved countryside both on Day 7 and Day 8.

Because of the infrequency of lodging near GR5, both days' walks are necessarily short, so the walker can enjoy the reserves at leisure. Domein Bokrijk, the goal for today's stage, is one of the most popular recreation areas in eastern Belgium and offers much more than just a nature preserve. There is an open-air museum featuring authentic reproductions of historic buildings of earlier times, an arboretum, an animal preserve, gardens, restaurants, and playgrounds. The walker might plan to split this visit into an afternoon look at the end of today's stage and a more careful scrutiny at the beginning of Day 8.

Be aware, too, that between Lummen and Bokrijk there are few cafés or shops along the route—possibly at the Stokrooi bridge or the hamlet of Nieuw Veld, but your chances of reaching them at lunchtime closing are good. To be safe, stock up in Lummen and plan on a picnic in the De Platwijers reserve or alongside the Albert Canal.

The trail from Lummen starts out through lovely and now slightly rolling countryside. In the light fog that dogged us throughout Belgium, the fields, with grazing cows and rows of poplars, took on the soft edges supplied by mist and looked like a nineteenth-century painting of the perfect pastoral scene. The perfection was marred once by a large and quite truculent domestic goose, who barred our progress on the trail for a while as he eyed us suspiciously; then, having quite clearly intimidated us, he waddled off and let us proceed.

GR5 crosses the A 13 highway on an overpass and heads into woods, emerging at the paved-road dike of the Albert Canal. Memories of Dutch days enter your brain, through your feet, as you walk the flat, straight bank of the canal, but the passing boats, hauling huge loads in both directions, are a good distraction. At Brug Stokrooi, the GR5 crosses the canal and continues along the other side before turning—watch carefully for the turn—into the nature reserve called De Platwijers. Now a dirt track, GR5 moves through a regal woods and past a marshy lake on whose still, gray waters coots and ducks skim. The day we were there, a large heron stood nearby in high marsh grass; he looked like a Great Blue but was darker gray in color. We dubbed him a Great Gray Heron and later learned that the bird is simply called a Gray Heron.

Zigzagging to avoid private land, GR5 passes Nieuw Veld and shortly thereafter enters the confines of Domein Bokrijk. The trail winds among several lakes and ponds, beside each of which, the day we were there, fishermen sat quietly on lawn chairs. They were hoping, they told us, for carp, but there wasn't a thing in anyone's basket—a situation it is best not to discuss with a fisherman. Past the fishing area, GR5 enters the park and museum section of the Domein. Follow signs to the modern, 120-bed youth hostel, or proceed out through the Domein to the highway for a hotel.

Day 8: Domein Bokrijk to Zutendaal (ca. 22 km, 5-½ hr)

A noontime start allows time enough for arriving in Zutendaal, especially if you have called ahead for a hotel reservation. Part of the walk there traverses the exceptionally beautiful De Maten, a sand-dune reserve and bird sanctuary, and the approach to Zutendaal itself passes through pleasantly lush meadows and woods. But in between, GR5 works hard to skirt the city of Genk, the most important industrial center of Limburg and a crossroads served by the Albert Canal and major highways. The effort does not always succeed, and this part of the walk never manages to get all that far from highway, electric wire, and industrial sites, as the walker marches on paved roads through numerous suburbs. Perhaps the effort to avoid urban blight should not always succeed; urban blight, after all, is as real a fact of Flemish life as the Kempen moors, and American walkers are no strangers to it themselves.

Start the day with some time in the living history museum of Domein Bokrijk. Here, in authentic materials, are the houses, barns, farmyards, and artifacts of country people at various stages in Belgian history, all carefully collected and rebuilt. Guides dressed in authentic period costume provide information on the thatched huts, the mills, the churches and barns open to display.

Leaving Domein Bokrijk, GR5 wanders hither and yon among heide and dunes, then stretches for about a kilometer along the Albert Canal beside one of the locks that accommodate the huge barges and canal boats. It enters the Maten nature reserve, thick with Scotch broom and meadow birds. Part of the reserve, in fact, is fenced off for breeding birds, and the trail follows along the edge of this area—not as scenic a walk as it might be unfenced, but good for the birds.

Closer to Genk, the walker finds himself among prosaic suburban homes, a sharp contrast to the lovely old brick houses of the countryside. In one of these suburban areas, we entered a grocery store and asked for Limburger cheese. We were met with a blank stare. Several cheeses were then brought forward for us to smell; the last, prepackaged in a foil wrapper, passed the smell test with flying colors. In Limburg, we were told, such cheese is simply called cheese of Belgium. The grocer seemed quite enchanted to learn that Limburger cheese has a special reputation elsewhere.

Out from the clutter of Genk's environs at last, GR5 heads through woods and across meadows thick with tiny wild pansies—yellow and deep purple like the garden variety. Here we saw signs for cross-country ski trails as the land rolled into Zutendaal.

Day 9: Zutendaal to Maastricht (ca. 30 km, 7-½ hr)

This stage ends with a detour into Maastricht, in Holland, but the walk is vintage pastoral Flanders—rolling, lush, and green. The route sticks close to the Albert Canal, crossing it at Gellik and Vroenhoven, descending gradually into the valley of the River Maas. Beyond Vroenhoven, where GR5 crosses the canal and where our itinerary splits off for Maastricht via highway, the Albert Canal and the Maas run parallel, meeting finally at Liège.

Leaving Zutendaal, GR5 passes through another nature reserve and bird sanctuary, De Hoefaart. Gellik itself, with cafés, grocery, and frituur, is a good bet for lunch.

Once across the canal and en route to Vroenhoven, the walker traverses open fields. On this our last day in Flanders, summer had finally arrived. We ambled along in the warm sun, suddenly aware that in two and a half weeks we had covered about 390 kilometers (242 miles) and had come nearly one-sixth of the way across Europe. There was ocean behind us and way, way ahead of us. We had done the dikes and polders of Holland, and now the flowering fields of Flanders.

Two and a half weeks of walking and we knew how it worked. We had gotten the hang of it, could pack up quickly in the morning and clean up quickly at night, and we were beginning to develop a good trail sense for following GR5.

9
Wallonie: Into the Ardennes

Maastricht, in Holland, may seem an illogical starting point for a walk across Wallonie, the French-speaking part of Belgium. But Maastricht—or more properly, the Maastricht Appendix, that cul-de-sac of Dutch territory dipping down between the borders of Belgium and Germany—is and always has been a crossroads. For that reason alone, Maastricht is a fitting symbolic gateway to the Wallonie section of the walk across Europe.

The entry into Wallonie represents a crossroads in two senses. First, this is the place on the route where the plain of Europe gives way to peneplain. At last—and from now on—the way leads up. Or up and down.

Second, here is the intersection, if any spot deserves the name, where the walker steps from the West Germanic world of Holland and Flanders into a new world dominated by the Latin heritage.

The city of Maastricht is an appropriate entry into Wallonie for other reasons as well. Although it is a Dutch city—and offers the walker a final, compressed look at things Dutch—Maastricht also makes the visitor acutely aware of a sense of borderlessness, or at least, of the capricious and arbitrary nature of boudnary lines on a map. In this part of the world, where one political border ends and another begins has been a matter of indifference to settlers, travelers, pilgrims, and armies for centuries. Maastricht thrives today, to a great extent, because it still serves in this crossroads capacity. It is a place on a thoroughfare where travelers from Germany, Belgium, and northern Holland can find every sort of accommodation. The town's merchants accept currency from these and other countries with equal contentment. Road signs accentuate the point, offering almost equal distances, if opposing directions, to Aachen, a stone's throw away in Germany, and to Luik, the Dutch word for the French-speaking city of Liège, a fast ride away in

Belgium. It is the geopolitics that begins to seem illogical—the historical vagaries that have created three nation-states out of two language groups on one piece of turf—especially since the national borders don't necessarily correspond to the language differences nor does the terrain change markedly the moment the borders are crossed. Much of the walk down the rest of Europe will confirm this impression of the ephemeral nature of borders, as you tread soil that has belonged to various nations.

Other signs in the center of Maastricht point north to Eindhoven, Nijmegen, Arnhem, and south to the Ardennes—place names that resound with echoes of World War II. It is a short excursion from Maastricht to the American military cemetery, 6 miles out of town, or to the caves of Mount Saint Peter, where you can still see the preparations that were made for sheltering 50,000 civilians from bombardment in 1944.

One of the realities about being a crossroads is that not everyone who passes through comes in peace. In the walk across Wallonie, that reality is brought vividly to life.

The Flemish word for Wallon, *Waelsch*, derives from the same root as the word *Welsh*; the root word means "foreign." True Walloons are said to descend from the Celts, who spread across Europe from the British Isles into Spain in prehistoric times. A lot has happened since then to mingle and commingle the blood of Wallonie several times over.

Today's Walloons speak a French that only a Frenchman would consider substandard. Lightly but distinctly accented, Walloon French contains some of the same peculiarities as Swiss French—for example the use of *septante, huitante,* and *nonante* for France's cumbersome *soixante-dix, quatre-vingt,* and *quatre-vingt-dix.* Many Walloons also speak a dialect resembling the French of a thousand years ago, but not derived—as any Frenchman will quickly tell you—from the Ile-de-France dialect, which became the model for the language of France. The Walloon dialect is spoken in the home—if it is spoken at all—and is consciously preserved by many as a token of cultural identity.

The walk across Wallonie will take nine days—including a detour to see Liège—and will cover around 180 kilometers. It is energizing walking—a pattern of ascending a plateau, striding across it, dipping into a valley to pass through a village or two, them climbing the next plateau. This new form of exercise will in fact provide relief to the flat-walking muscles that have worked without surcease to carry you across Holland and Flanders. It is good preparation for the Vosges, Jura, and Alps to come.

The route through Wallonie crosses the heavily industrialized valley of the Maas, which you can now call, in French, the Meuse. It then enters the Ardennes, at different times following beside or crossing the Ardennes rivers that help to feed the Meuse: the Amblève, the Warche, the Salm—the valley of each a world unto itself. GR5 exits Wallonie—and Belgium—through the German-speaking Cantons of the East.

It is a varied walk, inlcuding a diverse and sometimes curious landscape, a succession of towns and one large city, and a passage through the world-famous forest of the Ardennes.

The walker will cross the Hautes Fagnes, the boggy peat plateaus of the Ardennes heights—vestiges of the ice-sheets that chugged slowly down from Scandinavia and left these tundras at their outside rim.

The detour to Liège provides time for a layover, so that the walker may see the sights of the city that has been called "a priest's paradise, a man's purgatory, and a woman's hell." We women found it to be a lively town whose populace seemed to enjoy living there.

The names of many of the towns the route traverses echo arcane and archaic dialects—Ninglinspo, Hockai—and the route passes through one town so famous its name has become a definition for watering places all over the world: Spa.

Spa, Pearl of the Ardennes, was also a headquarters town for the armies of both sides in both world wars of this century, and it is the fact of war that haunts all other impressions of the walk through Wallonie. So many battles have been fought in the Ardennes, so many times, for so many centuries, at so great a price, that even on a quiet summer day, strolling beside a river or across a field or along a forest road, the walker becomes suddenly aware that the place he is in once rang with war sounds, and that the ground under his feet has been soaked with blood—over and over and over again.

The word *ardenne* comes from a Celtic root meaning dark or obscure, and the Ardennes forest has been a battleground at least since the beginning of recorded history, and probably for a good while before. Caesar described the Ardennes as being of immense size; he was reluctant to send his troops there in pursuit of a fleeing enemy who might easily find a defensive position in some "hidden valley or wooded area or ensnaring marsh."

The Ardennes was pivotal to the Schlieffen Plan for the German advance during World War I. Toward the end of August, 1914, two German armies and two French armies met head-on in the midst of the forest, fighting fiercely among villages and along wooded lanes. GR5 follows some of those lanes and passes through several of the hamlets where French soldiers fell back before the German onslaught.

But it is the war that followed the "war to end all wars" that really comes alive in the Ardennes region, particularly for the American walker. Spa. Malmédy. Stavelot. Vielsalm. How the names of these Walloon villages reverberate in American ears!

All across Wallonie, Belgians reminisced with us about the harsh winter of 1944 and about the bravery of the American GIs. Forty years after that winter, General James Gavin of the Eighty-Second Airborne Division recalled in an interview the great kindness of the Belgian people toward the GIs. "They gave the men their bedsheets," Gavin said. "They made them into smocks the soldiers could wear over their tunics as camouflage in the snow."

It was, indeed, the American GI's battle. Hitler had assumed that the heterogeneous American society, with the presumed weakening effect of its ethnic diversity, could not possibly produce an effective fighting force or effective fighting men. Hitler was wrong. The massacres, the tenacity, the colossal mistakes, and finally the heroism played out in Wallonie are all part of what Winston Churchill called "the greatest American battle of the war and . . . an ever famous American victory."

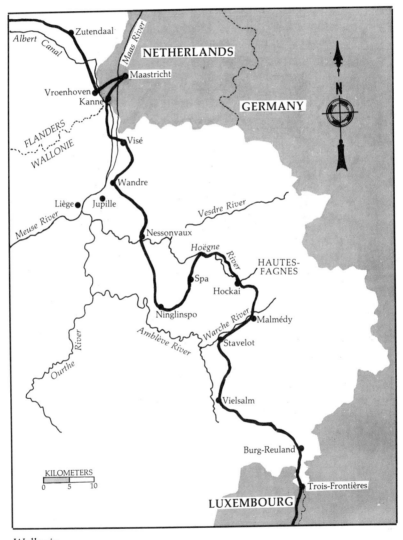

Wallonie

Wallonie

Day 1	Continuing from Maastricht (Holland)		
	to Kanne	6 km	1-½ hr
	Kanne to Visé/Liège	16 km	4 hr
		22 km	5-½ hr
Day 2	Liège (layover)		
Day 3	Liège/Visé to Nessonvaux	29 km	7-¼ hr
Day 4	Nessonvaux to Ninglinspo	19 km	4-¾ hr
Day 5	Ninglinspo to Spa	16 km	4 hr
Day 6	Spa to Hockai	27 km	6-¾ hr
Day 7	Hockai to Malmédy	15 km	3-¾ hr
Day 8	Malmédy to Vielsalm	26 km	6-½ hr
Day 9	Vielsalm to Burg-Reuland	26 km	6-½ hr
		180 km	45 hr

Day 1: Maastricht to Visé/Liège (ca. 22 km, 5-½ hr)

The first day in Wallonie begins in a Dutch-speaking provincial capital in Holland and ends in a French-speaking provincial capital in Belgium. Only a five-and-a-half-hour walk and a short bus or train ride separate the two. The walk is mostly along GR5, taking the walker up and over the smokestack-filled valley of the Meuse. You can leave Maastricht in the late morning and be in Liège in time for dinner in any one of a variety of restaurants—Italian, Greek, Portuguese, Indian, Chinese, and of course, Belgian.

Maastricht deserves a few hours of sightseeing. Originating as a Roman garrison protecting a ford over the Maas (Traiectam ad Mosam), Maastricht has been a fortress town ever since. As a result, it has been dutifully besieged by almost everyone in Europe.

Today the city is an attractive cluster of crooked roofs and gables, of ramparts and gates dating back to the twelfth century, of delightful squares and alluring shops.

Maastricht straddles the Maas—the river Jeker also flows through it—and it is on the quay known as Maasboulevard, near the Saint Servaas bridge, that the VVV is located. The staff of the VVV, pleasant, informative, and English-speaking, can provide a map and brochure outlining a walking tour of the city. There are few better ways to see any town in a few hours, especially if you can leave your pack at the VVV, or, as we did, at a friendly café.

To leave Maastricht, find the road named Mergelweg and head south along the Jeker towards Kanne. It is possible to follow Mergelweg directly into Kanne. Maastricht's sprawl ends abruptly, and Mergelweg becomes a pleasant country road that had more walkers than cars the day we were on it. Or, pick up GR5 where it crosses Mergelweg at Dalings Weg. The latter route is circuitous and irregular, but it follows the border for a while and traces some of the east bank of the Albertkanaal. In either case, when you arrive in Kanne, you have crossed the border back into Belgium.

Commuters from Kanne to jobs in Maastricht cross the border regularly, and notice it as much as we did—not at all. One such commuter is composer Willem Kersters, who, while teaching once a week at the Maastricht Conservatory, regularly stayed at the charming Hotel Limburgia in Kanne. Here Kersters wrote an opera, *Gansendonk*, first performed in 1984 in Antwerp. A page from the autograph score of the opera adorns one wall of the hotel's cozy lobby.

It was an unusually warm, sunny day when we passed through Kanne, and we stopped for cool refreshment in the Limburgia's bar, where we were befriended, in English, by a middle-aged Dutchman whose accent sounded more like Kansas than Kanne. Indeed, he had fled Holland for the United States in 1943, via Switzerland, Portugal, and England. In the States, he joined the Marines, hoping to return home in glory to fight his country's oppressors. He served with the Marines all right, for five years. In Guam.

Our friend advised us to investigate the town; it was the feast of Pentecost that day, and two events celebrated the fact—an open-air mass and a flea market. The latter was like flea markets everywhere; with packs on our backs, we were not about to buy anything, though Susanna was tempted by a photo album recording the visit of Belgium's king and queen to their African colony, the Congo, in the 1920s. In the photos, king, queen, and entourage smiled pleasantly in their starched tropical whites; they made colonialism look benign.

On a nonfeast day, the sights of Kanne require only a short visit, unless the walker is interested in a guided tour to the underground grottoes; the tour leaves from the hotel Louvain. Kanne's most imposing sight is the delicately beautiful castle on the hill overlooking the town. The castle was once the seat of the fiefdom. After the Belgian-Dutch partition of 1830, the then-scion of the noble family that lived there chose to keep the *kasteel* in the family and stick with Holland. So the most notable building in Kanne is actually in another country.

GR5 leaves Kanne by crossing the Albertkanaal. The crossing marks the limit between the provinces of Limburg and Liège and is the official entry into Wallonie. Hedgerows here—beautiful and sprouting wildflowers—are an immediate reminder of the war. In the drive east, Allied tank crews reportedly affixed the twisted debris of battle to the prows of their tanks, using the burned or rusted metal as plows to uproot the hedgerows, which had proved to be lethal barriers to armored divisions on both sides.

A short detour off the route to the fort of Eben-Emael, just past Kanne, provides a futher reminder of war. Built in 1933 to protect the roads and bridges to its west, overlooking the Albertkanaal, Eben-Emael was ringed around by defense walls from which artillery could resist any attack from any side. It was said to be the strongest fort in the world; at the outbreak of the war, the Allies took for granted the absolute safety of Eben-Emael's circumferential strength.

The Allies had not reckoned with the top of the fort, above which German gliders floated, dropping bombs that destroyed the gun emplacements and made the fort's defenders virtual captives. The Germans pushed on into Holland. Today, a ruined bunker serves as a memorial to the Belgians who died defending Eben-Emael.

This is the valley of the Jeker (Geer, in Walloon); GR5 now crosses the river and ascends a slight ridge. The climb in itself is a fairly momentous event for veterans of Holland and Flanders, an event celebrated by the appearance of a curious monument: a four-cornered chateau meant to be an apocalyptic vision of the valley's natural environment. Cherubim adorn each corner of the work, which is constructed of the local silica.

The route descends through nettles and follows the stream into Wonck. You are now officially on French-speaking turf.

Outside of Wonck, the route climbs a real hill, the first true climb of the trip—enough of a climb to cause panting and even sweat. You then cross a wide plateau, used as a motocross practice area by locals, as was loudly evident the day we were there. The far side of the plateau is the sharp edge of a steep quarried cliff, from which the walker looks down onto the narrow valley where the Meuse and Albertkanaal meet, a valley where small patches of green interrupt only briefly a sea of industries belching smoke and grime. It is a disheartening sight.

The trail descends, then wanders along the valley floor, winding to avoid fast roads and unsightly factories, crossing, where possible, the tiny cultivated plots. Certainly, between agriculture and industry, not an inch of this valley is wasted.

GR5 then crosses the canal, follows the Meuse, then bridges the river to enter Visé. The town is bustling, and although there is plenty of accommodation, Visé is the departure point for the detour into Liège. There are frequent buses and trains into the city; the train and bus stations are near one another, just over the bridge across which GR5 enters Visé.

We hopped a bus, hugging our packs on our laps and provoking numerous curious glances, and followed the busy conurbation along the Meuse to the city that has given its name to the province.

The walker can also choose to continue from Visé on foot, on GR5 to Wandre, then along a GR5 variant right into Jupille, the birthplace of Charlemagne, now dedicated almost completely to the brewery of the local eponymous beer. Liège is just over the bridge, although it will be a sooty, noisy, traffic-ridden trek to the center of the city.

Day 2: Liège (layover day)

The historical core of Liège—the *vieille ville*—is a cluster of crowded, winding, often noisy streets and squares. The Liègois have done well by their past. Contemporary shops are now housed behind seventeenth- or eighteenth-century facades; the city's numerous churches are shrines of history as well as houses of worship; and a surprising number of museums hold superb collections—of Mosan (Meuse basin) art, of the arts and crafts of Walloon life, and of the several industries that have meant the fame and fortune of Liège: glass, the decorative arts, and above all, armaments.

Ringing the vieille ville are spacious parks, boulevards, and esplanades, dominated by the sleek complex of the Palais des Congrès conference center just below Outremeuse, Liège's left bank and home of the famous Sunday market on Quai de la Batte.

Liège takes seriously its status as the capital of Wallonie. The Walloon dialect is kept alive in place names on street signs, and the Walloon culture is celebrated in theater and the arts. Tchantchès, the Punch-like character who for centuries has embodied the impertinent but good-natured Liègois spirit, is celebrated in a museum in Outremeuse. A statue nearby, built in 1938, represents Wallonie as a woman dressed in coal miner's garb and holding up Tchantchès as a torch of freedom.

While Liège is certainly worthy of a detour for its own sake, it is also a good place for the walker to rest, regroup, and reprovision. The tourist office on the edge of the vieille ville has up-to-date accommodation lists and carries the *Tronçon Belge* topo-guide. Other important services are easily obtainable here, as befits a city of this size and importance: a large, albeit busy, post office for receiving or sending mail; good telephone service; bookstores with English books and American and British newspapers and magazines. The walker should keep in mind that it is a long way—about two weeks of walking—to the next town of any size, although Malmédy, five days away, and Vianden in Luxembourg, some ten days away, have good shops. While food is available almost anywhere along our route, money is not, and since Belgian francs are used in Luxembourg, it might be a good idea to exchange enough dollars in Liège to see you through for fifteen or more days.

Day 3: Visé to Nessonvaux
(ca. 29 km, 7-¼ hr)

Who would have thought it? Hidden behind the grime of the Meuse Valley smokestacks, just over the limestone ridge against which towns are huddled all in a row from Visé to Jupille, lies a great ebb-and-flow of rolling hills dotted with villages of stone houses trimmed with stone blocks. The stone is very gray, but almost every window holds a flower box filled with exuberant geraniums, and the walls are decked with vines.

Today is a necessarily long day. There are no hotels until Nessonvaux, so the goal is clear; take an early bus or train from Liège back to Visé and set off, taking care to turn left at Wandre so you don't head back to Liège.

You are in the region called Herve, a moist area of rich pastureland, known for its dairy products. We enjoyed an olfactory experience of the local fare in the town of Tignée. We asked a woman who was washing down the terrace of her house if there was a café nearby. "Why?" she asked, "Are you thirsty?" When we nodded yes, we were urged inside where cold drinks were produced and cheese offered. Though we declined the latter, we were tempted by the cheese's strong aroma. "Like Limburger," we told our hostess. "No, no," she insisted, "Herve." The walker should make a note to try some.

It is a walk that moves mostly across open fields. The walker finds himself gazing well ahead to find the next trail marker, or following along the fenced boundaries of these fields. It is lush here, a wide-open plateau, dotted with wildflowers—rows of trees in the distance. The Herve is a popular walking area; the red and white GR5 markers are accompanied by numerous other markers for the circular trail that loops the plateau and dips into the valley of the Saivelette.

This field walking offers numerous different solutions for getting over or through fences: narrow stiles (Ginger decided the best way through with a pack is to start off backwards), swinging gates, ingeniously wrought openings in barbed wire, and a fair amount of slithering under or between. At one such do-it-yourself portal, after a piece of wet and muddy track, Susanna was holding down the bottom rung of wire with her foot while trying to pull her sweater off a barb when she felt a terrific shock. It was a *fil électrique*, electric wire, which works quite well through sopping wet boots. Our topo-guide had warned of this, but strolling along contentedly, we had neglected to check the text or observe the fence very closely. Opgelet! as they say in Holland when they mean "watch out!" Electric fences typically carry small white nodes; proceed carefully when you see these.

The hills roll a little higher as the afternoon progresses. The villages roll by, too. Micheroux. Wegimont. Saint-Hadelin. All contain the characteristic stone houses, and all except Saint-Hadelin offer cafés. If you carefully follow the Megawalker's Absolute Law of Travel, "The unentered café is not worth the ground it stands on," you can stroll this wonderful countryside as we did, fueled by Belgian beer and Belgian chocolate, two of the finer things in life, available for a song in their native land.

Just beyond the narrow streets of Olne, at the end of a lane used by cows moving from one pasture to another, the walker suddenly overlooks a landscape of great beauty. Hills tumble down in waves. Where three hills meet, a church spire proclaims a small village. It is the definitive picture of the village nestled among hills.

The route heads down toward the village, striking out across trail-less fields of grass. The fields belong to local farmers, who frequently pointed us in the right direction. They were invariably astonished when they heard about our project, and many wished us "Bonne Promenade" or "Bonne Route"—good walking.

The route now climbs another hill, where the GR563, for the Herve region, turns off from GR5. Head down the ridge, cross the Vesdre River, and you have arrived in Nessonvaux.

It had been a long day for us, from Liège to Visé to Nessonvaux, and we were eager for dinner once we had settled into the hotel. But dinner was necessarily delayed while the chef and entire hotel staff watched Belgium play Yugoslavia in a football match (U.S. soccer) on television. Several spectators told us several times that the Belgian team was young and untested, with a number of the players competing for the first time in an international match.

Belgium triumphed, 2–0, and we sat down to a most welcome meal.

Day 4: Nessonvaux to Ninglinspo (ca. 19 km, 4-¾ hr)

This was the day on which we learned a hard lesson about route finding on Europe's Grandes Randonnées. The lesson is that not every red-and-white-blazed GR is *your* GR.

We made our first mistake with our first step. There is a sign in the center of Nessonvaux reading "GRV." We headed confidently along this trail, which unfortunately is not GR5 at all and in fact goes in the opposite direction from GR5. It was our *hôtelier* who straightened us out. He came running toward us carrying a map. He was, by the way, the first person we had met in Belgium, at least among people involved with tourism, who knew about the Sentiers de la Grande Randonnée; indeed, his hotel sold maps outlining numerous hikes in the area, including GR5. The GRV, the hotelier informed us, was the trail of the Grande Randonnée de la Vesdre; we had taken the V of Vesdre for a Roman numeral, assuming that the new marking was a quaint Walloon touch. Assume nothing from now on; the GR trails proliferate as you keep walking across Europe.

The correct way out of town leads up a hill to overlook the Vesdre, then across a plateau, then down, and up again. There are even views as you top a plateau, looking down on what a moment ago was completely hidden—a valley, farms, a village of houses and buildings clustered around the ubiquitous church spire.

It was just before Banneux-la-Chapelle that we made our mistake. Following the topo-guide text religiously and studying its not-very-helpful map, we turned left at a chapel and strolled happily along a trail that the topo-guide warned us was *peu marquée* (not well marked). This was true. The trail we followed was *not* well marked; it was also the GR573, and we ended up, in pouring rain, in the town of Pepinster. As compensation for this lost day, our wrong walk was beautiful and our few hours in Pepinster delightful.

The correct GR5 turns left for Banneux after the chapel, onto a trail that is quite well marked indeed. It leads, in little over a kilometer, to Banneux Notre Dame, or Banneux-la-Chapelle.

Banneux is a pilgrimage center. In 1933, twelve-year-old Mariette Beco saw eight apparitions of the Virgin Mary here. The Blessed Virgin commanded that a chapel be built to mark the spot and promised that the local waters would prove to have healing powers. Numerous religious institutions have been established here since. The main street of the town is a line of religious shops, hotels, and restaurants. One restaurant, Le Ruth, is run by a family related to the proprietors of the famed LeRuth's in New Orleans. The Banneux version is a good deal cheaper, and the cuisine is correspondingly less haute. And although Banneux is a good place for a refreshment stop, save lunch for a while. After some 6 or 7 kilometers of beautiful walking through woods and along country lanes that wind among loaflike rolling hills, the trail emerges onto the La Reid road. Just a few steps away is Le Menobu, an inn with a wonderful restaurant. Not an inexpensive place, but delightful, welcoming of walkers, and a good place to get in out of the Belgian weather.

The trail then ascends the Bois de la Porallée, a huge forest and firebreak created on land that had once been a fallow, desolate place swept by harsh winds. From here, it descends gradually to the Ninglinspo stream, one of the most torrential—at times—of the Ardennes waters. A sharp right at the stream leads to a cluster of hotels and restaurants called Sedoz-Nonceveux, at the point where the Ninglinspo flows into the Amblève River.

Day 5: Ninglinspo to Spa
(ca. 16 km, 4 hr)

A shorter day today, so as to have some time in Spa.

The trail wanders up the Ninglinspo, at one point climbing quite steeply to offer a view before reaching a meeting point of two valleys, Ry du Hornay and Ry des Blanches Pierres. There is an almost Byronic quality to the walk along this stream, as if wood and water nymphs were hiding behind trees and among the stream's rocks. On the day we were there, the contemporary equivalent of these nymphs showed up instead: two groups of young hikers—a herd of boys coming from one direction, a crowd of girls following our route. "How many kids are there?" we asked one of the adult counsellors. "One hundred and fifty," she replied. She raised her eyes to heaven as we lowered ours to the stream where the kids seemed bent on getting as wet as possible while testing their high boots in the water. In a narrow valley, one hundred and fifty teenagers seem like ten thousand. We threaded our way among them to climb out of the Porallée and into silence.

Once out of the forest, the trail goes along pleasant country roads, from which you can look back across the valley to where you have been and forward to where you are going. A good hint about the terrain here is in the village of Basse Desnié: a ski lodge, for *ski à fond*—cross-country skiing—for which these low, flat-topped hills are ideally suited.

Up, down, up. Wide plateau gives way to valley from which the walker ascends another plateau. It makes for an easy rhythm, conducive to daydreaming.

Through forests of deciduous trees beneath which forget-me-nots grow in profusion, GR5 leads to Spa. Surrounded by wooded ridges, Spa has been known since Roman times for its waters, allegedly curative, which the crowned heads of Europe and thousands of other people have been taking for centuries. The thermal establishments, the world-famous casino, the palatial hotels of Spa, today wear a weary, ever-so-slightly-shabby look, though the town has revived itself with a series of music festivals and with the development of various tourist services.

In the center of the town is a monument, in English and French, expressing gratitude to the Americans who liberated Spa from the Germans on September 10, 1944. Our presence in a restaurant that evening sparked war stories from the locals, and an argument ensued as to who was the best general among the big three, Patton, Clark, or Patch. In Spa at least, Patton won, hands down.

Day 6: Spa to Hockai
(ca. 27 km, 6-¾ hr)

Having dined on *jambon d'Ardennes* the night before, we were encouraged to try two more local foods today—*gaufres* (hot Belgian waf-

Heading for the Ardennes forest, Wallonie. Photo by Susanna Margolis.

fles) and *tarte au riz* (pie filled with rice pudding). A superb breakfast, though it burdened somewhat the switchbacking climb you take out of town.

Atop the plateau, there are GR markers aplenty, so careful attention is required. Across the plateau, the route plunges downward again, following the Chawion stream. It crosses the stream at a fishing pool, climbs again, stretches through woods, and eventually emerges to pass under the sweeping viaduct of the A27 autoroute.

The walker would do well to detour from GR5 here, crossing the Hoëgne River to enter the town of Polleur, a charming place of stone and brick. The church, with its belfry like a flattened spiral, dates from the fourteenth century; the stone bridge, now restored, dates from 1767. Both are worth seeing, and the shops offer plenty in the way of provisions for a picnic on the bank of the picturesque Hoëgne.

Recross the river to pick up GR5, dipping through the hamlet of Neufmarteau before paralleling the stream, then crossing it, recrossing it, and crossing it again.

The trail enters woods shortly after Moulin de Jalhay, woods filled with the song of cuckoos and wrens but also, the day we were there, noisy with—and redolent of—motorbikes. The latter are used in a pervasive pastime that doesn't do much for the tranquility of the countryside or the condition of woodland trails.

GR5 presses on through the woods to emerge at the Auberge Hertogenwald at the town of Charneux. This hostel-like establishment with dortoir (dormitory) is popular with cross-country skiers in winter and caters to numerous school groups studying the natural history of the Ardennes in spring and summer. It is a good place to buy refreshment and perhaps talk with the gardienne (the custodian), as we did. We remarked with some astonishment that the VVV in Spa made no mention of the auberge when we inquired about lodging and food along the GR5—that, in fact, the VVV knew virtually nothing about the GR5. "There are not many hikers through here," the gardienne agreed, "and you are certainly the first Americans."

From the auberge, the route marches straight down a series of fields, sometimes cutting across them, sometimes following the fences. Then it crosses the valley floor before climbing again. Look behind you as you climb; extraordinary views stretch over the valley of the Hoëgne and beyond to the plateau of Herve. You are looking back across the Wallonie you have traversed.

Thick woods of fir trees as much as two feet across are followed by another crossing of the Hoëgne at Pont de Belleheid, an intersection of restaurants. We arrived there on an election day Sunday. The balloting was for Belgium's representatives to the European Parliament. Voting in Belgium is mandatory, and, among other things, this is excellent for restaurant business. "What else will people do after they vote?" as one restaurateur put it, though she added that the hoteliers were furious because no one was able to leave home for the weekend.

The trail now follows the Hoëgne, along one of its most rapid sections. The route here is rocky, rutted, with treacherous roots underfoot. Where the waters finally calm, you come to a small bridge, Pont du Centenaire, then climb among fields to arrive at the Auberge de Hockai, one of numerous hostels across Europe run by the Amis de la Nature. Here, you are also quite near the village of Hockai with its varied services and accommodations, and you are on the edge of the Hautes-Fagnes.

Day 7: Hockai to Malmédy
(ca. 15 km, 3-¾ hr)

A day of desolate wilderness and lush, cool forests, from the wild heights of the Fagnes to the minty gorge of the Tros Marets stream, to arrive at this city renowned for the destruction it has suffered throughout centuries of war.

The Hautes-Fagnes, with its bogs and marshes, harsh climate, and almost Alpine flora, is the highest region of Belgium. Signal de Botrange, Belgium's highest point at 694 meters, is in this region, although not along GR5.

For the walker, crossing these moors can be slow going. On a sunny day, the heat is intense, while underfoot the soggy soil is easy to sink into and the grassy tussocks are hard to step over.

But there is a special feeling to this place, as you pick your way hopefully from one clump of earth to what looks like the next clump that can hold you. A special silence prevails here, different from the pastoral quiet of the agricultural countryside, or the calm of densely wooded hills, or the tranquillity of sparsely populated villages. For the first time in this journey, you have the sense of wildness; it is an impression not easily come by in Europe.

Yet there are parts of the Hautes-Fagnes where one can see ruins of Roman roads. Vast sections of it have been designated *réserves naturelles* for the animals and plants that procreate here. And naturalists from all over the world are drawn here for study and research.

The GR5 passes no Roman ruins, nor did we see any naturalists at work when we were there; indeed, we saw no one at all as we followed the route across the Fagne de Lonlou and the Fagne de Fraineu to cross the brook of Tros Marets.

The trek across the Fagnes ends when you cross this lovely stream, which GR5 then follows, first along its bank, then climbing high above it, now descending again along a spectacular corniche path. Three times you cross the Tros Marets, until finally you ascend the opposite bank. The steep, narrow valley of the brook is a paradigm of blue-green coolness—stark contrast to the Fagnes.

Proceed along a forestry road to emerge at Ferme Libert, a well-known hotel, downhill ski resort (!), and restaurant specializing in gaufres with fresh cream. The view downhill to Malmédy in the valley of the Warche is stupendous.

From here, the route heads down to the town, crossing fields and strolling lanes. You are in Apollinaire country; Guillaume Apollinaire lived briefly in Stavelot and celebrated this area of Belgium in numerous poems, including one about the Fagnes. Just outside Malmédy, there is an impressive monument to him.

But on the day we were there, war was on our minds, not poetry. All along our route, especially in that fortieth summer after D-Day, Belgians had been reminding us of the role U.S. soldiers had played in their country's history. In the rain in Flanders, we were told, "You think this is bad? You should have seen the weather your soldiers had to contend with in '44!" In Wallonie, it seems there is no one of a certain age who did not personally meet George Patton and show him the route to Germany.

Malmédy holds a particularly dark place in U.S. military history, for it was at a crossroads near this town that German SS troops rounded up more than a hundred American captives, mowed them down with machine-gun fire, then shot through the head any who still breathed or moaned. The massacre reputedly did much to stiffen Allied resistance to the great German counteroffensive that Hitler himself had named Wacht am Rhein, "Watch on the Rhine." The plan of the attack was to push out of the Ardennes to Antwerp. It was in the towns you are about to pass through that the attack was stopped.

Before it was all over, however, the center of Malmédy had been completely destroyed by aerial bombardment. That is hard to imagine as you stroll toward the town through sleepy yet prosperous-looking countryside. Signs announce the pleasures that await the visitor to Malmédy: skiing, excursions, restaurants, and hotels. GR5, in fact, would avoid the center of town, turning right before the bridge over the Warche to pass the tanneries and paper mills that are also part of Malmédy's fame.

Instead, you must detour across the bridge to reach the central square of town. Street signs are in French and Walloon, and many signs are in German; Malmédy is only a stone's throw from the Cantons of the East, the German-speaking region of Belgium, and very near the Eifel forest of Germany whence the Wacht am Rhein was launched against Belgium.

Day 8: Malmédy to Vielsalm
(ca. 26 km, 6-½ hr)

Pastureland, thick forest, and many more reminders of war mark this day's route.

From Malmédy to Stavelot, you walk with rivers, following the Warche to its confluence with the Amblève, then along the Amblève into Stavelot. The walk is previewed in a spectacular view of the Warche valley from the Rocher de Falize, just outside Malmédy. Bucolic is the word. Cows graze, hogs feed, and tractors drive around the fields in ever smaller circles mowing down the sweet-smelling hay.

For us, the tranquillity of our walking was shattered—as it had been for several days—by low-flying fighter jets out on practice runs. As we approached Stavelot, these ear-splitting flights became more numerous. We were aware that NATO is thick in these parts, and, given the facts of history, the locals may be comforted by the presence of these defenders. But their sudden, darting forays startled us each time, and Ginger took to shaking a fist skyward when one passed.

At the entry into Stavelot is the historic Abbey, with remnants dating from the eleventh century. Still standing are several eighteenth-century buildings, which now house the town hall and a regional museum of religious art.

Wander through Stavelot; it is a good place for lunch, especially if you find a restaurant that serves the salad called *frisée à lardon*—escarole with Ardennes ham in a sauce. The town is small and sleepy, and its cobblestone streets contain old houses with interesting slate facades, and pleasant fountains that still serve the populace. In 1899, Guillaume Apollinaire lived briefly in the Hôtel Le Mal Aimé, which is still a hotel, and Stavelot seems never to have gotten over the fact. Apollinaire memorabilia are everywhere.

But mostly, of course, it is war memorabilia you see. In the main square of the town is a small stone which reads, "Ici fut arreté l'envahisseur, Hiver 1944-45" (Here the invader was stopped, Winter 1944-45). On the bridge over the Amblève, as you leave town, is a memorial, with letters missing, to 131 Stavelot citizens gunned down on the spot during the German offensive. Across the bridge, another memorial lists

One of the quiet, timeless hamlets of Wallonie, Belgium. Photo by Susanna Margolis.

the names of 26 victims massacred on "ces rivages de l'Amblève." "Souvenez vous," the memorial commands the reader; Remember! It is hard not to in this part of Belgium.

The trail climbs out of Stavelot—take care at the intersection of GR5 and GR-A (Amblève)—and again stretches through forest. In less than 7 kilometers, you arrive at Les Gattes, the charming chalet run by Les Amis de la Nature at Logbiermé. A forty-four-bed, do-your-own-cooking auberge, the place caters particularly to weekending or vacationing Liègois. On one wall of the cozy dining room there is a snowshoe which once belonged to a Canadian soldier; the snow in that winter of 1944–1945, we were told, was four feet deep.

Several Liègois couples—all friends—were arriving at Les Gattes just as we did. Many said they had been coming here since it was founded in 1956. They told us of the deer and fox that used to roam freely in these woods. One of them once saw a wild boar; he cheerfully admitted that the sight nearly scared him to death. But many of these wilder animals haven't been seen since the twenties or thirties; industrial and agricultural development have pushed them east into the forests of Czechoslovakia and Poland.

Take some refreshment at Les Gattes before pressing on to Vielsalm along more fields and through more forests. The slate you see on the houses and barns around here once provided Vielsalm its major industry—whetstones. Synthetic production has nearly destroyed the industry, but a large piece of local slate in Vielsalm's wedge-shaped square is today a memorial to General Hasbrouck and the American Seventh Armored Division, which defended the town before regrouping to participate in the Allied counterattack that would finally end the Battle of the Bulge.

Day 9: Vielsalm to Burg-Reuland (ca. 26 km, 6-½ hr)

Today's route enters the German-speaking Cantons de l'Est (Cantons of the East) and the Luxembourg Province of Belgium.

The route out of Vielsalm moves past slate quarries before entering woods which give way to meadows. The steep plateaus of the last several days seem to have smoothed out; the walk here is mostly along rural lanes and passes through few villages, although you can see a number of hamlets across fields.

The Cantons of the East—Eupen, Malmédy, and Saint-Vith—were returned to Belgium by the Treaty of Versailles in 1919. The German-speaking area here constitutes one of the four official language zones of Belgium, and the first German-speaking town you come to is Braunlauf, quietly agricultural. The route follows hayfields—new-mown when we were there—to the intersection called Schirm-Grufflange on the Saint-Vith–Luxembourg road. Someone had marked up the

French spelling of Luxembourg on the sign so that it read "Luxemburg."

On through plantation timber forests and out into fields; the valley of the Ulf River is at your feet. Down to the village of Bracht, then up again, and down at last into Burg-Reuland, where you must detour from GR5 to find a hotel for your last night's sleep in Belgium.

10
Riverbanking in Luxembourg

"Mir woelle bleiwe wat mir sin" reads the national motto of Luxembourg: "We wish to remain what we are." The question is, what *are* they? What is this little tiny country, known to many Americans as a place you take a train out of after your transatlantic flight lands there? Or as a banking center, a tax haven, or the seat of the Secretariat of the European Parliament, where the Council of Ministers of the European Community meets for three months of the year.

Few people know that tiny Luxembourg is the most motorized country in Europe, with the largest number of cars per capita of any European nation. Nor do they guess that Luxembourg's 775-kilometer network of marked walking paths is the densest in the world, as is its percentage of youth hostels. This incongruity, well hidden to both walkers and drivers, is only the first of many incongruities Luxembourg presents.

"Mir woelle bleiwe wat mir sin"—the words are in Letzeburgesch, the medieval Germanic-Dutch dialect that is the everyday language of most Luxembourgers, although it was not declared the country's official tongue until 1984, when its grammar and spelling were standardized. The words come from a song, composed in the nineteenth century to protest the arrival of railway lines from Paris and Brussels. But if Luxembourgers fear that foreign intrusion will dilute their cultural identity, it is also true that nearly one-fourth of the nation's population consists of foreign workers, whose labor helps ensure the highest standard of living among the countries of the European Economic Community. Meanwhile, the bureaucracy of the EEC has been given a welcome home in Luxembourg, where staff activities provide some 10 percent of the Grand Duchy's income.

So much for influx. As for outgo, it is said that there are more Luxembourgers in Chicago than in Luxembourg.

Although Letzeburgesch is the true native language, its use is officially optional. French is the language of administration and the one in which schoolchildren are taught. Newspapers are in German, except for selected articles on culture, which are in French. English is also recognized as an official language, but do not count on this as you walk the GR5 through Luxembourg.

Luxembourg's history is even more difficult to follow than its use of languages. An ideal buffer state, it has been conquered, partitioned, exchanged, and overrun by virtually every European power that ever existed; it has been in somebody's way in virtually every major war ever fought in Europe. First emerging as a political entity in the Middle Ages as a fief of the Holy Roman Empire, Luxembourg later gained the distinction of supplying rulers for other European powers—among them the House of Nassau, ruling family of the Netherlands. Like the other Benelux countries, Luxembourg has enjoyed Burgundian, Habsburgian, Spanish, and Austrian rule. It was under French rule twice, though it is said that when Napoleon swept Luxembourg into his net and was offered the key of the capital city, he returned it with a smile, telling the assembled citizenry, "The key is in good hands; take it back."

The Congress of Vienna in 1815 created the Grand Duchy of Luxembourg, but gave it to King William I of the Netherlands; a Prussian garrison was positioned in the capital. When Belgium gained independence from the Netherlands in 1830, a portion of Luxembourg was part of the deal: the Belgian province of Luxembourg, from which the GR5 walker has just arrived.

It wasn't until 1867 that Luxembourg was granted recognition as an independent and neutral grand duchy, and it wasn't until 1890 that its very own Grand Duke was appointed, Duke Adolf of Nassau (off a collateral branch of the Dutch royal tree). Adolf was an enthusiastic sovereign, who declared that "from this day forth I am, like you, a Luxembourger." The new Grand Duke promised to work for the development of the nation's "free institutions, as well as for the consolidation of her autonomy and her independence in the sight of Europe."

That autonomy was violated by the Germans in two world wars. In the second, Grand Duchess Charlotte and her son, Jean, who later succeeded as Grand Duke, went into exile. Jean served in the Irish Guards and was among the first Allied soldiers to enter a liberated Luxembourg in 1945.

The liberators were American soldiers and George Patton, who blunted von Runstedt's winter offensive on the soil of Luxembourg just before Christmas, 1944. The U.S. troops suffered extremely heavy losses— some 9,000 men. Most of them are buried in Luxembourg's U.S. military cemetery in Hamm, just outside Luxembourg-Ville, the capital city. Among the graves there is that of Patton himself. Though he died after the fighting was over—ironically, in a car accident near Luxembourg-Ville—his wish was to be buried with the soldiers of the Third Army.

Luxembourg today is ruled by the constitutional monarch, Grand Duke Jean, who is also Duke of Nassau and Prince of Bourbon Parma, but who lacks any political power. The country's government is a de facto rotating coalition between two of its three main parties. As a prime minister put it, "In so small a country, the room for political controversy is limited."

Luxembourg is not so small a country when you walk it, and when you do, you become keenly aware of the diversity of the terrain, climate, and vegetation. The northern part of the country, the schist- and slate-bound area known as Oesling, is a riven plateau that extends the Belgian Ardennes, joining it to the Eifel. The area is called the Ardennes Luxembourgeoises.

The southern region, Gutland or Bon Pays, a softer sandstone massif, is geologically a northern extension of France's Lorraine.

Local descriptions of the landscape confirm the impression that there is no such thing as a quintessentially Luxembourgian topography; rather, pieces of the country take their identity from comparison with other places. Where the rough Oesling meets the gentler incline of Gutland, erosion has created a more or less east-west chain of abrupt cornichelike ledges and ravines, forested with beech. This area, which the walker comes upon near Beaufort, is called Petite Suisse (Little Switzerland), while the vine-covered banks of the Moselle are often referred to, understandably, as the Midi of the Benelux.

With this topographic hodgepodge comes a corresponding diversity of climate and therefore of flora. Walking through Oesling, you see species of Atlantic, even oceanic, vegetation. Heading south, rugged mountain elements show up. Among the vineyards of the Moselle are plants one associates with a Mediterranean climate and the dry soil of the South.

But despite the associations to other, more dramatically identifiable places, Luxembourg is not any other place. It isn't the Midi, or Switzerland, or an offshoot of Belgium. It is what it is—quietly autonomous, free from any illusions about the realities of its history, highly literate, extremely prosperous, comfortable with its own incongruities. If that is what Luxembourgers have wished to remain, then, by hook or by crook, through a tortured history, precariously balanced between great powers to east and west, they have managed it very well.

One thing Luxembourg certainly is: a wonderful place to walk. Its very diversity makes it so—that and the look of the place. If the towns and villages seem a set from a Sigmund Romberg operetta, the countryside of Luxembourg looks like a Walt Disney fairy tale—castle ruins on hilltops, misty forests that follow meandering rivers, vineyards lined with lime trees.

The largest of the five small independent European countries, Luxembourg is nevertheless only 82 kilometers long as the crow flies. The GR5 route, however, does not fly as the crow but wanders and hedges, primarily to avoid the highways on which, presumably, all those car-owning Luxembourgers are driving. South/southeast, south/southwest, due east, due south, south/southwest again—the crow's 82 kilometers become the walker's 211 kilometers.

The walk takes nine days, but two additional days are recommended for the stay in Luxembourg. For the megawalker, a layover day is in order, and Echternach, a pleasant place, a good provisioning stop, and about halfway through Luxembourg, fits the bill. In addition, no one who comes to Luxembourg should miss Luxembourg-Ville. It is easily reachable by bus, train, or hitch from virtually any town in the country—we went there from Echternach—and is worth at least a day's sightseeing. It is the last day of the itinerary in Luxembourg.

The Luxembourg itinerary can be divided into three parts—or three rivers. GR5 takes the walker down the Our, which forms the border with Germany, as far as Vianden, then cuts across country to meet and follow the Sûre, here flowing east. The route then travels with the Sûre till it falls into the Moselle—also the border with Germany—and finally heads south, up-river, along the Moselle's left bank.

The Our Valley is a forested plateau cut by many feeder streams. Wooded hills alternate with narrow valleys through which the streams run; for the walker, it is a trek of relentless ups and downs. It was in the Our Valley that we first came upon the topo-guide phrase, *couper un méandre*—literally, to "cut a meander," something GR5 often does along that wandering waterway. Shortened and Americanized—as in "to coup" or "I think it coups a meander here"—the phrase found permanent acceptance in the vocabulary of our trip.

After cutting overland from Vianden to follow the Sûre, GR5 for the most part crosses pleasant fields before coming to the jagged faults and folds of Petite Suisse. Here—around Beaufort, Grundhof, Berdorf—you enter a world that is dark green in color and jagged in appearance. You climb in and among the deep, narrow declivities to the accompanying music of swiftly cascading brooks. The rocks and cliffs are covered with moss and ferns; a dense forest canopy preserves the cool, moist feeling of the place.

The last river is the Moselle, and the walking here is like strolling along a balcony overlooking a stage set of vineyards—pleasant, winding walking along well-worn *chemins viticoles* (vineyard service roads) as you contour the hillsides, then dip down to a fairy-tale village on the river's edge.

The tag end of the walk through Luxembourg is a westward trek across grain-field plateaus and through the country's industrial and mining basin—a prelude to Lorraine.

In practical terms, the most serious task confronting the GR5 walker in Luxembourg is keeping track of the trail markers. Forget the red and white stripes you have been following these last weeks; Luxembourg has its own varied way of guiding you, and the walker would do well to keep in mind from the start the names of the towns or areas where the markings change.

Right away, at the border, the red and white stripes disappear and a yellow disc (*boule jaune*) takes over. Follow this to a point just beyond Rodershausen on the hill called Geislay, where you pick up another trans-Europe trail, marked by a green triangle on white background. After Echternach, you pick up the trail of the lower Sûre and Moselle, marked with a yellow rectangle. At Remerschen, it's back to the *boule jaune* you started out with, except that near the Parc Merveilleux it is accompanied by the yellow triangle of the Sentier du Sud (Trail of the South). Take heart: the moment you cross the border into France, the familiar red and white markers reappear; after walking Luxembourg, you need to get used to them all over again.

In Luxembourg, we formulated four more guidelines for walking Europe from top to bottom. The first is the Law of the Weekly Market: "If the hiker comes to a town with a weekly market, it will have been held yesterday." The second law, similar but more complex, is the Law of Evening Entertainment: "The hiker will arrive in a town either the evening before or the evening after the town holds a concert or theatrical entertainment." The third law is of the same nature again, but can cause much more trouble. It is the Law of Financial Embarrassment, sometimes called the Money Law: "The hiker will run out of local currency

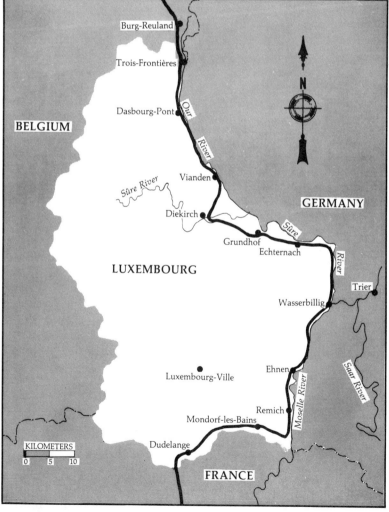

Luxembourg

on a Friday on which his route passes through villages too small to have banks and/or where local merchants will not cash traveler's checks." The fourth guideline is the all-important Principle of the Perfidious Ignorance of Locals: "Absolutely certain information offered by the indigenous population (in answer to such questions as 'Is there a restaurant in this town?' or 'Where is the nearest café?') is invariably wrong. Trust your instincts."

The Law of the Weekly Market remained unbroken throughout the rest of our trip across Europe. The Law of Evening Entertainment was broken only once. The inexorable working of the Money Law forced us to make a half-day detour in Luxembourg, and while the Law worked for one or the other of us on virtually every Friday of our trip, we were always able to manage. We ourselves failed to heed the Principle of the Perfidious Ignorance of Locals on numerous occasions; we were always sorry.

Luxembourg

Day 1	Burg-Reuland (Belgium) to		
	Trois-Frontières	13 km	3-¼ hr
	Trois-Frontières to Dasbourg-Pont	16 km	4 hr
		29 km	7-¼ hr
Day 2	Dasbourg-Pont to Vianden	27 km	6-¾ hr
Day 3	Vianden to Diekirch	17 km	4-¼ hr
Day 4	Diekirch to Grundhof	23 km	5-¾ hr
Day 5	Grundhof to Echternach	11 km	2-¾ hr
Day 6	Echternach (layover)		
Day 7	Echternach to Wasserbillig	25 km	6-¼ hr
Day 8	Wasserbillig to Ehnen	28 km	7 hr
Day 9	Ehnen to Mondorf-les-Bains	28 km	7 hr
Day 10	Mondorf-les-Bains to		
	Dudelange/Luxembourg-Ville	23 km	5-¾ hr
Day 11	Luxembourg-Ville (layover)		
		211 km	52-¾ hr

Day 1: Burg-Reuland (Belgium) to Dasbourg-Pont (ca. 29 km, 7-¼ hr)

The way out of Belgium proceeds more or less along the Our River, but first GR5 sees to it that you visit the sights of Burg-Reuland; namely, an eleventh-century chateau, from whose tower there are beautiful views up the valley of the Ulf. The route turns down-valley to the western bank of the Our, along which it remains all day. This is particularly important to remember when leaving the town of Stoubach (good refreshment stop), where the route seems to veer left; if you follow it, you would cross the Our, so look for a right turn leading uphill out of Stoubach.

The climb out of Stoubach leads to a plateau where GR5 actually touches the Luxembourg border; a stone plinth marks the dividing line, and the town of Leithum, in Luxembourg, is less than a kilometer away. GR5, however, descends slightly eastward, heading across open fields where you must check every shed and outhouse for the red and white markers. Just before Ouren, GR5 heads up through a church graveyard along a prominence featuring the Twelve Stations of the Cross; there seems no other reason for this deviation, and those of little faith may wish to plod on into Ouren via road.

There is a long afternoon ahead, and not much chance of refreshment along the way, so do not leave Ouren without being well fed.

The border is 1.2 kilometers away. It is a place where three nations meet. A footbridge crosses the Our, narrow at this point, into Germany. Another small bridge jumps the Ribbach brook into Luxembourg. The site is marked by a monument to what has thus far proven an elusive hope—a united Europe.

We were the only people at the site the day we passed through. The monument is not mentioned in the topo-guide, nor in the Michelin guide, nor in any of the tourist brochures we had collected along the route. Nor is there a customs control office or a border guard to stamp passports.

Just step across the stream into Luxembourg.

A deadly quiet four-hour walk follows, from the Belgian border to Dasbourg-Pont. It is a spectacularly beautiful walk, enhanced by the quietness. A very real sense of remoteness pervades this walk; the only other humanity we saw was a trio of kayakers on the river below.

The first couple of kilometers, as you set off to follow the yellow disc road, are an easy amble along the river bank. The area is accessible to cars and furnished with picnic tables for the fishermen who stand at regular intervals above the lazy river.

The leisurely walking is deceptive. The route leaves the road and begins to climb through dark forest as the Our cuts the valley more deeply, with abrupt twistings and turnings. You climb, contour along a ledge—sometimes looking through foliage to the swift river below, sometimes gaining a view straight across to the German bank of the Our—then descend a gully to climb again. It is good, hard walking through an almost magical forest.

Now hugging the river, now cutting its meanders, the route comes to Kasselslay, a regal prominence dominating the river. The yellow-disc GR5 winds halfway up Kasselslay; it is well worth it to drop your pack and sprint up to the top for the view. The detour trail to the viewpoint—and the pack-dropping-off point—are well marked, and the panorama up and down the Our Valley is staggering.

The trail cuts another meander shortly before Dasbourg-Pont. Be sure you are going uphill (right, away from the river); Dasbourg, only a few hundred meters farther, will soon be in view.

Dasbourg-Pont is a customs point. Luxembourgian *douane* and German *zoll* stare at each other from opposite ends of the bridge. The café there offers lodging as well as meals, at which you might as well start ordering the wines of the Luxembourg Moselle. Further back on the highway, toward Belgium, there is a caravan campsite; enterprising hikers might be able to talk their way into renting a caravan for the night.

The customs guards regularly stop trucks crossing the bridge and occasionally stop cars. Walkers pass with impunity, so you can stroll over to Germany for an after-dinner walk. The German side of the Our, like the Luxembourgian side, is a narrow riverbank backed by a steep cliff.

Day 2: Dasbourg-Pont to Vianden (ca. 27 km, 6-¾ hr)

A long day of meandering with the river or climbing heights to cut its meanders. The walking is too lovely here to try to make time, but get an early start so you can enjoy a leisurely evening in Vianden, a town of exceptional charm.

The route starts out along the highway, the N10, as far as Rodershausen. If the shop is open, and if the weather bids fair, this is a good place to buy provisions for a picnic, though there is also the possibility of lunch-with-a-view in Untereisenbach or Wahlhausen—both of which, however, come a bit too soon for a midday meal.

It is also possible to get to Rodershausen along the German side; this detour affords a look at some ruins of a Siegfried Line bunker. You cross back to Luxembourg on a wooden footbridge, arriving at the southern end of Rodershausen, just at the point where the yellow discs head uphill.

Wild daisies and foxglove line the path up to Geislay, where there is a fine view of the valley and where the GR5, known as E-2, meets the E-3, the trail leading from the Atlantic through the Ardennes to Bohemia.

The joint trail leads now up and over a meander-slicing cliff to Obereisenbach, then climbs again to reach Untereisenbach. Ubereisenbach, largest of the Eisenbachs, is mostly across the river in Germany. But Untereisenbach offers a set of terrace restaurants that afford views of the river and its opposite bank. If you're ready for lunch, this is the spot; it is at least worth a refreshment pause. Beer lovers should try Bofferding, which we discovered in the Eisenbachs.

Up again now as the trail takes a great leap away from the river and follows back roads into Wahlhausen. At 499 meters, Wahlhausen is one of the higher points in Luxembourg and offers excellent views of the Our Valley. Wemperhardt, *not* on GR5, at 559 meters, is the official apex.

The trail leads down among fields and forest, goes along the N10 for a while, then climbs and descends into Stolzembourg, a small village under a ruined castle on the hill. The simple church, with its gray exterior and folkloric reliefs depicting the Stations of the Cross inside, is worth a look. We were there on the day before Luxembourg's National Day (June 23 is the holiday), and the horizontal tricolor that is the national flag bedecked the interior.

National holidays may inspire national pride; in any event, we got a taste of the latter in a café in Stolzembourg. Chatting with the customs agent we recognized from Dasbourg-Pont, we asked if French or German were his first language.

"Luxembourgeois!" was the almost indignant answer (in French).

"That's a German dialect, isn't it?" we continued.

"C'est une *langue*," came the answer, in a solemn voice and accompanied by a rather stern look. "It's a language."

We apologized; the customs man wished us "Bonne Promenade"; an incident was averted. We found the natives of Luxembourg in general to be less cheerfully friendly than the Belgians, and it was the one place anywhere on our trip where a hotelier upped the price of rooms when he heard we were American. But the Luxembourgian sense of irony, which they direct at themselves more than at others, has its charms. The overcharging hotelier, by the way, couldn't do enough for us once he had stiffed us.

From Stolzembourg, there is a long climb up to one of Europe's most powerful hydroelectric plants atop Mont Saint Nicolas. Hidden from view until you're right at it, the plant was one of the first in the world to make use of a very simple principle: store energy when demand is low, then feed it back into the system when demand is heavy. The huge pumps of Mont Saint Nicolas draw water from Our Valley reservoirs during off-peak periods; the water is stored in the hilltop reservoir GR5 passes. When demand rises, the water stored atop Mont Saint Nicolas is converted into energy and flows back into the valley reservoirs again.

Mont Saint Nicolas is something of a tourist attraction; this means that there are a couple of cafés right near the *bassin*, the artificial lake, which is worth a look in any event.

The trail heads downward, offering a splendid view of the curious peninsula that projects into the Our from the Luxembourg side. Then it climbs to the charming chapel called Bildchen, climbs again to the pavilion above Vianden, and descends underneath the chairlift to arrive at the chateau, one of Europe's most striking fortresses.

Victor Hugo, who came to Vianden in 1871 as part of his self-exile from France, called the town a "jewel set in splendid scenery" and named as highlights the "sinister ruin" of the castle and the cheerful nature of the people.

Vianden has been playing host to other voluntary exiles—namely, tourists—for a long time, and boasts a wealth of hotels and restaurants of every category as well as a large, comfortable youth hostel.

The town and its castle are worth more than a quick look; save the following morning for sightseeing.

Day 3: Vianden to Diekirch
(ca. 17 km, 4-¼ hr)

Among the sights of Vianden are the house (now a museum) where Victor Hugo wrote *L'Année Terrible* and much of his best poetry; the ancient ramparts; the double-nave parish church, built in 1248 and one of the oldest religious buildings in Luxembourg; the Trinitarian cloister (restored) with its tombstones on the graves of Vianden nobility; and an interesting folklore museum.

But the town's chief sight—and absolutely not to be missed—is Hugo's "sinister ruin," less a ruin since restoration work was set in progress, and sinister only in recalling some of the unpleasant things that might have gone on during the fortress's thousand-year history. A hexagonal hole in the middle of the chapel floor, for example, opens downward to the dungeon, which is indeed sinister. On the other hand, the Knight's Hall, reputed to have been able to accommodate 500 warriors, is quite grand. Mostly, the view of this castle from without, and especially as you head for Diekirch and put some distance between you and it, is a vision of something quintessentially European and highly theatrical. Under the spotlights that illumine the castle on a summer evening, or even in the middle of a gloomy and overcast day, the corbelled turrets and gables of Vianden's castle, perched on its craggy hillside, present a fairy-tale appearance the walker will not soon forget.

The fairy-tale castle of Vianden, Luxembourg. Photo by Ginger Harmon.

What the tourist office probably will not tell you about the castle is that not all of its ruination was due to natural causes. In 1820, one of the city administrators bought the castle for himself. Times were hard, and to help make ends meet, the new owner spent seven years selling off bits and pieces of the castle for building material: the entire copper roof, all the wooden beams, and even portions of the wall. Though this is no different from what happened to most of Europe's great monuments of antiquity—and no worse—the authorities do not give much play to the scandal. The restoration work, in any event, makes the point moot.

The walk from Vianden to Diekirch takes about four hours. GR5 in fact does not go through Diekirch, but it is the appropriate stopping point if you devote some time to sightseeing in Vianden, and Diekirch itself is well worth the short detour.

Leave Vianden from behind the youth hostel where GR5 climbs to meet the highway. There is a fine viewpoint and photo opportunity spot here, looking back toward the castle. The trail follows alongside and then actually on the highway into Bettel, a village offering both provisioning—*ravitaillement*—and a handsome modern church, with windows by Wilhelm de Graaff.

The trail heads towards Longsdorf along a back road, climbing well away from the river. At the sanctuary of Marxberg, you can visit the interesting Gothic chapel of Saint Mark, where the iron crowns that pilgrims put on to cure headaches are on display. Then away, along a country road, before stretching out along the fields and woods of the plateau.

The countryside here makes a subtle shift from schist formations to sandstone; at Bettendorfer Berg, you can see limestone quarries where marine fossils have been found. You can also look down onto the valley of the Sûre River, enroute here to the Moselle from its source near Bastogne in Belgium. GR5 now descends to the river, which it will cross into Gilsdorf. The pretty route into Diekirch is over the river and to the right along its bank. Or, you can continue along N19 for some twenty minutes into town.

Diekirch brews the most commonly served beer in Luxembourg, Diekirch beer. The town is a major commerical center and, given its location, a major thoroughfare. On the Sûre, it lies on the main east-west axis of the country; it is also the dividing line between Oesling and Gutland. Perhaps to save the charm of the town from the traffic, the historic center has been turned into a pedestrian mall. We were there on National Day, and the squares and winding streets of Old Diekirch were hung gaily with flags and filled with holidaymakers.

There are several worthwhile sights in Diekirch. The church of Saint Laurent has a Roman right nave (built on a Roman structural foundation) and a Gothic left nave. It is in the heart of the old center, whose streets and lanes are fun to explore. In this nation so rich in Gallo-Roman remains, the walker should not miss the Roman mosaics from a third century villa discovered in the 1920s along what is today the

Esplanade. The mosaics are housed in the Municipal Museum on Place Guillaume, outside the pedestrian center. The highlight of the mosaics is the head of Medusa, which shows different faces when looked at from different angles. The villa was evidently substantial, if not lavish; the three skeletons found there, the absence of articles of real value, and the presence of ashes have led scholars to surmise that it was destroyed by invading Franks.

A monument from even further back in time is just outside the city (follow signs marked Promenade H). This is the so-called Autel du Diable ("Devil's Altar"), a Celtic megalith believed to be of neolithic origins.

Day 4: Diekirch to Grundhof (ca. 23 km, 5-¾ hr)

Welcome to Little Switzerland, the Petite Suisse Luxembourgeoise.

Grundhof, on the Ernz Noire stream, is the heart of this region and is a good stopping point for the night after a walk of nearly six hours.

It is a varied walk—woods, fields, streams, and the sandstone formations that are the hallmark of Little Switzerland.

Head back from Diekirch to the Gilsdorf crossing on whichever side of the river you prefer. GR5 traverses Gilsdorf, then cuts up a field— fine views backward to the Sûre—and enters a long forest trail that crosses the top of the plateau.

Emerging from the forest, you can see Eppeldorf in the distance, but you must dip down and up again across fields before entering this small, quiet village, where a café and shop offer refreshment. We seemed to be the only creatures moving in Eppeldorf the day we were there. As we emerged from the eighteenth-century village church, however, two dogs came snarlingly toward us. They were called off by a young woman who, it turned out, ran the local café. Over a sandwich and beer, she entreated us, in a combination of halting English and almost as halting French, to try to understand the diversity of Luxembourg.

You see more of this diversity as you leave Eppeldorf, zigging west then zagging east to avoid highway, and stretching along a stream lined with curious rock formations before coming to the two chateaux of Beaufort.

The chateaux are the imposing ruin of a twelfth-century castle and the elegant seventeenth-century building next door. The twelfth-century chateau may—and should—be visited. (Packs can be left behind the ticket window.) It is a maze of dungeons, torture chambers, and various living rooms. Watercolors hung in each room depict how life may have been lived in that room six or seven hundred years ago.

The chateau next door can be seen from the balconies of the older fortress. Its graceful facade, tastefully opulent, fits perfectly its current use as a concert hall. There was a concert in progress the day we passed through, and Handel's "Water Music" floated over to us as we stood on a twelfth-century parapet looking out over the wooded park of Beaufort. You need to climb (via staircase) the ancient ramparts to enter the town of Beaufort itself. It is a charming town, with restaurants, cafés, hotels, and a youth hostel.

The official GR5 skirts the center of town, going around the swan-filled lake across from the chateaux, then stretching along the brook called Hallerbach. This stream is said to have a thousand small cascades; its rapid flow makes it a good spot for observing water ouzels. We saw one bobbing along the stream, then quickly submerging to chase insects or whatever was on the menu that day.

Another species in evidence along the Hallerbach is the fisherman, usually stationed in an area marked Pêche Privée, *privée* to one or another of the nearby hotels.

The banks of the Hallerbach present the walker a moist, green canopy of beech and paths that wander among fragrant pine trees, but the banks are also lined with the ornate sandstone rocks typical of the area. The paths here are accessible and hence well traveled; the walker might feel more as if he is in a wooded park than in countryside.

The trail emerges onto a highway, which it tracks toward Grundhof. But GR5 turns right, over the Ernz Noire stream and up a hill, without actually following the road to the center of Grundhof where the Ernz Noire meets the Sûre. Detour here, staying on the road and proceeding toward the Sûre riverbank; it is lined with hotels clustered near the bridge. Grundhof is a walker's center, offering numerous excursions for hikers, so it presents the walker the chance to meet like-minded Luxembourgers.

Day 5: Grundhof to Echternach (ca. 11 km, 2-¾ hr)

A short day today, through dark, moist woods and among sandstone chasms and gullies, to arrive in time for some sightseeing in Echternach, a beautiful and ancient (restored) town that offers the walker abundant facilities for provisioning and other errands.

Backtracking out of Grundhof along Chemin Rural 121, the walker reaches the small bridge crossing the Ernz Noire creek. The path across it is marked Promenade B-2 as well as GR5, and it leads uphill toward the viewpoint of Kasselt.

From Kasselt, the trail stretches above the Ernz Noire Valley alongside a balcony of marching cliffs, many of them split to form narrow gorges—the Seven Gorges and the Zigzag Gorge, in particular. Berdorf, to which the route leads, has a climbing school, and it is on the vertical sandstone cliffs of this valley that the *escalade* students practice; the names of the climbing routes are painted on the faces of many of the rocks. The day we walked among them was a wet one, and the combination of slippery sandstone and slippery moss, which covers the rockfaces, seemed to present some tricky climbing. Nevertheless, despite steady drizzle and occasional downpours, there were climbers hanging from one cliff or another all along the route.

Berdorf is another tourist center, one of the principal ones in Luxembourg, not least because of the walking and climbing possibilities that abound here. The town is on a wide tableland in the midst of the valleys of the Ernz Noire, the Sûre, and the Aesbach stream. The area as a whole is also known as the Mullerthal, and it is the picturesque heart of Petite Suisse, the eroded midrib between Oesling and Gutland.

We did indeed meet hikers in Berdorf, of a very special stripe, who both gave us a foretaste of France and introduced us to an important segment of European outdoors people. They were a group of French walkers, some thirty strong, from Metz, where they formed a chapter of the Club Vosgien called the Troisième Age (third age), equivalent to American golden age clubs. Hikers all their lives, these people were no longer able to do the rigorous Alpine climbing of their younger days, but they were not about to give up the out-of-doors, so they arranged bus tours to areas providing gentler walking, such as here in Luxembourg, with lunch stops in restaurants like the one in which we met them, where they were finishing up a lavish, wine-filled lunch with large glasses of cognac.

We found this lively group delightful, and frankly, the feeling was mutual. They showed us maps, warned us that the trail markings for the GR5 in the Vosges were not very good (which we discovered to be true, in spades), hefted our packs, wished us "Bon Courage," a phrase we were to hear more and more as we headed south. They looked the picture of European hikers; although some of the women wore wide, flowing skirts, almost everyone else was in knickerbocker pants, with high socks and high boots, and all carried walking sticks. A spry eighty-seven-year-old, with only two teeth left, sang to us—inspired partly, no doubt, by the cognac he had been imbibing—first, a mountain song about "quatre-vingt chasseurs qui n'avaient pas peur" (eighty hunters who had no fear), then a love song. He also kissed our hands before departing. A Frenchman, after all, is a Frenchman. Even in Luxembourg, and even at eighty-seven.

GR5 traverses Berdorf and heads across a field toward woods. There are a number of trail markers here, and the effect is confusing. Head *down* to the Aesbach brook. The trail follows beside the brook, passing among ferns, under overhanging rocks, through a dark green beech forest with a decidedly primeval feel to it.

Through these woods, the trail comes to the Gorge du Loup, or Wolfschlucht, a doleful chasm cut between two high cliffs. Staircases enable exploration of this site; one leads to the viewpoint of Bildscheslay, from which there is a fine view down to the Sûre. As the trail leaves the Gorge du Loup, note the natural formation called Cleopatra's Needle.

GR5 continues to climb, emerging from forest at another viewpoint called Trooskneppchen—a bit more citified, with a pavilion and café. From here, it is an easy downhill stroll into Echternach.

Day 6: Echternach (layover day)

This is the city of the Benedictine Abbey founded by Saint Willibrord, who came from Britain's Northumberland in the seventh century and Christianized northern Europe, effecting an alliance between the Carolingian dynasty and the Papacy. The saint's remains are in the crypt of the Echternach Basilica, the most important religious building in the Grand Duchy.

The basilica and most of Echternach were in fact destroyed in World War II during the von Runstedt offensive when, from October of 1944 to March of 1945, the town and the surrounding area constituted a no-man's-land between armies. After the war, Echternach was rebuilt in only three years: the basilica was reconstructed; other ancient buildings were restored; and today again, thanks to twentieth-century technology, the town brims with medieval atmosphere.

In the summer, Echternach caters to hordes of pilgrims and tourists who come for the famous *sprang prozession*, a danced pilgrimage to the tomb of Saint Willibrord, held on Whit-Tuesday. With its origins shrouded in mystery and conjecture—some connect it with the Saint Vitus Dance; others say it started as a murderer's successful ploy to evade punishment—the Echternach procession combines religion, merrymaking, and Moselle wines in a day-long homage to Saint Willibrord. It is one of the major folkloric festivals of Europe.

Even if your timing is not right for Whit-Tuesday, there is much to see in Echternach. The town hall on the market square, the patrician façades along the narrow streets, the abbey with its *orangerie*, the park with its pavilion, the restored Roman villa—all these make Echternach a pleasant place to pass time.

The megawalker can take further pleasure from the fact that he has come about 400 miles from his starting point in Holland and is more than one-quarter of the way down Europe. This fact, and the numerous shops and facilities of Echternach, make it a good resting place.

We parked ourselves here for two days. We had made Echternach a poste restante, so one day was spent in collecting and answering mail, with time out for feasting on the *Herald Tribune*, *Time*, and *Newsweek*; shopping for depleted supplies; seeing some sights; and getting haircuts.

Day 7: Echternach to Wasserbillig (ca. 25 km 6-¼hr)

This final day along the Sûre is a walk of almost wild zigzagging up and down through cool, deep forest, with occasional descents to riverbank villages. The day ends where the Sûre ends, in a lively and much-frequented city on the banks of the great Moselle.

It is a very green day, through forests—primarily of beech—whose high canopy was thick enough to shield us from frequent rain the day we walked through. There is the green of the leaves, the green moss hugging the tree trunks, thick green undergrowth, green reflecting back on green from forest floor to ceiling. The Californian member of our partnership, admitting that, to her, grass is normally yellow, routinely referred to these woods as rain forest. To the New Yorker among us, they were reminiscent of the hills and sudden gullies of the Catskill range, or the lower slopes of the Adirondacks.

GR5 is marked by the yellow rectangle on this stage; it is the path of the Basse-Sûre (Lower Sûre) and ends at the confluence of the Sûre and Moselle at Wasserbillig. Leaving Echternach, the route goes along the river in the town's park, then leads up the rise of the riverbank and away from the town.

The trail goes through quiet beech forest made dramatic by flamboyant rock formations, here of limestone. Some of the formations are cut with steps, which form part of the trail; the rock shapes themselves have names: Veitcheslay and Roudeschleff.

It is beautiful walking among these trees and rocks, over a thick, soft ground cover of leaves—but beware of the nettles and thistles that occasionally make the walker's passage a prickly one.

The trail descends into Rosport, for which Rosport water—the local sparkling water—is named. It then ascends along the Dickweiler road and again enters forest, which it follows to Girsterklaus, with its charming twelfth-century chapel. Shortly afterward, GR5 traverses two beautiful ravines—Girsterbach and Girstergriecht—loping down one side, then ambling up the opposite bank before heading down again to the town of Born.

GR5 contours the riverbank until Moersdorf, again clambering up and down little gullies, stretching under beech trees, with lots of ivy underfoot and pink primroses along the path. It zigs and zags away from the river, down toward it, then back up, along the first vineyards of the Moselle and into Wasserbillig.

Here the Moselle River receives its tributary, the Sûre. Across from Wasserbillig is Germany; Trier is only 15 kilometers away. The result is that Wasserbillig is an important junction point for roads, rail lines, and water traffic, both tourist and commercial. Not too far from here, up-river, is Mertert, the major port of the Moselle and its network of canals. Along this water route flow barges piled high with coal from Germany's Saar region as well as such typical Luxembourgeois exports as flowers, especially roses, and the affordably priced Rieslings and Sylvaners of the Moselle vineyards. It makes Wasserbillig a busy town; keep in mind as you search for a hotel that truck and car traffic along the main drag lets up very little at night.

Wasserbillig is also in the center of some outstanding Roman ruins. Trier, in Germany, is easily accessible by train from Wasserbillig, if you have the time and inclination. Founded by the Romans as Augusta Treverorum in 16 B.C., Trier was later the capital of the Roman province here and is today a treasurehouse of ancient Roman remains, including the famed Porta Nigra, the imposing Imperial Baths, and a Roman bridge. (Karl Marx's birthplace is another of Trier's monuments, from a later era.) Only 3 kilometers from Wasserbillig, also in Germany, is the Roman colony of Igel.

Day 8: Wasserbillig to Ehnen (ca. 28 km, 7 hr)

The Moselle River—the name derives from *Mosella*, the Gallo-Roman word for "little Meuse"—is at times 100 meters wide in its 512-kilometer passage (320 miles) from northeastern France to the Rhine. The GR5 walker tracks a bit more than fifty of those kilometers, where the river constitutes the border between Luxembourg and Germany. Those two countries and France signed a postwar agreement to improve the Moselle's navigability; the work was completed in 1964, and two of the facilities built then—the *barrages* (dams) at Grevenmacher and Stadtbredimus—are along GR5.

But it is wine for which the Moselle valley is best known, and GR5 passes through the three principal centers of Luxembourg's viticulture industry: Grevenmacher, Remich, and Wellenstein. In these towns, and in many others along the riverbank, the GR5 walker will want to sample the local product: white, dry, typically fruity. The soil and the variety of grape here give Luxembourg's wines a distinctive bouquet, and the acids and organic salts of the grapes give them a fresh taste. The most popular of the Luxembourg Moselle wines are Rivaner, made from a cross between the Riesling and Silvaner grapes, and Elbling, a simple white wine, nicely dry. The fruity Auxerrois makes a nice aperitif; the Pinot Blanc is a particularly suitable accompaniment

Luxembourg, among the vineyards of the Moselle. Photo by Susanna Margolis.

to the fish dishes that characterize the local cuisine; Pinot Gris is good with meat dishes; Riesling and Traminer go well with dessert. And don't miss the sparkling demi-secs, as pretty to watch as they are delicious to drink, with their buzzing flume rising persistently up the middle of the glass.

The itinerary affords the GR5 walker two full days among the vineyards and river towns of the Moselle, rich in history and celebrated in song. There have been vineyards here for a very long time; they were already a well established fact of life when Ausonius, the decidedly minor Latin poet of the fourth century, wrote his lengthy poetic tribute, *Mosella*. The route mostly contours the hillside, usually along a chemin viticole, a service road used by the vintners to tend their vines. Be aware that the network of chemins viticoles frequently changes as fields are reconfigured. If the markers disappear suddenly, or if, as happened to us, the *trail* disappears suddenly, do not panic. Consult maps, and head for the next town as best you can. In most cases, the town will be visible below you, and you will be able to see plainly how to work your way along some other chemin viticole to get there.

At regular intervals, G5 dips down to a town on the river's bank, and while the walker should of course carry food for emergency purposes, lunch with wine overlooking the Moselle is a pretty safe bet— and a good one.

The route out of Wasserbillig is, in fact, the Sentier de la Moselle— still marked by a yellow rectangle. GR5 climbs away from the river in a wide loop—the port of Mertert is thus avoided—to the height of Boxberg, where there is a splendid panorama over the Moselle, the Sûre flowing into it, and, further east, the confluence of the Moselle and Saar across the border between Wasserbillig and Trier.

At Boxberg, GR5 plunges into forest, continuing its wide loop up and away from the river as far as Manternach, where it descends sharply to the river and the town of Grevenmacher. Grevenmacher calls itself *the* wine center of Luxembourg; the *caves* (wine cellars) of the town may be visited, and the narrow streets with shops selling the various appurtenances of the wine trade are also worth a wander. Grevenmacher has other claims to fame as well. A plaque on the town hall recalls Goethe's passage here enroute to and from the battle of Valmy in 1792. Another plaque on the same wall commemorates the arrival in Grevenmacher, on October 9, 1804, of Napoleon, then the Emperor of the French. He was greeted, the plaque states, "by the authorities of the city . . . having at their head the Mayor . . . and he was acclaimed by an enthusiastic population."

GR5 climbs the church steps to leave Grevenmacher, striking out amongst the vineyards along the crest of the hill, or at times about two-thirds of the way up the hillside. This vineyard walking is like having a box seat in a theater. Onstage below, the river, the barges plying their elongated way north and south, the villages, the vines carpeting the hillsides on both sides of the river, the ribbons of highway and railroad all perform for the walker's entertainment.

Down to Machtum. It was here that we experienced the final straw that led to the official formulation of the Principle of the Perfidious Ignorance of Locals. Two Machtumers took one look at our backpacks and told us there was absolutely no restaurant in the town. Despondent, we rounded a corner to find a charming restaurant overlooking the river. The food was excellent, the prices high, and the wine list was six pages long.

The trail heads up again, bordering a forest of boxwood (a touch of the Mediterranean) under chalky cliffs, to Ahn, to Wormeldange—capital of Riesling wine—up again to Upper Wormeldange, then along the river to Ehnen, a town ringed by vine props.

It is a town of many other attractions as well. The old quarter, with its hilly streets; Luxembourg's only circular church, built in 1826 and dedicated to Saint Nicolas; the wine museum (in a sense, the entire town is a wine museum); and the fine cuisine of its restaurants, most notably that of the Hotel Simmer, to which eager gourmets come from all over the world. GR5 gourmets will note that pike and trout are local freshwater specialities.

Day 9: Ehnen to Mondorf-les-Bains (ca. 28 km, 7 hr)

Another day of leisurely vineyard crawling and traverses of the rose-bedecked villages of the Moselle Valley. GR5 climbs up from Ehnen to meet the by now familiar chemin viticole, stretches along the side of a hill, then dips down to Greiveldange, set back from the Moselle, where you cut a bold meander of the river. The route heads up yet again before descending into Stadtbredimus. Nip down to the river here; if you are lucky, you may see a barge moving through the locks. It is fascinating to watch these over-long canal barges, and it is sobering to think of the skill that must be required to steer them from a point at the stern of the boat that seems miles from the bow.

At Stadtbredimus, the GR5 departs temporarily from vineyards and treks through forest before descending to Remich. Called the Pearl of Luxembourg's Moselle, Remich is another wine town worth exploring a bit; wander among the narrow streets lined with old buildings entered through sculpted oaken doors, and have a look at the church with its ancient tower. As in all the towns along the Moselle, virtually every bit of garden in Remich bursts with roses, and there are rose-covered terraces of cafés where you can taste the local wine.

Just across the Remich bridge in Nennig, Germany is another ruin of a Roman villa with fine mosaics. On foot, this would be a substantial detour; you might try to walk across, then hitch to the site.

From Remich, it is back onto chemins viticoles, along the hillside, then down into Wellenstein, up the hill and back into vineyards. The trail descends a relentless staircase into Wintrange, then climbs again to Kapberg, where a cross dominates the vantage down to Remerschen.

At Remerschen, E-3 departs from GR5 (E-2); the former will lead south to Schengen (and on to the Black Forest of Germany and into Czechoslovakia), while GR5 heads west, leaving the Moselle at last—that is, until we meet it again in Lorraine.

Just after climbing a steep staircase out of Remerschen, the trail is once again marked by the yellow disc. Follow it across the wide plateau to the border town of Mondorf-les-Bains, a spa whose waters are said to cure afflictions of the liver, gall bladder, intestines, and stomach, as well as all forms of rheumatism.

Triva buffs will rejoice to know that John Gruen (1868–1912) was born and raised in Mondorf and is buried here. Gruen once held the world's record for weightlifting—four thousand pounds. Among his more theatrical feats were his horseshoe-breaking exhibitions, his lifting of a platform holding twenty-five people, and the raising, by hand, of two horses plus their riders.

Day 10: Mondorf-les-Bains to Dudelange/Luxembourg-Ville (ca. 23 km, 5-¾ hr)

This last walking day in the Grand Duchy provides a foretaste of France; indeed, the landscape is routinely described as *paysage Lorrain*, and it presages both the wide plateaus of France's Lorraine and the industrialization of the region.

From Mondorf, GR5 climbs to plateau and winds among broad grain fields. It is a quiet, pastoral walk, with occasional villages dotting the landscape. The latter part of the day's walk, however, perforce enters the industrial heart of the Grand Duchy, and for us, this proved a most frustrating afternoon.

In the summer of 1984, virtually the entire section of trail near Dudelange, our destination, was undergoing rerouting, and we were hardly ever sure of our direction. The reason for the rerouting has its origin in politics.

In the nineteenth century, Luxembourg's more powerful neighbors imposed upon the Grand Duchy the so-called Treaty of Perpetual Neutrality. German armies violated the treaty twice during the twentieth century, and after World War II, Luxembourg decided to abrogate the treaty entirely and cast its lot with the North Atlantic Treaty Organization.

With a standing army of just over six hundred soldiers, and with a land mass of just under one thousand square miles, Luxembourg's contribution to the collective defense of Europe necessarily took on a particularly Luxembourgian character. Specifically, the country became a storage depot for military equipment that would theoretically be used to replenish supplies lost during the opening stages of a conventional East-West conflict on European soil.

Two huge supply depots were built in the Bettembourg area, one of them precisely in the path of GR5. In the summer of 1984, this "theater reserve depot," as it is known in NATO parlance, was being expanded. In addition, a new Luxembourg-Metz highway was being constructed nearby. For us, this meant that GR5 simply disappeared some 5 kilometers before Dudelange; lengthy consultation with the map eventually enabled us to improvise our own route to this industrial town.

In Dudelange, the walker sees the first evidence of the decline that has afflicted much of Europe's coal industry. The industry got its start in 1842 with the discovery of minette, an oolitic iron, the kind found in limestones and dolomites, that is rich in oxides and phosphorous. The supply has always been known to be limted and was estimated to last only until the early years of the twenty-first century. Yet most of the mining around Dudelange has stopped already. Several locals we talked to told us that what put the mines here out of business was Canadian iron ore, which is of a higher grade. In any event, unemployment is high in the town, and its tourist attractions—remains of the former castle on the hill, and paintings in the church by Dom. Lang, considered one of Luxembourg's great painters—do not exert a great pull.

For the walker, this is the place to find public transportation, or perhaps a lift, to Luxembourg-Ville, less than 15 kilometers away.

Day 11: Luxembourg-Ville (layover day)

City dwellers will feel a rush of familiarity on entering Luxembourg-Ville. Everything is relative, of course, so that Echternach seems big after Grundhof, but the capital of the Grand Duchy *feels* like a capital city. The air here clicks and the streets hum rather more than in Bergen-op-Zoom or even Liège, the other big cities along—or near—the GR5.

Two Roman roads once met at this site: one linked Metz to Aix-la-Chapelle, one ran from Trier to Reims via Arlon. Today, the city's Grand Rue follows the course of the Trier-to-Reims road.

The city's site is imposing: the summit of a sandstone cliff traced by two rivers, the Alzette and the Pétrusse. The ravine of the Pétrusse separates the old city from the new city to the south; numerous bridges link the two. To the north, the city connects with the height of Kirchberg via the bridge named for the Grand Duchess Charlotte, which crosses the Alzette. Kirchberg contains the several edifices dedicated to European unity. It should be noted that Robert Schuman, the great statesman of France (and briefly its premier), was born in Luxembourg. Schuman is perhaps best known as one of the architects of the idea of a united Europe, now embodied on the Kirchberg.

Given its situation, it is not surprising that, by the tenth century, Luxembourg was one of Europe's strongest walled towns—so threateningly strong that the terms of the 1867 Treaty of London required that the fortress be razed. Today, the remains of the city's massive fortifications have been turned into parks with pleasant walking paths, among them the famous Chemin de la Corniche, unique in Europe and affording wonderful views downward.

Another interesting remnant of the fortress is the network of underground passages known as the Bock Casemates. Hewn out of the rock by the Austrians in 1745, the casemates later served as bomb shelters during both world wars. A section of these passages can be toured. The walker will also want to have a look at the Grand Duke's palace, standing at street level right in the center of things and distinguished, not by a lavish park or ornate gate, but by the presence of a single soldier in his sentry box. The cathedral, the Place Guillaume, the Place d'Armes, and the museum are other worthwhile sights. Place d'Armes is the place to sit in a café and people-watch. The museum, with its superb Gallo-Roman collection, should be of particular value to anyone whose interest in the rich culture of Roman Gaul has been stirred by the walk through Luxembourg.

In addition, Luxembourg-Ville is filled with shops, restaurants, hotels, and of course, banks. These fortresses of Luxembourg's contemporary strength line the newer boulevards of the capital, a collective tribute to the Grand Duchy's cunning holding-company laws, its liberal foreign exchange system, and its easygoing regulations governing the exchange of stocks and securities.

Lest you think you are in a city of philistines, music lovers should take note: Franz Liszt reputedly gave his last recital in the casino of Luxembourg-Ville.

11
France
as Far as
the Alps

The France of the GR5 from the Luxembourg border to the north shore of Lac Léman (actually to la Cure; the next five hours to the lake are in Switzerland) represents a very small sliver of a rather large nation—the largest in Europe.

The route hugs the eastern border of France. Indeed, of the eight nations with which France shares borders, GR5 has already passed through two, Belgium and Luxembourg, and now proceeds to cling to the frontiers of two others, Germany and Switzerland. (Crossing the Alps, GR5 will touch Italy; a short detour from Nice brings the walker to yet a sixth border, that of Monaco. Only the France-Spain and France-Andorra frontiers are off the GR5 route.)

This is marginal France, in more ways than one. In the twentieth century alone, Lorraine and Alsace have been German, in two separate shifts, for a total of nearly one-quarter of the century's passage. The Jura has been so isolated by topography, climate, and sheer cantankerousness that, until the highways and trains and airports of this century, most Frenchmen never gave it much thought; even today, it is hardly a preferred area for French vacations.

Marginal or not, this *is* France. Sliver or not, the GR5 from Luxembourg to Léman delivers to the walker an enormous diversity of the richness of France. Lorraine, the Vosges of Alsace, and the Jura are all different from one another in ways both obvious and subtle; these differences the walker gathers step by step.

Lorraine, despite its hyphenated attachment to Alsace, is a whole other world from the ridgetop of the Vosges Mountains tracked by GR5. Lorraine is a rolling plain that leans west; its villages tend to be dour and utilitarian. Alsace is the first step of the GR5 into real mountains, with a lavishly rich lowland to the east and villages extravagantly bedecked with flowers and Rhenish in appearance. The Jura is something else altogether—a high, wide plateau cut by brilliant waterways, a place whose people huddle in small villages or under low roofs to keep the weather at bay.

Modern France derives from some two thousand years of contacts with Celts, Romans, and innumerable barbarian tribes. The resulting mixture of practices, institutions, and peoples was more or less unified by about the fifteenth century—at least into a fairly definable territory—but the diversity persistently peers out from behind the harmony and often causes a certain pleasant orneriness. It is nice to think, for example, that the name France comes from a Latin word describing the land of the Franks who were a Germanic people.

Within the frontiers that were more or less set in the Middle Ages (with the notable exception of some of the territory GR5 will pass through) are wide differences of terrain. France, in fact, is sometimes described as a microcosm of Europe because the three major types of European landforms are all represented here. In fact, they are all represented in the France of the GR5 as far as the Alps.

For sedimentary basins and lowlands, take Lorraine and the Plain of Alsace, just across the Vosges Mountains from one another.

For worn-down Hercynian mountain blocks, remnants of ancient mountains formed during the Carboniferous and Permian periods and eroded before being uplifted during the Tertiary period, take the Vosges, with their thin soil and underlying granite and crystalline rocks.

For younger, folded mountain belts, take the Jura. For although the Alps are the prime example of such mountains, the lower, less rugged Jura range is in fact a component of the Alpine chain.

Thus, in the 860 kilometers from the Luxembourg border to the start of the Alps, the GR5 walker experiences the topology of Europe in one fell swoop, although a walk of 860 kilometers may not seem like a swoop to the walker.

From the border to the Alps, GR5 marches through a changing France—agricultural and industrial landscapes, waterways, forests, hills, cities, and towns.

Agriculture remains a major industry of France, and many of its major agricultural products are in evidence along the GR5 route as far as the Alps—most notably: dairy products, beef, wine, hops, and orchard fruits.

In Lorraine, GR5 crosses an area that was once mined extensively for its underground riches—coal and iron ore. The outsized industries spawned by these mineral deposits are a far cry from the minutely precise and painstaking industries carried out in the Jura: watchmaking, woodworking, the creation of delicate precision instruments.

France is drained by some of the most famous rivers of Europe; in its passage to the Alps, GR5 crosses the continent's divide between the north-flowing and south-flowing basins. At the bottom of the Vosges, traversing the Belfort Gap, the walker leaves behind such rivers as the Moselle, the Seille, and the Ill that flow to the North Sea, and enters the region where streams like the Doubs will mingle their waters with the Saône, the Rhône, and eventually the Mediterranean.

France is a wooded land, and the walker will pass through both planted and natural forests on plains, plateaus, and the slopes of mountains. French forests are either *domaniale* (belonging to the state), *communale* (belonging to the local *commune*), or *privée* (privately owned). The National Office of Forests manages the *forêts domaniales*, regulating the amount, type, and age of wood that may be cut. *Bornes*—boundary markers, often of stone—divide and identify numbered parcels of forest. The trees are classed and marked. The legend "A.F." on a tree (for Administration Forestière) means that the tree has been approved for cutting; other marks classify trees as dry, broken, uprooted, and the like. It is said in France that these official state markers are backed by as much legal protection as that accorded a bank note.

The cities that lie near the GR5 here are probably, except for Strasbourg, second-string attractions for tourists from overseas, although in fact, Metz, Nancy, Montbéliard, and Besançon are treasures of their separate regions and of the French Republic. But the life of France that GR5 shows the walker is in the small villages that lie along the route, villages that in a number of instances have been left behind by time or economic change. To many of the people in many of these villages, the appearance of a pair of walkers is a major event—especially if they are Americans, an exotic breed in these parts, but a pervasively influential people about whom everyone in France has an opinion.

As he proceeds south, the French-speaking walker will note changes in the language, in the sound of the accent, and in local usages. In Alsace, he encounters an entirely new dialect. From the top of France to the bottom, however, the walker is likely to be wished farewell with the words *Bon Courage*. This phrase does not translate well into English. "Good courage" doesn't at all have the fusion of congratulation and good wishes for the future that the French conveys. *Bonne Route* and *Bonne Promenade* wish you a good hike, but *Bon Courage* tells you you're pretty plucky to have come this far—keep it up.

12
Paysage
Lorrain

In Lorraine, fields and woods alternate in quick succession. The pattern is punctuated by villages, each one filled with houses decked with flowers, each house with its tiny vegetable patch, and in the midst of a cluster of houses, the church.

It is fitting to find this kind of walking here, for it is the same sort of walking the megawalker has done since setting out from the North Sea coast, distilled here in Lorraine. Think of *paysage lorrain* as perhaps the apex of generally flat walking across a pastoral landscape; from the Vosges forward, it is all hills.

Lorraine is two river valleys and a plateau. The Meuse and Moselle valleys, with their high escarpments, form the western half of the region, while the famous Plateau Lorrain constitutes the eastern half.

Lorraine leans westward toward the Parisian basin. The wide plateau sweeps downhill from the Vosges, caught between the sandstone curve of the Vosges massif to the south and the hills of the Ardennes to the north. The waterways of Lorraine follow this inclination, but in fact flow into the Moselle and the Meuse, thus eventually heading north to the North Sea.

Lorraine's regional park, Parc Naturel Régional de Lorraine, reflects these two predominant topographic facts, being divided into a western portion including the Côtes (banks) de Meuse and Côtes de Moselle, and an eastern portion embracing the plateau. The GR5 in Lorraine gives the walker a taste of both, taking him south along the Côtes de Moselle, then eastward across the plateau to bump up against the Vosges.

Both the escarpments and most of the rolling plateau to the east are of limestone. Only at the edges of the Vosges on the southern and eastern borders of the plateau is there a transition to sandstone, and eventually, to the granite core of the sandstone massif.

Underground are the rich deposits of iron ore, coal, and rock salt that have long been the wealth of Lorraine. The walker first enters Lorraine in the Pays du Fer, the iron fields that stretch southward along the Moselle as far as Nancy (and extend northward into that industrial core of Luxembourg the walker has just left). Longwy, Thionville, Metz—these cities not far from the GR5 route were the great steel towns of the area, while to the northeast, along the border with Germany's Saar region, are the coal fields. In the middle of the Lorraine plateau, where GR5 moves from west to east across the valley of the Seille, are immense deposits of salt, mined here since before Roman times.

Only the salt industry is still vital, and it is a cottage industry compared to the massive, thriving activity that once characterized the steel industry here, which made Lorraine the industrial heartland of France. Ask five different people and you will get five different answers as to why this region now suffers severe economic depression, why the mills are closed and the jobs gone. It was management's fault for failing to modernize. It was the government's fault for failing to force management to modernize. It was the fault of the Japanese because they knew how to modernize. Whatever the cause, the result is painfully obvious to the megawalker as he trudges through one lifeless village after another, past one decaying mill after another.

But industry in Lorraine, even failed industry, is far from all-pervasive. Wood was once an important crop, used to provide firewood for home, foundry, forge, and glassworks. While its use has declined, many of the planted forests remain. There were once vineyards in Lorraine as well, lost, around the turn of the century, to the disease of phylloxera. Still, the broad sweep of fields and woods offers the walker a palette of shades of green. Grasses and grains grow on the less fertile prairies. And while meat and milk products predominate, accounting for some 75 percent of Lorraine's agricultural revenue, the orchards in the valleys produce pears, apples, and the famous mirabelle plums—not always eaten but often saved for liqueur.

Cuisine in Lorraine goes well beyond the famous quiche. There is a great variety of superb *charcuterie* (meat products)—especially of pork and veal, and desserts that the walker may not walk off till he has reached Nice. Among these are *madeleines* (shell-shaped cookies), *tarte aux mirabelles* (plum tart), and the caloric disaster known as *vacherin* (crystallized fruit, ice cream, whipped cream, and meringue). It is perhaps not surprising that one writer has dubbed Alsace-Lorraine the "Dominion of Fat"; the walker should be forewarned that the Alsatian food to come may prove even fatter than the culinary temptations of Lorraine. In any event, the cuisine of Lorraine tends to be "northern": good cold-weather food with plenty of fat, butter, and cream to keep you warm.

After Julius Caesar had conquered Gaul and made it a Roman province (or provinces), the Moselle region became an important center for trade and commerce between southern Europe and the lands to the north. What is today Lorraine was literally in the middle of this, crossed by the main traffic routes linking the lowlands, Germany, France, and the way south.

Lorraine first takes on a distinctive identity with the treaty of Verdun in 843, when Charlemagne's empire was cut up and bequeathed, in thirds, to his grandsons. Lothaire received what was left after Charles got the west and Louis got the east. His portion—Lotharii Regnum, or Lotharingia—was thus from the beginning the place in the middle. For centuries, it was the scene of tug-of-war battles between the regions flanking it, while at the same time it struggled to retain its independent identity. In 959, the kingdom of Lotharingia was split into the duchies of Lower and Upper Lorraine, and from then until the thirteenth century, the dukes of Upper Lorraine—the present-day region— strove to remain free of the Holy Roman Empire while they battled within to unify the duchy. Afterwards, Lorraine had to contend with the rule of the Habsburgs, then with Prussian dominance. Over the centuries that followed, Lorraine fell more and more under the political influence of an increasingly powerful France. It was annexed to France by the Treaty of Ryswick in 1697 and officially incorporated into the French nation in 1766.

That was hardly the end of the story, however. Both Alsace and Lorraine were transferred by treaty to Germany in 1871, after the Franco-Prussian War. They were restored to France in 1918, and they again fell under German rule from 1940 to 1945. Today, both are French. The GR5 passes through numerous towns and across several battlefields that have repeatedly been tossed back and forth between France and Germany. The American walker will not be unaware that American troops fought in Lorraine in the last two of these struggles.

In the walk across Lorraine, GR5 goes through the *départements* (departments) of Moselle and Meurthe-et-Moselle. (In France, a department is the basic unit of political administration; a province consists of departments.) Each of these departments can lay claim to owning the capital of Lorraine. Metz, the administrative capital, with one of the most beautiful cathedrals in France, is in Moselle. Nancy, the historical capital, a center of art and learning as well as of commerce, is in Meurthe-et-Moselle. Both cities began as route centers and fortresses defending gaps in the ridges.

The walk takes twelve days—including a full day in Nancy, which is well worth the time—before arriving at the slopes and sudden, fresh forests of the Vosges. The route moves south at first, along the Moselle's west bank, in the industrial Pays de Fer. Here, GR5 keeps mostly to the deep, quiet woods, just brushing the somewhat drab industrial cities and towns of this famous and once-prosperous area.

At Ars-sur-Moselle, GR5 follows the riverside escarpment, the Côtes de Moselle. It enters the western zone of the Parc Naturel Régional de Lorraine, an area of grasslands, forests, and tiny villages between Meuse and Moselle. This is the famous Petite Suisse Lorraine—it has by now become clear to the walker that all nations claim a Little Switzerland—a countryside which, for all its natural beauty, will reveal to the walker the scars and trenches of Lorraine's many wars.

At Liverdun, on the outskirts of Nancy, GR5 turns abruptly east, crosses the Moselle River at last, and gradually ascends the plateau in the direction of the Vosges. Entering the eastern zone of the Parc Naturel

Régional de Lorraine, the GR5 passes through the famous *pays du sel* (land of salt) and, to cut the taste, the *pays d'étangs* (land of lakes). It is a quiet walk as you traverse the plateau, a ramble through fairy tale villages, magical woods, wide fields—quite peaceful, almost timeless.

These are twelve days of easy and delightful walking in a region of restrained charm. Even the industrial scars of Lorraine have a kind of instructive beauty.

There are, however, two significant problems associated with the walk across Lorraine. First, lodgings along the GR5 here are few and

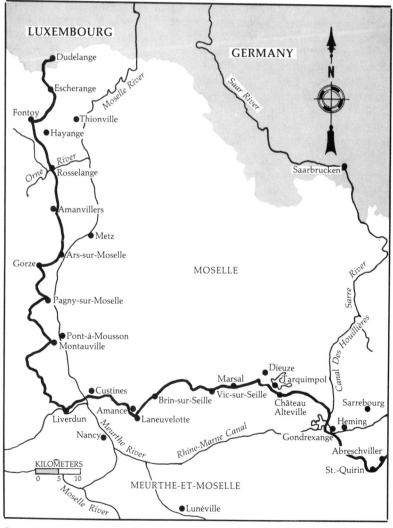

Lorraine

far between. It is frequently necessary to walk, hitch, or bus well off the trail to some town or other for a place to stay. On two occasions, we have turned this necessity into opportunities to see two beautiful cities of France—Metz and Nancy.

The second problem is the *balisage*, as it can be called now that we are in France—the trail marking of GR5. Sections of the Club Vosgien are in charge of trail blazing along this section, and Club Vosgien has numerous sections. One result is that the quality and consistency of the balisage vary widely; another result is that there are often gaps— presumably no-man's-lands where one section's marking ended before another section's marking began. We found this frustrating indeed, although it sharpened our skill at sniffing out where the GR5 might be, while also inspiring our best route-improvising efforts. At least in Lorraine, we learned we weren't the only ones having trouble along GR5. In fact, the very first other hiker we met on our journey was a young Dutchman here in Lorraine—and he was lost.

We were now a month and a half into our journey. Here in Lorraine, we were to suffer a short-lived bout of homesickness when the Fourth of July came and went with no fanfare. For compensation, Bastille Day lay just ahead—and so did the halfway point of the walk across Europe from top to bottom.

Lorraine

Day 1	Dudelange (Luxembourg) to Fontoy	31 km	7-¾ hr
Day 2	Fontoy to Amanvillers/Metz	26 km	6-½ hr
Day 3	Amanvillers/Metz to Ars-sur-Moselle	11 km	2-¾ hr
Day 4	Ars-sur-Moselle to Pagny-sur-Moselle	24 km	6 hr
Day 5	Pagny-sur-Moselle to Montauville	17 km	4-¼ hr
Day 6	Montauville to Liverdun	23 km	5-¾ hr
Day 7	Liverdun to Amance	25 km	6-¼ hr
	Amance to Laneuvelotte/Nancy	3 km	¾ hr
		28 km	7 hr
Day 8	Nancy (layover)		
Day 9	Nancy/Laneuvelotte to Fleur-Fontaine	4 km	1 hr
	Fleur-Fontaine to Vic-sur-Seille	21 km	5-¼ hr
		25 km	6-¼ hr
Day 10	Vic-sur-Seille to Château Alteville	21 km	5-¼ hr
Day 11	Château Alteville to Gondrexange	22 km	5-½ hr
Day 12	Grondrexange to Abreschviller	22 km	5-½ hr
		250 km	62-½ hr

Day 1: Dudelange (Luxembourg) to Fontoy (ca. 31 km, 7-¾ hr)

The day that starts in Luxembourg's Dudelange and ends in France's Fontoy is an exceptionally long one. It is made even longer by the bus ride (or hitch) the walker must take at day's end to find lodging. There were no hotels in Fontoy the summer we were there, nor anywhere between Dudelange and Fontoy, nor for several hours after Fontoy. But a ride to a variety of places from ten minutes to forty-five minutes distant will get the walker a bed for the night—and a dinner and next morning's breakfast to go with it.

GR5 leaves Dudelange along the Kayl road, then pops up away from the highway to the height of Galgebierg. The soil here is red—evidence of the iron that, until recently, was the mainstay of the area's economy.

The route then heads down to Tétange, a pleasant town and the last in Luxembourg—a good place to provision yourself with ravitaillement if you have not already done so. Head out of town along the Rue de Volmerange—uphill—then proceed into woods. Very soon, the GR5 crosses the point where the Sentier du Sud's yellow triangle departs downhill to Rumelange; GR5 continues straight ahead.

Suddenly there is an abrupt change of markers; the familiar red and white stripes reappear. In the thick foliage of these cool woods, you have arrived in France. We saw no frontier marker to announce the fact, so we did so ourselves by proclaiming "Lafayette, nous voici!"

From the woods, GR5 debouches into quintessential paysage lorrain. Vast fields stretch before you. The alternating squares of grains and grasses create a patchwork in shades of green, spotted with smaller patches of dark-green woods—forest green in color, to be exact. Bright red poppies, dazzling blue cornflowers, and all manner of little yellow flowers grow along the edges of the fields and lanes.

GR5 crosses the D15 highway, and a pleasant walk ensues—fields and woods, woods and fields—to the curious town of Escherange. Just east of the town, on the slope of a small valley, is a portion of the infamous Maginot Line. (The ruins of it will be visible as you leave town.) Built in France before World War II, the Maginot Line was a system of linked fortifications—underground and above ground—along the eastern border of France between Belgium and Switzerland. The guns were directed in a limited arc toward Germany, the traditional enemy, but they could not be rotated to face the opposite direction. Yet the Line was considered so impregnable a defense that it was believed the German armies would not even attempt a breakthrough. Indeed, they did not. Instead, in 1940, the armies of the Reich invaded Belgium, then bypassed the Maginot Line entirely, crossing into France from the north.

The people of Escherange, however, were evacuated in 1939 and sent en masse to Vienne. War was certainly approaching, and it was assumed that the town would be an important position to be manned by the

French armies. The French armies never got the chance to fight from Escherange; the Germans destroyed the village entirely. When Escherange was liberated in 1945 by the American Third Army, the people returned and entirely rebuilt the small, slapdash village.

We asked one of the inhabitants, an elderly woman standing before her house, if she would give us some water. This she did most willingly, inquiring who we were and where we were headed. There ensued an intense discussion about our route—not with us, but between the woman and her fragile-looking husband, who had suddenly appeared. Both insisted vociferously that we couldn't go "par là," where the trail marker directed us, because it was all "terre militaire" and "absolument" forbidden to pass there. It was a "centre nucléaire." Soldiers with dogs patrolled there. We would be hauled off to prison.

We went there anyway, though with some misgiving as we moved into suddenly deep woods. However, no shots were fired. No dogs attacked. No tanks rolled by. We did see a small sign saying "Route Militaire—Accès Interdit," but the "interdit accès" was the road going the other way. Confirmation again of the Principle of the Perfidious Ignorance of Locals; never believe what the natives tell you.

GR5 descends through the woods to the crossroads of Bellevue, where the D14 and D57 highways meet. From here there is a striking view down to the plain of Moselle and the industrial city of Thionville, the *Métropole de Fer* (city of iron), in the heart of the pays de fer.

The trail heads south, however, leading downhill, skirting the town of Algrange on a route that passes the entrance to several mines. Then it climbs again to the plateau and continues into Fontoy, a city that traces its history to Roman times. Buses to Knutange, Hayange, and Thionville leave from the town square about every half hour, and all three towns have lodging. Knutange is some ten minutes and Hayange about twenty minutes away. Thionville is a forty-five minute ride; nevertheless, we chose to go there.

It is an industrial city, once one of the largest steel-producing centers of Europe, now fallen on hard times. But the center of the city, the old town, offers some interesting sightseeing: a walk along the Moselle, here canalized for barge traffic; a wander among the narrow streets; a visit to the Tour aux Puces, the Flea Tower, a fourteen-sided medieval keep which houses the museum of local history.

We ordered quiche lorraine for dinner.

Day 2: Fontoy to Amanvillers/Metz (ca. 26 km, 6½ hr)

Another walk through wooded countryside, punctuated by occasional short spells in rather dreary industrial areas. The route traverses the plateau between the Moselle and the Conroy, a minor tributary of the Orne, then drops down to cross the Orne River at the industrial town of Rosselange. Between Rosselange and Amanvillers, the trail crosses yet another plateau, this one standing between the Orne and the Moselle. At Amanvillers, it is necessary to take a bus or hitch to Metz for the night.

We started the day with a bus ride as well, an early-morning opposite commute back to Fontoy. We disembarked in the square and made our way to an *alimentation* (food shop) to pick up trail provisions. Our presence in the shop caused more than the usual fuss. The proprietress was quite beside herself to see Americans in her store. To her, Americans meant Patton, tanks, the liberation of Fontoy. In 1940, she told us, "in an instant," Fontoy and all of Lorraine had *become* Germany. One day she and her neighbors were Frenchmen. Then the Nazi armies arrived, and overnight, they were declared to be Germans. The children in particular, our shopkeeper among them, were forced to learn and speak German.

So there was great joy when Patton's tanks rolled through Fontoy, the first of them pouring under the railroad bridge up the street at noon on September 10, 1944. Madame offered us candies while she went to fetch *quelque chose*. She returned with a photograph, obviously precious, of that event. There was the railroad bridge; there were the tanks, edging along in their bumptious way; there were the smiling GIs, helmet straps hanging, waving from the top of the tanks and strolling along beside them. Madame remembered it well, and we, she told us, were the first Americans she had talked to in forty years.

When we finally said our goodbyes to this woman and her story, we passed right under that very railroad bridge. It looked exactly as it had in the photo. Only two things were different: the weather (those GIs had been squinting from the sun, and we were in a cold, gray drizzle), and the reasons for crossing under the bridge in the first place.

And there, just past the bridge and along the slope of the hill, was the first other GR5 walker of our journey. Pieter, from Dordrecht, Holland, spoke perfect English in which he was able to impart a lot of information and advice about GR walking. He had walked all of GR10, in the Pyrenees, and was doing portions of GR5 during vacations from his work in urban renewal. Equipped with tent, stove, and sleeping bag, Pieter's practice was to camp in fields along the trail each night. He also carried a fine pair of field glasses, which he used, not for bird-watching, but for trying to find the next GR5 marker up ahead. This was our first inkling that we weren't the only ones having trouble following the trail.

Between Fontoy and Rosselange, however, such trouble is fairly minor. GR5 passes first through the dark woods of the Forêt Domaniale de Moyeuvre as far as the village of Neufchef. There is a right turn at the statue of Joan of Arc in the village—a statue that is virtually the only homage to Joan along all of the GR5 in Lorraine. Her native town of Domremy is along the Meuse, well west of here.

From Neuchef, GR5 proceeds into another forest, that of Rosselange, woods whose thick stands of beech and oak create such a heavy cover that the walker may at times feel he is in a tunnel. The trail emerges from the forest at the *cité ouvrière* of Rosselange, a large complex of worker housing built in the 1950s, when steel mills and iron ore mines were turning the Orne Valley into a major industrial center. Today, the cité is shabby and strangely quiet; old men tend the tiny garden patches behind their houses, in the shadow of the contorted pipes, ducts, and smokestacks of the steel mills they once worked. The stillness of these mills, silhouetted against the gray sky of Lorraine, gives them an eerie beauty. But by the time we had wandered around Rosselange, nearby Clouange, and Rombas a few kilometers further on, it had become evident that the *crise économique* of Lorraine had ripped the life out of towns, countryside, and people as well. Gloom and dilapidation were the rule. In the stores and streets and bars of these gray towns, there were no young people. The whole threadbare place seemed to echo with emptiness.

From the Orne Valley, GR5 again enters woods, the forest of Pierre-villers, where a sign warns about mining crevasses. In this forest, the GR5 winds and shifts frequently all the way to the D7 highway and Amanvillers. We had just managed to lose our way and were staring after some deer darting away from us when Pieter came crashing through the shrubbery, lost again, his field glasses proving of no use at the moment. Together, we made a route to the D7 highway (there are lodgings about 5 kilometers west along the highway at Sainte-Marie des Chênes), crossed it, and proceeded into Amanvillers. From here, there are buses to Metz some 15 kilometers distant. We easily hitched along the N43 highway.

The evening in this lively city will prove a welcome relief from the day's drab villages of the Orne Valley, and there will be time for sightseeing tomorrow before returning to Amanvillers and following GR5 to Ars-sur-Moselle.

Day 3: Metz/Amanvillers to Ars-sur-Moselle (ca. 11 km, 2-¾ hr)

Metz, on the confluence of the Moselle and the Seille rivers, between the Côtes de Moselle and the Lorraine plateau, is an ancient city whose gothic cathedral of Saint-Étienne is one of the most beautiful in France—indeed, in all of Europe. As the Roman town of Divodorum, it was at the intersection of two major Roman roads and became an important trading center of the Gallo-Roman world. It remained an important center of commerce throughout its history and up to the present day, when the canalization of the Moselle makes it a navigable port for traffic to and from the Rhine.

It has other claims to fame as well. The two-and-a-half-month battle of Metz in the autumn of 1944, between the German defenders and the American Third Army, was one of the most brutal in the Allies' eastward progress toward the Rhine.

The city, however, managed to retain its beauty—in winding, hilly streets; esplanades and squares along the riverbank; ancient churches and palaces; above all, in its cathedral.

Said to be the most luminous of all cathedrals in the world, the Saint-Étienne of Metz is often called the "apotheosis of light." It has 63,000 square feet of stained glass—including two exceptional windows in the 131-foot high nave, and contemporary windows by Marc Chagall in the left transept and ambulatory. The cathedral is in an appropriate setting—a wide square edged by buildings almost as impressive as the cathedral itself.

There are other sights worth seeing in Metz: the seventh-century church of Pierre-aux-Nonnains; the Porte des Allemands, a citadel which once guarded the ancient road to Saarbrucken; the museum with its Gallo-Roman collection; the Place Saint-Louis and other smaller, almost hidden squares the walker discovers in wandering this appealing city.

From Metz take a bus back to Amanvillers (ask for the *gare routière*, bus station) or taxi there to start the short walk—only about three hours—to Ars-sur-Moselle. GR5 heads first into the charming valley of Montvaux. Shortly after the ruin of an old wall, the trail turns left into woods and follows the Montvaux brook parallel to the highway.

At Châtel-Saint-Germain, the site of an ancient Roman *castellum* and later of a fortified chateau, GR5 crosses to the hillsides of the Moselle—the côtes. It wanders along the côtes, winding in and out of woods and villages, to the riverside Ars-sur-Moselle for this night's stay.

Day 4: Ars-sur-Moselle to Pagny-sur-Moselle (ca. 24 km, 6 hr)

As the names of the starting point and destination make clear, today's stage is a walk along the Côtes de Moselle.

In the character of the countryside, this is a subtly different Moselle from that of Luxembourg. These slopes are steeper than the riverbanks to the north. Fruit trees impart a lushness to the landscape, even though it seems drier, its grasses less intensely green. The villages are different, too. Nearly flat tile roofs seem almost Mediterranean—until the walker, grown vain about the miles already walked, remembers the distance still to be walked and realizes this can't be a hint of Nice. Not yet.

At Ars, the walker enters the western zone of the Parc Naturel Régional. GR5 ascends first among garden plots and parcels of orchard, then drops back to the river to pass beside an ancient Roman aqueduct. Built in the first century, the aqueduct once straddled the river, and today, sixteen arches remain on the east bank and seven on the west. In its day, the aqueduct brought water from Gorze to Metz. Today, Gorze is still the water source for Metz, although the water no longer runs there on this aqueduct.

GR5 proceeds past a miliary cemetery from the 1870 Franco-Prussian War before entering Rongueville. Here it turns and climbs steeply to a high forested plateau, where the Belvedere Varieux offers a broad view of the Moselle Valley. But the trail is insistent on forest path again, until it emerges above Gorze to a sweeping panorama of the green and gold hills behind the village and the village itself seemingly tucked into a cleft in the slopes.

GR5 crosses the Gorze declivity, then climbs up a field of red-gold wheat into the Bois de Prince, an ancient forest, much crisscrossed by trails and forest roads, and with scores of old bornes—stone markers that here identify ownership of parcels of trees. At a break in the forest, GR5 reaches the col de Rudemont—the first time along the route that the walker comes to anything called a *col* (mountain pass). As we arrived at this landmark, we met three elderly gentlemen, retired teachers, who told us they hiked together every day—except Sunday; "Never on Sunday."

"What happens on Sunday?" we asked.

"Sunday we consecrate to our wives," one answered. The others chuckled.

We walked with them for a while, then turned off with GR5 to descend into Bayonville and then Onville before climbing into forest again.

After an hour's walk in the shady forest, GR5 emerges, under a buzzing high-tension wire, on the slope above Pagny and the cool, green valley of the Moselle. Green as far as the eye can see. Susanna dubbed the GR5 in Lorraine an eye-ease trail. It descends now to a small shrine, with a statue of the Virgin, just above Pagny; do not turn right on GR5, but detour straight down into the center of the village.

At closer quarters, Pagny is a dismal town reminiscent of those in the pays du fer to the north. Railroad tracks cut the town off from the river. On the flat plain beyond, high grass only partially obscures the near-ruins of worn-out factories. Pagny's houses are gray and sooty; the brilliant roses looking out through garden fences seem out of place.

Day 5: Pagny-sur-Moselle to Montauville (ca. 17 km, 4-¼ hr)

Today's stage is both beautiful and full of interest, as GR5 takes the walker across a lush landscape that is rich in history. Perhaps of particular interest to the American walker is the crossing of a World War I battlefield, where some of the notorious trenches of that war, now overgrown, are visible. At Pont-à-Mousson, to which the walker must proceed from Montauville to find lodging for the night, the military history lesson continues.

From the shrine above Pagny, follow the route leading up the valley to Prény. Be sure to visit the village, dominated by the ruins of the chateau. Built in the ninth century, the chateau was for a time the principal residence, after Nancy, of the dukes of Lorraine, who expanded and fortified it. In 1636, on order of King Louis VIII, Richelieu's troops dismantled the chateau. Today, its ruins stand on private property, but the grounds may be visited, and from the 365-meter height on which the chateau stands, the walker sees clearly how Prény masters the valley, why the dukes chose to make it a fortress, and why a king who wanted to control the dukes decided it must go.

From Prény to Vilcey-sur-Trey, the route effectively zigs southwest as far as the farm of Sainte-Marie aux Bois, then zags southeast to Vilcey to cross the stream. Leaving Prény, head downhill across fields brilliant with poppies and make for the woods. The relay tower, *relais Hertzien*, is your landmark, although you will skirt it along a forest road, looping west.

The farm of Sainte-Marie aux Bois sits in a dip between two rolls of hills. The clearest directional signs we saw that day adorned its fence: "Private Property!" "Keep Out!" We lunched along the dirt road that passes the farm, waiting for the sagging barn roof to collapse, which it appeared it would do any second. However, it stayed on the barn throughout our picnic.

The route follows the road curving southwest, then turns sharply southeast through woods and down a field to Vilcey-sur-Trey. This minute, sleepy village had an eerie, Brigadoon-like silence as we entered it on a hot, sunny day, until we heard the sounds of conversation and looked through an open window to see three generations of women shelling peas. The elderly grandmother called out a greeting, and we asked for water. This the granddaughter was told to fetch, admonished by her grandmother to "make sure it is cold." She was pleased to see us and was surprised only by the fact that we were American. She had, she said, *l'habitude* to help hikers—what else did we need?

The route crosses the Trey stream, then climbs through woods, making twists and turns to the battlefield called Bois de Prêtre. Here, from a freezing cold January through to a brutally hot August in 1915, French and German troops contested the height-of-land inch by inch. Around the edge of the clearing are the trenches in which the soldiers huddled; kick away the overgrowth and you can see them clearly—a curious and moving sight for Americans, who, thankfully, have no World War I battlefields on our own soil. In the eight-month struggle, seven thousand were killed on each side and three times that number were wounded before the French prevailed, only to lose this desolate hill to Germany in the 1940 invasion. Today, again a part of France, the Bois le Prêtre is a clearing that hikers cross, and little else.

We stopped in the clearing to read a description of the battle in the topo-guide, how one side would gain a hundred meters in a day of fierce fighting and heavy losses, only to be repulsed the next day, forced to fight all over again for the same piece of ground with hand grenades, aerial torpedoes, land mines, rifles. There wasn't a sound as we read the description, except for the terrific humming of insects which made the air vibrate.

At the far end of the field is a monument to both the French and German soldiers who fought here. The route heads downhill from the monument into Montauville, whence the walker can proceed by foot, bus, or taxi to Pont-à-Mousson for the night.

Once known as the Athens of Lorraine because of the university founded here in the sixteenth century, Pont-à-Mousson more recently, in both world wars, was renowned for its role as a beachhead over the Moselle.

In September, 1944, the Germans were dug in to the west of the town when Patton's army arrived and began bombarding the German position. When the Americans entered the town, they found the bridge over the river destroyed and the Germans holding the opposite bank. For two weeks, Pont-à-Mousson was shelled by both armies, from opposing directions, until the Americans, establishing a beachhead further north near Thionville, could come down the east bank of the river and dislodge the Germans.

Despite the destruction, Pont-à-Mousson retains a good deal of its past and offers considerable charm. Its Abbaye des Prémontrés is a fine example of eighteenth-century monastic architecture, and the town's Place Duroc, bordered by sixteenth-century houses and arcades, is a beauty.

Day 6: Montauville to Liverdun (ca. 23 km, 5-¾ hr)

Enter Petite Suisse Lorraine, the valley of the Esch brook, where cool woods edge wide fields filled with wildflowers, across which the walker can see one, two, sometimes three small villages in one panning view. Underfoot, the trail is still scarred with the traces of trenches, foxholes, bomb craters—reminders that this amiable landscape was once—twice!—the front.

For us, this stage was a particularly spectacular day, as perfect summer weather made the fields a particularly brilliant green, turned the wheat particularly golden, made the reds and purples and yellows of the wildflowers stand out with particular intensity under a blue sky. Even the air seemed tinged with color.

So it was frustrating when one of the Laws of Inevitable Occurrences worked its will with particular vengeance. The law in question states that "sooner or later, something will break or rip." Its vengeful version is that "if something is going to break, it will do so at the worst possible moment." What broke was the doohickey for rewinding film on Ginger's camera. Which meant no color film. Which meant that this beautiful day had to be photographed by our minds and memory alone. Which may be sufficient.

Even the GR5 markings were cooperative this day when, for the first time in the journey across Europe, the walker meets *déviation* signs. These indicate marked itineraries that lead away from the GR5 to a village, gîte, or particular attraction. The two déviations we met but did not follow take the walker to Gouffre, a small village typical of the area, and along the Esch Valley to Mannonville; both offer an opportunity to see more of the Petite Suisse Lorraine.

Starting from Montauville, the route climbs through woods, then stretches southwest across high fields to Mamey, a sleepy hamlet whose church, just beside the trail, is worth a look. GR5 now edges a field that, on the day we were there, was so fraught with poppies it seemed half red. The trail again enters woods, where the walker sees more evidence of World War I trenches, then emerges into Saint-Jean.

This miniscule hamlet—total time to traverse it is probably under a minute—is one of the loveliest sights in all the walk across Europe. Tucked in a valley cleft beside the Esch, which runs swiftly and shallow at this spot, Saint-Jean is a little paean to tranquillity. Flowers sprout from every window ledge of the four or five antique houses that make up the town. On the corner of the last house in the village, an inscription reads: "In the name of the trinity and under the invocation of the Blessed Virgin Mary, this stone was placed by Mademoiselle Anne Thérèse Louise Félicité Willerot. July 24, 1788." The village is so small and the incised words so clear that Anne Thérèse didn't seem so far away or long ago as all that, and we wondered what event had caused her to place the stone. None of the six or seven villagers who had come out to greet us could answer, but a delightful couple wanted to show us another piece of local history, and walked us to the stream.

They were in fact from Nancy, but they came each weekend to Saint-Jean to set up their trailer in the field and *respirer*, as Madame put it. At the age of fifty-six (she looked forty; this is France, after all), the mother of six, complaining gently about a husband who "doesn't want to hike anymore," although he certainly was fit enough, she listened longingly to the story of our walk. She thought it was *formidable*—

A road through typical paysage lorrain. *The village is Mamey, France. Photo by Ginger Harmon.*

what she wouldn't give to come with us; she had even bought the topoguide for this stretch of the GR5 in a bookstore in Nancy.

"Come with us then," we offered, and we thought she hesitated for just a moment before shaking her head and turning back to the trailer.

Her husband took us up to the bridge over the Esch and pointed to a stone serving as a conduit for the well that feeds the brook. On it were the insignia and name of the One Hundred Twenty-eighth Territorial French Army—and the date, 1915. Monsieur described the fighting: up on the slope were the Germans; there in the valley stood the French, while volleys of gunfire burst back and forth across this now quintessentially peaceful tract of land.

GR5 plies the field to Martincourt, then follows the D106 highway for a spell, crosses more fields, and again jumps the winding Esch. Now it climbs, edging another wide field that can be seen in tantalizing glimpses through the trees, before emerging from the woods at Rogéville.

Rogéville has only houses, no shops, so we were delighted, as we entered the town, to see the circuit grocery truck—half convenience store, half neighborhood deli, all on the back of a van. We ate our purchases on the prairie beyond Rogéville, with a view that sloped down toward it.

It is all field walking from here to Rosières-en-Haye, as GR5 climbs gradually to the height of land for a view southeast to Mont Saint-Michel, a flat-topped summit that stands above the city of Toul, not far from Nancy.

From Rosières, the route again alternates between woods and fields, then heads down a low gully under thick foliage—a humid and buggy walk the day we passed through. Just before emerging out of woods at the Moselle, GR5 passes a most impressive junkyard—a veritable wall, perhaps a kilometer in length, of dead cars, refrigerators, and stoves. It's an appropriate way to exit the western edge of the Parc Naturel Régional.

The trail now runs along the river to Liverdun, a sizeable town which seems to spill down the hillside to an oxbow meander in the Moselle. It is a popular vacation spot, and a frequent weekend retreat for Nancy urbanites. This makes the hotels, mostly on the outskirts of town, fairly expensive. A wander through the old part of the city, with its hilly streets and thirteenth-century church, is an agreeable stroll.

Day 7: Liverdun to Laneuvelotte/Nancy (ca. 28 km, 7 hr)

GR5 changes direction at the start of this stage, striking out generally eastward across the plateau Lorrain and leaving the Moselle at last. We have recommended cutting back to Nancy at the end of this day's stage because of the paucity of hotels along this stretch; that is, since you have to leave the trail for a night's lodging anyway, you might as well go to Nancy.

From Liverdun, GR5 heads uphill and follows through woods above the town of Pompey—a long strip of houses and villas and an increasingly industrial appearance.

The trail drops down to the river at Custines and crosses it, then climbs out of town to look back over the valley once again. The view is something of a paradigm of Lorraine: there are the villas of Liverdun and there a giant steel mill. It still puffed some smoke into the atmosphere the day we were there, but we had learned that it was barely in use anymore and that thousands had been laid off. Ironically, two new plants were under construction, and we could see the shells of them abuilding—a Japanese electronics firm and a German soft drink company. All this industry—the dying steel mill and the factories being born—is set in a landscape of antique villages and wooded hills among which snakes the *boucle* (the curve) of the river. We evinced no small amount of wistful sentiment in saying goodbye to the Moselle.

GR5 heads into woods, the Bois de Faulx, and follows an old military road from World War I. It is easy, restful walking, but don't fall asleep entirely because the trail does make some turnings, although not for about an hour and a half. We missed one turning entirely; crossing a clearing, we simply forged straight ahead, following logic, when we should have cut obliquely across it, following GR5. We disobeyed our own rule about turning back if you don't see a marker for 200 meters, wandered around in the woods for half an hour, and finally crawled abjectly back to the clearing and did it right.

GR5 proceeds into the lush Bois de Blanzey. The trail winds down into a gully, along it, then across a clear-cut area, and up to a road that edges the hill and offers glimpses of the next open valley of fields and towns through the trees. It emerges from the trees above the farm of Blanzey, and now there are splendid views across the valley to the hills of Grand Couronné and Amance. The buildings of Blanzey, including a twelfth-century crypt in the chapel, make this tiny farm hamlet a true gem of Lorraine, and GR5 passes right under the covered archway to the farm compound. (Unfortunately, the GR marker is on the keystone of the arch.)

GR5 heads into Moulin, a pretty village that scatters itself downward along the winding main street. We asked for water at a house at the top of town, a suburban ranchstyle spread, with a pool and landscaped yard, looking more Californian than French. In fact, the young housewife gave us a bottle of Vittel and shrugged off our protests that all we really needed was some tap water to fill our canteens. Hospitality in the high-rent districts has its good points.

At the bottom of Moulin, GR5 crosses the N413 before making a dusty climb up to Amance. Arriving at the top, the walker finds himself on the lower spine of the ridge; from here, the views go on forever to the valleys both north and south. Farther along the GR5, in the center of town, there is another fine view from the yard of the thirteenth-century church.

From Amance (or from just before the town), take the D37 downhill to Laitre-sous-Amance and on to Laneuvelotte for the bus to Nancy.

Day 8: Nancy (layover day)

Curiously, it was a Pole, not a Frenchman, who was responsible for the dazzling central square that is the heart of Nancy—the exquisite Place Stanislas. The Pole was a dethroned king, Stanislas Leczinsky, a loser in the Wars of the Polish Succession (1733–1738), who was given Lorraine as a consolation prize by his son-in-law, who just happened to be King Louis XV of France. Stanislas was to be the last Duke of Lorraine; a condition of the gift was that upon his death, Lorraine would devolve to France.

Stanislaus showed his gratitude by creating a square called Place Royale, with a statue of Louis in the center. During the French Revolution, the statue was ripped down, to be replaced, years later, by a statue of Stanislas himself, in whose honor the square was then renamed.

It is the work of the architect Emmanuel Héré and the ironmaster Jean Lamour. Together, they created a perfectly proportioned square surrounded by classical pavilions and enclosed by wrought iron archways and railings ornamented brilliantly in gold leaf. You can sit in one of the sidewalk cafés that front the square for a long time without getting bored, so harmonious and elegant is this spot.

On the side of the Place Stanislas opposite the elegant *hôtel de ville* (city hall), a triumphal arch opens into yet another spacious square, the elongated Place de la Carrière, enclosed by handsome eighteenth-century houses.

One corner of Place de la Carrière leads to the gothic Ducal Palace of Nancy, dating from the thirteenth century and today housing the historical museum of Lorraine, with exhibits from two thousand years of history.

Another corner of Place de la Carrière leads to the Parc Pépinière, fifty-seven acres of tree-lined paths, lawns, formal flower gardens, pools, fountains, cafés, a bandstand, and a zoo. In the evenings, people stroll here to the music of Viennese waltzes piped over loudspeakers.

Nancy is situated on the confluence of the River Meurthe and the Rhine-Marne Canal. First settled in the seventh century, it became the capital of the duchy of Lorraine in the fourteenth century. A natural crossroads, in a valley lying virtually at the geographic center of Lorraine, Nancy has long been a commercial and government center as well as a center of government, education, and culture. It was badly bombed in World War I, and in World War II was a major center of the Resistance, whose partisans fought with Patton's soldiers in the city's liberation on September 15, 1944.

There are countless sights to see in Nancy, and many of them are found in a walk through the vieille ville, the old quarter, the original Nancy dating from the tenth century and filled with ancient residences, many of them now serving as shops or restaurants.

For the megawalker, Nancy offers a good deal more than sightseeing. It is a big city and a fine place for all kinds of provisioning. It is even possible to find some GR topo-guides here, though mostly for nearby regions. But several bookstores have English-language books and periodicals, and the *International Herald Tribune* is available right in the Place Stanislas, as well as elsewhere.

Indeed, as we tore around the city replacing socks, repairing camera doohickeys, loading up on books and magazines, and playing tourist, we considered how woefully meager was the amount of rest achieved during our rest days along GR5. In any event, the change of scenery and the freedom from a backpack make those days refreshing to the soul.

Day 9: Nancy/Laneuvelotte to Vic-sur-Seille (ca. 25 km, 6-¼ hr)

This long stage requires a very early start by bus from Nancy back to Laneuvelotte. Here the walker may either climb back up to Laitre-sous-Amance and Amance, or make his own route by way of back roads to meet the GR5 between Fleur Fontaine and Bois la Dame.

From here, GR5 passes through the Forêt Domaniale d'Amance, a popular walking, cycling, picnicking area—especially along the lake of Brin. The trail emerges from the forest to cross a field to Brin-sur-Seille. It was a very hot day when we were there, and we had looked forward to the café promised in the topo-guide. But when we arrived and asked some *pétanque* players how to find it, they informed us it was closed, the proprietor on vacation.

What about the hotel, also promised in the topo-guide?

Also closed—and permanently, a few years ago. Would the *marcheuses* like a cold drink?

The marcheuses would, so we repaired to the amazingly messy apartment of one of the pétanque players, where we were treated to deliciously cold beer and a show, on an ancient and broken videomaster, of stereopticon views of France.

Pétanque is the game Italians call "boccie," a form of bowls; it is clearly a primary occupation in Brin-sur-Seille, where little else seems to happen.

From Brin to Vic-sur-Seille is a long and quite beautiful walk through what the walker has now come to recognize as typical paysage lorrain—field and woods, woods and field. In the distance are the villages—red-tile roofs and a single church spire poking up from tucks in the rolling hills. The broad fields of grain, hay, and corn truly undulate across the horizon. Poplars line the country roads that link the villages, and here and there is an orchard, usually old, with gnarled trees.

Just before arriving at Vic, GR5 enters the eastern zone of the Parc Naturel Regional de Lorraine and the region known as the pays de la Seille et du sel—country of the Seille River and salt. Since prehistoric times, people have mined salt here in the valley of the Seille. Today, two-thirds of France's industrial soda, used in manufacturing chemicals and textiles, still comes from the salt deposits of the region.

Vic-sur-Seille, in the heart of the region, claims a history dating back

2,500 years, but its appearance is primarily medieval, especially the machicolations of the fortifications, the fourteenth-century church, and the splendid Hôtel de la Monnaie, the mint, constructed in 1456 and decorated with richly carved wooden railings, windows, and doors.

Day 10: Vic-sur-Seille to Alteville (ca. 21 km, 5-¼ hr)

Only once in this book do we recommend a specific hostelry by name, and it is the Château Alteville at the end of today's stage. It is recommended as much for what it is and for the family that runs it as for its considerable charm and comfort, and the walker is well advised to phone ahead from Vic, just to be certain that the Barthelemys have room. (You need to contact the Château Alteville, c/o Livier and Marie Barthelemy, Tarquimpol, 57260 Dieuze; telephone (8) 786-92-40.)

Château Alteville comes at the end of a day in which GR5 traverses the heart of the pays de la Seille et du sel, moving steadily eastward, gently ascending the gradual uptilt of the plateau—a hint of the Vosges only two walking days away. From Vic, GR5 heads upward. Turn for a last look at the tile rooftops of this charming town, then head east among green and yellow flowering fields. Along the horizon are the tiny villages of Moyenvic, Haraucourt-sur-Seille, and Marsal, which GR5 now enters via a drawbridge and an impressive gate built by Vauban. Sebastien Le Prestre, seigneur de Vauban, to give him his just due, was born poor in 1633. He became a military engineer and a marshal of France, and in the process, he strengthened the nation's frontiers, designed and built 33 major fortifications, and repaired 300 others. Throughout the walk across France, and particularly in the Alps, the megawalker will see the fruits of Vauban's extraordinary genius. Yet despite his success and prestige, Vauban died in disgrace. In the last years of his life, he penned a treatise calling for equality of taxation, thus bringing down on his head the severe disapproval of Louis XIV, who dismissed Vauban in 1707. He died the same year.

Vauban's gate house in Marsal is today a museum housing exhibits on the history of salt in the Seille region. We were almost glad it was closed the day we passed through Marsal; in what was now generally agreed to be a ferocious heat wave, even the thought of salt made us thirstier than we already were. We headed instead for the café across the town square to cool off with cold drinks in the shade of a brightly colored umbrella and to watch, from our front-row seat on the square, the very lazy progression of life during a heat wave in Marsal.

From here, GR5 proceeds along a quiet country road. Again, in the distance in all directions are the church spires of the small towns: Saint Médard, Mulcey, Juvelize, Guéblange-lès-Dieuze. The trail passes through the hamlet of Blanche-Église, then enters the cool Bois de Morsack—a welcome relief to us after the open road where the heat seemed to rise up from the hay strewn alongside. Once in the woods, a sign proclaims the area a military firing range; we picked up speed at that, and again when we debouched onto the D999 highway—a hair-raising kilometer's walk, during which the breeze provided by the trucks speeding by was cancelled out by the sweat of terror.

Then it's back into woods to emerge just above the huge Étang de Lindre. Across its waters, on a peninsula, is the ancient village of Tarquimpol, distinctive for its high round turret with dunce-cap roof. Tarquimpol, as its name suggests, dates back to the most ancient Roman era. GR5 passes it on the road, which then leads to Château Alteville.

The Château Alteville, classed as a *gîte rural*, is a large, stately Renaissance mansion, the home of Monsieur et Madame Livier Barthelemy. It is at the center of a large farm whose main products are grain and cattle.

This is a working farm; Livier Barthelemy is no gentleman farmer, though he is very much a gentleman and very seriously a farmer. The property has been in his family since 1900. In the library of the chateau is a rendering showing the original main building and the added flanking wings—plenty of rooms and apartments here of various sizes to accommodate a variety of purposes: a night's sleep, a wedding, a meeting, an extended stay of six months or a year.

We were sweaty and not exactly fresh-smelling when we arrived, but the Barthelemys greeted us by leading us into the elegant reception room, seating us on chairs that had to be precious antiques, and pouring out tall glasses of *citron pressé*. When considering the contributions of France to Western civilization, altogether too many people overlook this drink. Its genius lies in its simplicity: a large carafe of water and ice, a glass of fresh lemon juice, a bowl of sugar. Mix to taste, and *voilà*! The perfect summer thirst quencher.

In our view, French civilization reached its apex as we sat in the cool elegance of the Château Alteville, sipping citron pressé out of crystal glasses and making the acquaintance of the Barthelemys. They are not only friendly and kind; they are also knowledgeable about the history and culture of Lorraine. And they are very, very funny. It made for a delightful evening.

We dined *en famille*; the Barthelemys offered us the choice of this or being by ourselves, and we instantly decided it was no contest. At the table were Monsieur's mother, a resident; Madame's parents, here from Paris to await the birth, said to be imminent, of another grandchild; one of the Barthelemy sons and one of his friends—handsome and charming young men. A beautiful three-year-old grandchild popped in from next door just as dessert was being served, and his father (also the father-to-be) came by to fetch him. This gentleman had actually been invited for our benefit; Alsatian by birth, he told us very simply that the Vosges were beautiful mountains, but he liked the farmland of Lorraine.

The three-wine meal, one of the best we had in Europe, consisted of purée of fresh green bean soup, carp from the nearby lake in a sauce of cream and mustard, ham, potatoes, salad, bread, cheese (a strong, semihard called Cantal, provided by the cheesemaker himself, the friend of the Barthelemy son), and dessert—virtually all of it homegrown and homemade.

Day 11: Alteville to Gondrexange
(ca. 22 km, 5-½ hr)

Into the *pays des étangs*—land of lakes—to end at one of the biggest in Gondrexange, from which, however, the walker must detour for a night's lodging.

GR5 continues on road to Assenoncourt. Although it is only 2 kilometers from the Château Alteville where we had just finished a lavish breakfast, the day was already so hot and muggy that we stopped for refreshment. A decrepit but talkative little lady ran the café. "Ran" is an excessive word; the service was extremely slow as she hobbled on a bad leg to serve us, but she used her cane to good effect to open the shutters, shoo the cat, and point to the list of ice cream flavors and available drinks. We were, she said, the first Americans she had seen on the GR5—most foreign hikers were Dutch—and she promised us we would soon be "dans la forêt" and cooler.

The forêt was not really that much cooler. We repeated to one another that the heat would have to break sometime. Even the lakes and ponds the GR5 wanders among helped only a little.

The towns along this stretch are typical farm villages—houses and barns all pushed together in a communal row, with the fields out beyond the town. Yet the lakes have brought some tourism to the area—albeit seasonal tourism. Past Fribourg, for example, on the Étang de Stock, is the restaurant of the Ferme des Bachats—a good lunch spot for this day.

From here forward, GR5 is definitely in the midst of a water sports area. Summer bungalows, trailers, and campsites abound, and we found it curious that most of the license plates on the cars were German. The trail goes along the road that leads to Diane-Capelle, but it turns off before the town to follow the Canal des Houillières. It is a long, flat walk along this still waterway—shades of the good old Dutch days—till the trail nips up the dike for a view west to the Étang de Gondrexange, east to Le Petit Étang, ahead to the junction with the Rhine-Marne Canal.

GR5 meets and goes along the canal; pleasure boats are at anchor here, and we heard the gleeful sounds of swimming children from the Petit Étang. This was the first time all summer we had seen swimmers and sunbathers.

From Gondrexange, the walker has two choices for lodging. One is at Heming, only 3 kilometers away. Ten kilometers distant, however, is Sarrebourg, and we had an ulterior motive for heading there by taxi: the famous Chagall stained glass window in the Chapelle des Cordeliers. It seemed a shame to be so near and not take a look.

Livier Barthelemy had told us the previous evening that he disapproved of the window—not of the work itself, which he found beautiful, nor of the artist, but of the fact that an ancient building had been lopped in half to make room for the window, and of the city fathers who had allowed that to happen. Maybe, but the brilliantly colored window, "Paix," designed by Chagall and executed by Marq, is quite overwhelming in its beauty—in our view, worth the detour.

That night, the heat wave did indeed break. The heavens opened with a burst— wind, fierce rain, hailstones the size of jelly beans. All of this took only a few minutes, but the screaming sounds of rescue sirens went on for quite a while. Over the next few days, we would see the widespread damage caused by this sudden, intense *ouragan*.

Day 12: Gondrexange to Abreschviller (ca. 22 km, 5-½ hr)

From Gondrexange, GR5 turns more nearly southeast, heading straight for the midsection of the curving range of the Vosges.

Still traversing fields, the route passes through the small hamlets of Landange and Aspach into the Bois de la Minière. Emerging from the woods, the walker has his first view of the Vosges in the distance, weather permitting. Then it is down into Fraquelfing for the last push across paysage lorrain, just as the terrain changes from limestone to the sandstone of the massif.

On through Niderhoff to Métairies Saint-Quirin, where GR5 turns up into forest. As we made that turn, one of a group of men standing in a doorway called out to us: "Où est-ce que vous allez?" (Where are you going?)

"To Nice," we answered, and they nodded—as if it were the destination of most people strolling through this minute hamlet.

The road climbs to the top of the woods, where we swore we caught the edge of a change in the air: the cool, minty smell of mountains. There were a lot of fallen trees. Some seemed snapped in two; others, mostly sycamores, were uprooted. As we descended the road, there were more and more of these downed trees; we had to climb over and around several that blocked our path. It was our first inkling that the storm of the night before had been more than just a local cloudburst.

GR5 emerges from the forest and heads down the road into the lovely village of Saint-Quirin. For us, it was a perilous walk. Electric wires were down, snaking across the road. Precariously balanced half-fallen trees lay against others, equally precarious, along the edge of the road. We carefully skirted or climbed over these scary obstacles.

Saint-Quirin was a town cleaning up. At the restaurant where we lunched, the storm was all anyone talked about. L'ouragan had lasted five minutes, we were told; its fierce winds tore holes in roofs, knocked over trees, and blew out the power, which was still out. Madame worried about the food spoiling in her now useless refrigerator.

The walker should not miss the fifteenth-century church of Saint-Quirin, with its two bulbous spires; we made a point of passing it, though even here, crowds of townspeople were abuzz with talk of the storm.

GR5 climbs out of the town into woods. There we saw what the force of the storm had been. The upper slope of the hill was nearly denuded. Giant trees had snapped apart; falling, they had taken others with them, uprooting some, breaking others. The lovely, long, slender bodies of fir trees tumbled down the hillside like so many pick-up sticks, while their implanted bases stood forlorn, with ominous, jagged tops. At the top of the forest, at Deux Croix, a group of forest workers stood assessing the situation. They warned us not to follow the trail to Abreschviller but to take the road. The trail was too dangerous, one said; many trees "had not yet finished falling." He estimated the winds of the brief storm at 150 kilometers per hour (about 90 miles per hour) and pointed out to us the worst-hit slope, now a gaping hole in the forest. The last storm like this, he told us, was one hundred years ago. All the trees would have to be cut, and the wood, having split and cracked, was useless. It broke his heart, he said, to see such damage.

We followed the road into Abreschviller. Susanna wanted to ride the famous Chemin de Fer Forestier, a steam train ride through the woods, but the storm had closed it down. Workers clambered over the church. The storm had knocked out some of its windows, torn tiles off the roof, and, above all, tipped the weather vane off the very top of the steeple. It teetered, perilously awry, one leg barely attached, while the other flew into the air. The year before, a woman told us, lightning from a storm had knocked it off entirely. This year, l'ouragan.

So the formidable power of nature was much on our minds as we slept, for the first time on our trip, in real mountains.

13
Uphill:
The Vosges Mountains
and Alsace

It is mountain walking all the way to Nice, starting now—in the Vosges, GR5's mountainous route through Alsace.

The 120-mile-long chain of the Vosges Mountains separates the Plateau of Lorraine from the Plain of Alsace. To the west, the slopes of the mountains rise gradually from Lorraine up to the crest, but the eastern flank of the Vosges is a sharp drop down to the rich alluvial farmland of Alsace, bordered further east by the Rhine Valley and Germany's Black Forest.

Mountains, narrow valleys, and the vineyards of Alsace along the famous Route du Vin: in traversing all this, the walker is in a relentlessly up-and-down world. He will stay in that world, virtually without relief, until the Mediterranean. As the experienced hiker knows, what would seem to be the boredom of mountain walking (you go up, you come down, you go up again) is actually its charm: you cannot see and do not know what is over the next hill, except, to be sure, another hill.

The Vosges is the first of the three great mountain chains the GR5 crosses in the walk down Europe. Of the three, it is the range that lies most nearly north-south, actually paralleling the Rhine for some 170 kilometers. GR5 heads pretty much southward down the Vosges, although it loops east to visit the vineyards of the plain and to catch some of the lovely valleys further south. The walker thus experiences a little bit of everything Alsatian: mountains, vineyards, forest, plain, valley— and people. The Alsatians *are* different.

To begin with, there is their language. Don't call it a dialect within the hearing of any Alsatian, and especially do not call it a German dialect, but that is what it is—a Germanic dialect from the same group that produced Swiss German. You will hear it in everyday speech, and you will see it in the family names of the people and in the place names of villages, streets, and natural features.

Alsace was first invaded by Germans in 58 B.C., then again in the fourth century, the ninth century, the tenth, the nineteenth, and the twentieth. From 1871 to the end of World War I, it belonged to Germany, and in 1940, it again fell under German domination for five years. Yet German possession of Alsace has always met with resistance, and the province's ties to France, even among the most independently minded regional chauvinists, remained strong. Of his great general, Kleber, Napoleon said, "He speaks German, but he rattles his saber in French." What accounts for this devotion to France as much as anything were the periods of German domination, 1871–1918 and 1940–1945. The more recent of these was particularly persuasive. As one Alsatian woman told us, "In three months' time, Hitler turned the Alsatians into the best Frenchmen in the world."

In the Franco-Prussian War of 1870, as well as in both world wars of this century, the front line of fighting stretched down the Vosges along what is today more or less the GR5. In 1914, the Germans invaded through the Vosges and took up positions along the crest, which they maintained throughout the war. It worked the other way around during the Allied offensive of 1944. The Americans under Patton and Patch were to the north, the French under General de Lattre de Tassigny were to the south. Their joint line moved east—through Saverne, Strasbourg, the pocket of Colmar, Rouffach, Mulhouse—across the Alsatian plain to the Rhine and onward into Germany.

At the war's end, Alsace and its great city of Strasbourg became the headquarters of the postwar Council of Europe. Strasbourg is today known as the capital of Europe, a reference to its role as headquarters of the European Parliament, a well-intentioned if somewhat toothless body. It has even been suggested that people become candidates for the Parliament because victory means that you get to come to the heart of Alsace three times a year to eat and drink yourself silly at taxpayer expense.

There are three groups of Vosges: Vosges du Nord, or Basses Vosges; Vosges Moyennes; and Hautes-Vosges. GR5 ignores the Vosges du Nord, which are separated from the middle and high Vosges by the Saverne Gap, an important east-west link through which a major highway, a railway line, and the Rhine-Marne Canal all pass.

Instead, GR5 follows the Vosges Moyennes from Abreschviller loopingly south to Haut-Koenigsbourg, then picks up the more Alps-like Hautes-Vosges. Geologically, they are two different kinds of hill.

The middle Vosges, like the Vosges du Nord, are a sandstone massif, often called the Vosges Gréseuses. The massif consists of a core of ancient crystalline rock covered by sedimentary deposits from the Permian and Triassic periods. These are wooded rumps of mountains that rise and fall across a vast granite dome. The highest point of the middle Vosges is the peak of Donon, 1,009 meters (3,329 feet); GR5 climbs to it on Day 1 of our itinerary.

The Hautes-Vosges, the Vosges Cristallines, are formed of granites and gneiss vigorously eroded by glacial activity and fast streams. Cirques filled with lakes, moraines, jagged rock outcroppings, the flower-filled high meadows known as *chaumes*, even the blanket of conifers, combine to produce a feeling that, for want of a better word, is called Alpine. It is not Alpine; it is distinctively Haute-Vosgienne. Along the crest of the massif are the highest summits of the Vosges Mountains, as well as a highway, the Route des Crêtes, which allows multitudes of people to reach these summits. The highest point in the Vosges is Grand Ballon at 1,424 meters (4,699 feet), reached on Day 11 of our itinerary. The third highest point in the Vosges is also its southernmost summit, the Ballon d'Alsace (1,247 meters; 4,115 feet), reached on the final day of our walk here.

Down from Ballon d'Alsace, the walker enters the so-called Porte de Bourgogne of the Territoire de Belfort, the corridor between the Plain of Alsace and the Saône-Rhone furrow, and the divide between central Europe and the Europe of the Mediterranean.

The slopes of the Vosges are richly forested, thick with wildflowers and plant life, and are home to a variety of birds and forest fauna.

At the lower elevations, the forest is primarily of beech, oak, maple, and sycamore. You climb into conifers: Sylvester pine, with bundled needles; the hangdog spruce—*épicéa*—with its drooping branches and cones; the fir with its high horizontal branches—*sapin* in French, the king of the forest.

Among wildflowers, look particularly for foxglove, which likes to grow near both beech and fir. Campanula in the meadows, anemone among the glacial rifts, heather, wild raspberries, and aromatic herbs are all to be found here.

Le grand tétras (the wild grouse) is often flushed from this vegetation, and the villages of the middle Vosges are said to play host to storks, though we never saw one. But we did see deer, which are not uncommon in these high, forested hills. The famous chamois, however, which once roamed here freely, has been pushed back to the higher elevations of the Alps.

The narrow valleys and thickly forested hillsides of the mountains support only a small population. There is some hard-scrabble farming in the valleys, but the soil is poor, and yields do not come easily. Cattle grazing, however, both in the valleys and up the slopes, provides a variety of dairy products, most notably the superb cheeses of Alsace.

The forests are also a source of economic wealth. Timber is harvested for lumber, for furniture making, and for paper. Textile production, a valley industry since the eighteenth century, is today served by the hydroelectric projects that seem to line the crest of the Vosges from glacial lake to glacial lake. From the high streams of these mountains rise four great rivers: Moselle, Meurthe, Saar, and Ill.

One of the great industries here is tourism, year-round. In the winter, there is both downhill and cross-country skiing. In the summer, eating and wine tasting, sightseeing, and hiking are popular—in about that order.

The wine tasting proceeds along the world famous Route du Vin (Michelin three-star rating), a 180-kilometer drive among the vineyards and wine-producing towns of the Alsatian plain just at the foot of the Vosges. It is a little frightening to think of all those people driving from village to village, stopping for a glass or two of Gewurztraminer, Sylvaner, or Riesling, then getting back in their cars and back behind the wheel to drive on to the next town.

If it were true that eating while drinking prevents drunkenness, that might be some consolation, for eating in Alsace is a constant pastime—justifiably so. The gastronomic specialties of the region are so well known it is only necessary to remind the walker of a few of the most famous: the *patés* and *terrines*, *choucroute* (sauerkraut, sausage, and potatoes), *coq au Riesling* and *truite au Riesling*, *tarte a l'oignon*, *kougelhopf* (a raisin sponge cake dessert baked in a pottery mold).

The walker in the Vosges has a special advantage when it comes to eating: the frequent appearance of a uniquely Alsatian institution, the *ferme-auberge*. As the name implies, the ferme-auberge is a farm and it is also an inn. There is a requirement for the fermes-auberges that everything served there must be homegrown and homecooked. Almost all fermes-auberges keep small herds of cows and goats and produce their own cheeses—especially Munster, which you can buy by the round or portion of a round. In addition, the fermes-auberges tend to be situated on hillside meadows, and from their terraces, the walker can enjoy a panoramic view down to the valley and out to the mountains just crossed or those to come.

The Megawalker's Absolute Law of Travel ("The unentered café is not worth the ground it stands on") underwent an important emendation in ferme-auberge territory—to wit: "Stop at every ferme-auberge you pass at least for cheese or a drink, but whatever you do, eat lunch at a ferme-auberge at least once, even if you must detour from the trail to do so." Happily, signs aplenty along GR5 advertise the nearby fermes-auberges, so you can easily make your way to one when the need arises.

The gastronomic dilemma of Alsace focuses on the drinking. Since it is probably impossible and certainly unwise to partake fully of both the renowned wines and the renowned beers of the area, some compromise must be forged. We solved it by drinking wine in the wine towns and beer up in the mountains, except sometimes when we switched, or simply drank both.

The most famous of the beers is Kronenbourg, but there is a goodly variety of mostly dark, burnished brews that are worth investigating. Wine has been produced here since the third century, toward the end of the Roman epoch. In the sixteenth century, a law was promulgated limiting the varieties of wine grapes of the region. Wines "a l'appellation d'origine controlée" are Sylvaner, Riesling, Gewurztraminer, Muscat, Pinot Blanc, Pinot Gris or Tokay, and Pinot Noir or Rosé d'Alsace. These wines are bottled in long-necked green *flutes d'Alsace* and are customarily served in green-tinted, long-stemmed glasses.

From Abreschviller to Giromagny, GR5 covers 287 kilometers (178 miles) in thirteen days. Almost all of one day and half of another are given over to city sightseeing in Strasbourg, the head and heart of Alsace and one of the great cities of Europe, and in Riquewihr, the quintessential wine town within whose walls are concentrated—perhaps just ever so slightly self-consciously—all the history and picturesqueness of the Route du Vin.

From Abreschviller, the route moves south and east across the Vosges Moyennes to the wine villages of Barr, Andlau, Châtenois, and Ribeauvillé—four flowering towns. GR5 then continues south up to the crest of the Hautes-Vosges, striking in a southeast direction far enough that it must loop back west/southwest to continue along the crest to the southernmost Ballon d'Alsace.

The trail marking in the Vosges departs from the official GR standard. Several different patterns are used, most typically a red rectangle on either a white disc or a larger white rectangle. These are the markings of the Club Vosgien, who put this trail here long before there was a continent-wide organization to set standards, and whose local route 1-A the GR5 mostly follows.

But in the summer of 1984, the Club Vosgien's markings were not always as complete or as effective as they might have been. We had been warned of this by the Troisième Age crowd way back in Luxembourg, so we were not too surprised when route-finding problems arose. Under the circumstances, it is useful to carry the *cartes des Vosges*, excellent maps, published, ironically enough, by the Club Vosgien. Four of the 1:50,000 maps cover the GR5 route and are obtainable along the route and certainly in Strasbourg: Sainte-Odile/Vallée de la Bruche, Sélestat/Ribeauvillé, Munster/Gerardmer/La Bresse, Thann/Guebwiller.

For us, the walk through Alsace was marked by a number of highlights. First, we were in the mountains at last, laboring uphill and looking out on breathtaking scenery from top-of-the-world vantages. Second, we met numbers of other hikers and were able to begin to share the camaraderie of the trail—the instant rapport felt among people whose idea of a good time is to throw thirty pounds of weight on their backs and head uphill. Five of these other hikers were following the same route we were walking and were keeping to the same daily stages. For a week, we seven were companions, although when they left to return to their separate homes, and we all exchanged addresses and made the usual vows to keep in touch, we probably didn't believe we would. But we did.

Third, it was in the Vosges that we passed the halfway point of our trip, both of us sound of foot, body, and mind.

Finally, in doing the Vosges of Alsace, we crossed a true continental divide. We had now traversed that portion of lowland Europe whose rivers drain into the North Sea. At the southern edge of the Vosges, we changed basins, dropping into a river valley that drains southward to the Rhone and, eventually, the Mediterranean. Although we were heading south in a straight line, it felt like turning a corner.

Day 1: Abreschviller to Plate-Forme du Donon (ca. 24 km, 6 hr)

The walk across Europe dispenses with any sort of middling introduction to climbing—unless you count Holland, Belgium, Luxembourg, and Lorraine—and starts right in with a 709-meter (2,340-foot) elevation gain up to the summit of Donon, followed by a steep descent of some 300 meters (1,000 feet) to the Plate-Forme.

GR5 departs Abreschviller (passing épiceries and alimentations where

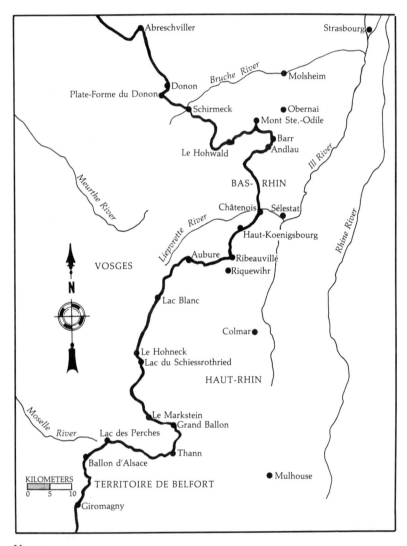

Vosges

Vosges

Day 1	Abreschviller to Plate-Forme du Donon ... 24 km	6 hr
Day 2	Plate-Forme du Donon to Schirmeck ...... 8 km	2 hr
Day 3	Schirmeck to Le Hohwald .... 24 km	6 hr
Day 4	Le Hohwald to Andlau .... 25 km	6-¼ hr
Day 5	Andlau to Châtenois .... 30 km	7-½ hr
Day 6	Châtenois to Ribeauvillé .... 20 km	5 hr
Day 7	Ribeauvillé to Aubure .... 14 km	3-½ hr
Day 8	Aubure to Lac Blanc .... 25 km	6-¼ hr
Day 9	Lac Blanc to Lac du Schiessrothried .... 20 km	5 hr
Day 10	Lac du Schiessrothried to Le Markstein .... 23 km	5-¾ hr
Day 11	Le Markstein to Thann .... 29 km	7-¼ hr
Day 12	Thann to Lac des Perches .... 21 km	5-¼ hr
Day 13	Lac des Perches to Giromagny .... 24 km	6 hr
	287 km	71-¾ hr

the walker should definitely stock up on food) and heads for Lettenbach. This pretty but minute village has two curious and quite striking structures: a corner building that was built to be a corner building, with a flat façade and diagonal wings; and a bulb-steepled church with a lovely clock, surrounded by lunettes, on the metope.

From here, the route turns upward, a walk that was a nightmare the day we were there because of the fallen trees blocking our way. Still, someone had been there before us, and there was the faint trace of a way through. We climbed among branches and found half a *baguette* (the long, slender French bread), perhaps fallen from our trailblazer's pack. Ginger held on to it in case we overtook the unfortunate hiker whose lunch this was to have been.

GR5 achieves a forest road that climbs gently among conifers. The storm's debris seemed to be behind us here, and we even saw some logging activity underway. Atop the ridge, at Belle Roche, the walker has a wide view east over the valley of Saint-Quirin and south along the ridge he is about to follow. On a ledge just below the Belle Roche summit is a grotto, marked by a skull-and-crossbones flag. Some young people were gathered around a fire there, and we asked if they were missing a baguette, but they had climbed up another way and were well provisioned with all manner of bread.

Still climbing, GR5 comes to Borne-Brignon, where the walker passes a series of Gallo-Roman milestones, a reminder that a Roman road once passed through the col du Donon and that Celts, Romans, Franks, and later armies at one time or another all fought over this strategic pass.

The route dips and climbs—to the Tête de la Croix-Simon, down to its col, up to the top (nearly) of Malcôte. From here there is a vast panorama down a clearing. In the distance, Donon, with its transmitting tower, dominates the landscape. A nip up to the Sac de Pierre takes the walker past a fenced Roman milestone, its inscription entirely worn away. Now GR5 levels out to reach the D44 road, which it follows briefly to the col de l'Engin. Where the GR53 takes off for Wissembourg, the walker has a splendid view out over the valley of the Bruche before GR5 mounts gently to the col between the two Donons, Haut and Petit. From the parking lot here, the trail ascends in switchbacks to the summit of Donon. The ascent itself offers staggering views, and the summit, with its temple-like *musée* and its orientation tables, provides a full 360-degree panorama. At the top of Donon, you bestride the sandstone massif that marks the border between Lorraine and Alsace, and between the department of Moselle in Lorraine and that of Bas-Rhin in Alsace.

There were two hikers at the summit when we arrived, a German and a Dutchman, conversing laboriously in fractured English. We asked about the morning's half baguette, and the Dutchman's eyes lit up; his name was René, and he was spending a couple of weeks hiking and camping in the Vosges. We were to see a lot of him over the next several days.

The Donon summit is a popular day-hike destination, and its far side is creatively crisscrossed with unofficial trails and cut switchbacks. Just keep going downhill in the opposite direction from the way you came up and you will arrive at the Plate-Forme du Donon.

As its name implies, the Plate-Forme is a flat area where a road can run between the hills. There are a few hotels, a few houses, and a war cemetery where the crescents on the graves of four Arabs and a Turk stand out among the crosses of the others *morts pour la France.*

In the bar of our hotel, we saw the handsome older couple we remembered from Abreschviller; we had been particularly resentful of the fact that Madame, although wearing, like us, heavy boots and floppy, worn-out clothing, nevertheless managed to retain a certain French chic we certainly did not feel we possessed.

We smiled at one another. "You must have come by car," we said.

"Comment?" Madame expostulated. "En voiture? Ah non! À pied!" And she pointed to hers to confirm the fact.

They too were walking GR5 for a while, to see the Vosges. Parisians, they had hiked almost everywhere else in France and were full of information, charm, friendliness, and admiration for our project.

We learned that their names were Henri and Monique.

Day 2: Plate-Forme du Donon to Schirmeck (Strasbourg) (ca. 8 km, 2 hr)

It is only a two-hour walk to Schirmeck and all downhill. A mid-morning arrival there leaves plenty of time to secure a hotel, change clothes, and hop the train to Strasbourg for a full afternoon of sight-seeing.

GR5's intention is to take you from the Plate-Forme to Schirmeck through thick woods, allowing only tantalizing glimpses of the valley of the Bruche. But a local promenade, marked by yellow crosses, moves right along the Framont stream, which will feed the Bruche, and passes a series of madly picturesque villages to arrive at the same destination. This is the perfect example of a case in which an American walker, as much tourist as hiker, might well want to edit the GR5 route.

Whether you follow the GR5 above the Framont or head along the stream's right bank through Grandfontaine, Framont, Vacquenoux, and Wackenbach, you and the stream both meet the River Bruche at Schirmeck. This is a popular starting point for hikes, and we saw several groups of promenaders in knickers and bright knee socks tossing their rucksacks on their backs and heading off for holiday trekking—it was Bastille Day.

Numerous other holidayers were on the train to Strasbourg, only an hour away across the flat Alsatian plain.

The name Strasbourg means "city of roads," and it has been a crossroads of Europe since Roman times. On the Rhine, traversed by the Ill, Strasbourg is linked to the west by the Rhine-Marne Canal and to the Rhone River and the south by the Rhine-Rhone Canal. It is a city with an outstanding history. Gutenberg started working on the printing press idea in Strasbourg, and Goethe was a student at the university here. The city today has a travel-poster appearance, a world-class culinary reputation, and one of the world's most beautiful cathedrals.

Built of pink Vosgien sandstone, the towering Cathédrale Notre Dame soars above the city. The statues and bas-reliefs of the façade detail Bible history from Adam and Eve to the Ascension of Christ. Inside, you walk the 103 meters of the cathedral's length between huge pillars in an awesome space (the nave is 32 meters high) lit through the half million pieces of stained glass that make up the windows. A curious astronomical clock is one of the cathedral's great treasures, not only for its decoration but because it is half an hour slow.

Strasbourg has a wealth of other churches and museums, including an excellent archaeological collection and an Alsatian museum devoted to the folk art and customs of the province. But a particular delight is to wander the city's streets, reeking of Rhineland quaintness, especially the quarter known as La Petite France. This was once the home of fishermen, tanners, and millers, and its movie-set appearance has been carefully preserved. Gabled, half-timbered houses bursting with flowerpots line the canal; covered bridges cross it; postcards are for sale everywhere.

Strasbourg's Bastille Day celebration, which included a contest of jousting off river sculls on the Ill, was well under way, and preparations were proceeding apace for the night's street dance and party. Rain threatened, however, and it looked like the festivities were going to get doused. We decided to head back to Schirmeck for a small-town Bastille Day.

The official ceremony was held at the town's memorial, a pylon flanked by two columns. The stone in the center is inscribed, "La ville de Schirmeck à ses morts. Guerres 1914–18, 1939–45." Under the right-hand column is an urn; under the left is a statue of a woman, representing France and bent double with weeping.

In the pouring rain, only a few people stood under umbrellas along the road. We, along with many others, watched from upper-storey windows as the parade came by: an Army drum-and-bugle corps in tan uniforms, then the fire brigade, then the honored veterans and assorted townsfolk.

A portly veteran was awarded two medals, with great ceremony. A brief citation was read as the first medal was handed over. The second and clearly weightier honor was presented after a lengthy exposition by a very old man. We strained to hear but caught only phrases: "urged the preparation for war in '37 and '38"; "Resistance"; "captured by the Germans." Kisses were planted as the medal went from its purple velvet cushion onto the honoree's chest to the accompaniment of the "Marseillaise." Flashbulbs popped. The band and the other legions regrouped, turned around, and marched off. Bastille Day continued in the taverns of Schirmeck.

We had some reason for national celebration of our own. That day in the Strasbourg train station, Susanna had seen an Italian newspaper whose headline blared that a woman—"an Italian-American woman," as she was proclaimed—had been nominated as the vice-presidential candidate on the Democratic national ticket. This was exciting news to two American women, though many of the people waiting for trains might have been a bit alarmed at Susanna's whoops about Gerry from Queens.

Day 3: Schirmeck to Le Hohwald (ca. 24 km, 6 hr)

This is a stage of stiff climbing and steep descent. On this day, too, GR5 takes the walker past Struthof, a Nazi death camp to which convoys of prisoners from all over Europe were brought. There is no way to avoid Struthof along this stretch of the GR5.

For us, happily, the day was almost equally memorable for the Alsatian picnic we happened upon. Several hours in the midst of generous, vital Alsatians was a good antidote to the morning's chilling history lesson.

Climbing out of Schirmeck, GR5 offers views through the trees back down to the valley of the Bruche as it enters the communal forest of Barembach. Signs here declare that the forest is rationally exploited, its harvesting carefully regulated. Fir and beech are cut when they have reached forty-five to fifty years of age; the spruce are not cut until they are at least eighty. Numerous paths wander this forest, including a "learning trail" for school children.

Struthof is another lesson altogether. More than 30,000 victims of the Nazis were exterminated here between 1941 and 1944; many died building the barracks and the road that leads up to the camp. In a small shower-house, an Alsatian doctor carried out gas experiments on Jewish women sent up from Auschwitz; the doctor managed to flee in safety as the war was ending. The camp today is preserved as a national memorial. It speaks for itself.

Just beyond Struthof, GR5 turns sharply to the left, off the road and down into a gully of forest. It was pouring rain as we descended, and the balisage seemed to run out on us. We knew the trail picked up the road again and that there was a *gîte-abri* (covered shelter) up there somewhere, so we simply pushed uphill to look for it.

We were right on the mark and headed for the shelter to get in out of the rain. It was filled with people who waved us in and handed us glasses of kyr—white wine with crème de cassis. The group was a labor union—we never learned what their labor was—celebrating the day-after-Bastille Day with a picnic that had to be moved indoors because of the weather. They had already invited in a Dutch couple, Jan and Renske, whom we had seen the evening before in Schirmeck; three German hikers; and a Parisian couple who were passing in their car.

The warm fire in the fireplace fueled a lot of cooking activity. The ringleader of the group was a cheerful, funny man with a heavy hand on the wine bottle he kept tilting over our glasses. The cooks wondered if we'd like a little snack and served us barbecued *saucisson* (sausage) and glasses of Pinot Noir. Then came something they called *farce*—lamb innards chopped up and soaked in the same kind of garlic-and-butter sauce in which escargots are typically served. This was poured onto hunks of french bread and handed over with more wine. Then came Camembert cheese, coffee, and more wine.

It was a jolly and generous crowd, all perforce squeezed into the shelter, although several of the children ran outside now and again to play. The Dutch couple finally got going, and the German hikers followed, and the Parisians waved goodbye from their car, but we stayed right where we were.

Political arguments proceeded fast, furiously, and with great humor, while the food just kept coming. As one woman explained to Susanna, "Left-wing or right-wing, one always eats well in France."

It turned out that all this snacking was simply to keep people alive until dinner was ready. We didn't stay for dinner, but we saw it cooking: a lamb (sans innards, we assumed) being turned on a spit over a bed of hot coals in front of the shelter.

We left reluctantly and on shaky legs. From the shelter, GR5 climbs to the Champ du Messin, then finds a forest road to the col de la Katzmatt. Turning south, it arrives at the viewpoint of the rock of Rathsamhausen, follows a piece of ancient Roman road, and crosses the D124 highway to just under the Champ de Feu. There is a magnificent view from the top of the Champ de Feu, which the walker can reach on the road; for us, however, given the still-dismal weather and our overstuffed condition, the climb was out of the question.

The route now takes a sharp northeast angle to cross three forest roads and arrives at the Hohwald waterfall. You then pass a stone celebrating the Great Spruce of Strasbourg before entering the lively town of Hohwald itself.

Day 4: Le Hohwald to Andlau (ca. 25 km, 6-¼ hr)

We had calculated that just before Barr, on today's stage, we would pass the halfway point of our top-to-bottom walk across Europe. Happily, the weather was superb, with a rain-fresh edge to the air.

GR5 climbs gently from Le Hohwald, contouring slowly and rising almost imperceptibly. The handsome Dutch couple we had seen in Schirmeck and again at the Alsatian picnic were ahead of us on the switchbacking walk, and we kept waving to one another across fields.

Wild foxglove and deep red columbine grow in profusion here along the path, while in clearings there are patches of bright pink epilobium, called fireweed for its ability to thrive where the soil has been damaged or cleared.

After the forest hut of Welschbruch, where the walker can find refreshment, GR5 continues its gentle ascent through the forest of Barr, among groves of high fir and pine, with oblique views from the hillside to the grand vista below. Shortly after the Carrefour (crossroads) de la Bloss, a highway intersection, the walker sees the first signs of *mur païen*, remains of a massive and extensive enclosure of large stones, on some of which depressions for embellishments are still evident. The wall is some 10 kilometers long and dates from the eighth century B.C., presumably constructed by a polytheistic people, though for what purpose remains a mystery. In the fourth century A.D., the Romans rebuilt the wall as part of the defensive system along the road whose remains the GR5 here crosses.

The trail climbs to the convent of Mont Sainte-Odile, the premier religious center and pilgrim's shrine of Alsace, for here are the remains of Alsace's patron saint, Odile. This is her story:

Odile was born in the seventh century in Obernai, daughter of Duke Étichon. As an infant, she was blind, infirm, and female—sufficient reason, in her father's eyes, for her to be ordered killed. Her nurse, however, whisked her to safety and raised her secretly. Time passed. Odile was baptised, regained her sight miraculously, and grew into a beauty. Her mother and brother decided to tell Étichon of her existence, but Étichon, instead of pardoning his daughter, murdered his son. Later, filled with remorse, he relented and decided to marry Odile to an eligible knight. She, however, wished only to consecrate herself to God; she fled, with Étichon in hot pursuit. The miracle that saved her was a sudden, inexplicable opening in a huge rock, which then closed before Étichon could pass through. Étichon now knew he was beaten. He accepted Odile's vocation and gave her his summer residence at Hohenbourg, where she created the convent. It is a compound of pink sandstone sanctuaries separated by pretty inner courtyards. From a terrace atop the wall, the walker has a panoramic view of the vineyards below and the tree-covered slopes of the Vosges. Of equal importance to the walker is the convent's cafeteria, where we met Jan and Renske, our Dutch cohikers, who told us they had seen a booted eagle in the forest. Later, as we were leaving the cafeteria, we met Henri and Monique on their way in. We were all getting to be pretty familiar to one another.

GR5 heads down from the convent to cross the plateau of Bloss to the lookout of Maennelstein. The fabulous view from here takes in the Rhine and its flat wide plain, the Vosges, and even the Black Forest beyond the river.

Downhill again, passing more mur païen before coming to Kiosque Jadelot. This round structure straddles the trail; its front porch indeed protrudes over the edge of the hill. The trail walks right through it, offering a fine view out the front window.

GR5 continues downhill past the romantic ruin of the chateau of Landsberg, just off the route and accessible by a side trail, and then emerges into a clearing where the Petit Kiosque, a kind of gazebo, commands another view of vineyards and plain.

Just above Barr, at a monument to a benign-looking gent named Edvard Héring, we crossed the halfway point of our sea-to-sea walk and scraped an X on the trail to mark the spot. (The GR5 designers avoid any sort of fanfare at this point.) We never did learn who Edvard Héring was. All the monument told us was that he died in 1893, but to us, his will ever be a famous name.

The trail now drops down pleasantly along a *chemin vignoble* (what we had learned to call a chemin viticole along the Moselle in Luxembourg) to Barr, one of the supreme vineyard towns on the Route du Vin—picturesque, quaint, and loaded with tourists. Barr is designated a *ville fleurie*—a beflowered town—by a national organization that promotes "the blossoming of France." Indeed, the number of blossoms put forth by the geraniums and petunias in the flower boxes of Barr seems incredible, and the flower boxes are everywhere—along the streets, in cafés, banked around fountains, and sprouting from every window ledge. This, plus the wine and the typically Alsatian architecture, make Barr particularly enchanting.

From here, GR5 follows another chemin vignoble, where vintners were hard at work the afternoon we passed through.

"Will the wine be good this year?" we asked.

"Toujours!" came the answer. "Our wine is always good."

In Andlau, another ville fleurie filled with wine vaults, we tested the vintner's declaration in a *winstube*—wine-bar—above an elegant restaurant.

He was right.

Day 5: Andlau to Châtenois
(ca. 30 km, 7-½ hr)

Carry sufficient food and water for this long day on which GR5 takes you back up into the Vosges to the viewpoint summit of Ungersberg at 901 meters (2,973 feet), before a long walk through woods and a descent to vineyards at Châtenois.

The route climbs past the backyard gardens of Andlavian houses through thick spruce woods to the Maison Forestière de Gruckert, a refuge run by the Amis de la Nature. It pushes on up to the col of Ungersberg, then climbs in easy switchbacks to the summit. Climb the ruined tower here—not so ruined that it's dangerous—for views of the villages up and down the Route du Vin and out toward the distant Black Forest.

At the Ungersberg summit, we were some two and a half hours out of Andlau and, according to topo-guide, just about an hour away from our next major landmark, the ruin of the chateau of Ortenberg. So we were surprised indeed to walk for some three and a half hours—up and down through forest, past the farm of Neumatten, across a highway, up the Dambach Forest to the Schulwaldplatz, along the road to Kaesmarkt, into the forest of Bernstein, past the *château-ruine* of Bernstein—before coming at last to the Ortenberg ruin. It was particularly confusing because at various places along this route, trail signs had disagreed among themselves about distances to various next stops.

The Ortenberg ruin, perched on a large clump of rock, standing isolated from the side of the hill, literally commands the valley of Ville and the plain of Sélestat below. There is another fine view further along at the Château-Fort de Ramstein, which is also fun to clamber around in.

GR5 descends from here into town.

All three of our Dutch companions were already gathered in Châtenois, and although René went on to find a camping place, we joined Jan and Renske for dinner—monumental platters of choucroute and a bottle of Tokay. There is nothing subtle about Alsatian food, and there was nothing subtle about our enthusiasm for it that night. In the middle of our meal, Henri and Monique arrived in town and we applauded them through the open window. Their plan was to hike the Vosges until, as Henri put it, "la fatigue dépasse le plaisir"—weariness overtakes pleasure. They had still not reached that point, even after this long, long day.

Less precious than Barr or Andlau, a little less publicly fleurie, Châtenois is a quiet town backed by a lovely mountain. Yet it still has flamboyant flowers in profusion enough, firewood stacked neatly behind wrought iron fences, elegant street lamps hung from curled flanges.

Of particular interest are its curious bell tower and a fifteenth century gate tower where storks are said to nest.

Day 6: Châtenois to Ribeauvillé (ca. 20 km, 5 hr)

A day of castles—four in all—perched on hilltops commanding the Rhine plain below. GR5 climbs from Châtenois to follow a winding mountain-and-forest route past these haunting fairy-tale castles before descending to the Route du Vin at Ribeauvillé.

This stage also marks the transition from the sandstone Vosges Moyennes to the granitic Hautes-Vosges, a transition marked by the stream of La Liepvrette, at the end of whose valley Châtenois lies. At Haut-Koenigsbourg, this transition is formalized as the walker leaves the department of Bas-Rhin and enters that of Haut-Rhin.

Leaving Châtenois, GR5 climbs the hill of Le Hahnenberg to the Maison Forestière de Wick. This is a spot accessible by car, with a busy restaurant-café and a monkey zoo. Some of the monkeys were roaming loose in the woods as we approached—a bizarre sight in the middle of Europe.

The route continues its climb to Haut-Koenigsbourg, a total of 562 meters (1,854 feet) above Châtenois. Situated atop a high peak that falls off sharply in every direction, the feudal castle that stands here now in restored splendor once commanded a superb defensive position over the plain below. It was destroyed by the Swedish in 1633 and remained a ruin until 1901 when the town of Sélestat, which couldn't afford to preserve the castle any longer, offered it to Kaiser Wilhelm II of Germany. He ordered its reconstruction, and today, little if any of the original castle remains. As a museum and for the setting alone, however, Haut-Koenigsbourg is hard to match.

GR5 proceeds down to the col of Schaentzel, then down again to Thannenkirch, known for the curative powers of its mountain air. The massif above the town, the 992-meter Taennchel, has been designated a zone of tranquillity as the result of efforts by a local Club Vosgien member, the very man in whose café we stopped and who told us of the trails he had cut on Taennchel. He urged us to detour to Ribeauvillé by way of his mountain, but we decided to stay on our route. It seemed ironic that, even on foot, we often had the regretful feeling that we were rushing through a place deserving of more time and exploration.

Château de Haut-Ribeaupierre is the highest of the three ruined castles of Ribeauvillé. A lone, turreted tower still stands there and offers fine views in all directions. Descending from Haut-Ribeaupierre, the walker passes Château de Guirsberg, an isolated ruin on an abrupt rock, and Château Saint-Ulrich—from below, a most imposing and grandiose sight.

For its castles, its famous Pfifferdaj folk festival (held in September), its beauty, and its production of Traminer and Riesling (the so-called sisters of Ribeauvillé), the lively tourist center of Ribeauvillé is justly famous. For us, it loomed particularly large in importance as a mail pick-up, our first since Luxembourg. Ginger, who had received less mail in Echternach than she had hoped for, was convinced there would be even slimmer pickings at Ribeauvillé and was all set to be furious with her friends and family—particularly her four children. In an attempt to lessen her ire with some sport, Susanna had offered to wager that there would be mail and that the children would come through. The stakes were a bottle of champagne.

We therefore hurried downhill into town, eager for news from home and bubbly wine. Susanna won the bet, and we proceeded to a café to drink her winnings. There, already hard at work on beer around a table, were all our Vosges companions: Jan and Renske, René, Henri and Monique. The very fine wine tasted particularly good shared among us.

Day 7: Ribeauvillé/Riquewihr to Aubure (ca. 14 km, 3-½ hr)

Before leaving Ribeauvillé, the walker would do well to spend a morning in nearby Riquewihr, where the quintessence of Route du Vin charm is concentrated at a world-class level. It is only 4 kilometers from Ribeauvillé—an easy walk or hitch or taxi ride.

To call Riquewihr quainter than quaint is by no means to question its authenticity. Set amongst sunny vineyards, this tiny walled gem of a village has kept its sloping-with-age, half-timbered buildings in a near-perfect state of preservation. Some of Riquewihr's buildings date from the thirteenth century, but most are of the sixteenth century. Since then, neither war nor technology has put even the slightest crease on Riquewihr's appearance. Flower boxes are of course everywhere. Huge wooden casks lead into dark, stone wine *caves.* Gothic German lettering on signs announces Winstub and Caveau and Tarte a l'Oignon and Souvenirs. Cars are not permitted in the old center of town, and every method is used to conceal other modern technologies applied to the production of the town's raison d'être—wine. Trucks carrying wine vats, we noted, pulled up to caves during the lunch hour, when hardly anyone is on the streets, so that even this hint that Riquewihr's vintner families are among the most productive, most savvy, wealthiest wine merchants on earth will go unnoticed.

We had brought our Michelin green guide and followed the tour it describes, as virtually everyone else was doing. We stopped at the wine caves for tasting, as virtually everyone else was doing. We lunched on onion tart and Alsatian Riesling, as virtually everyone else was doing. Then we went shopping. Virtually everyone else was doing that, too.

We each bought a handsome wine bucket, and Susanna also purchased a set of Alsatian wine glasses. The shop clerks boxed them all, and we hurried off to the Riquewihr post office to mail them home. Riquewihr post office closed until 2 P.M. We taxied back to the Ribeauvillé post office. Ribeauvillé post office closed until 3 P.M. We ascertained that there was a post office in Aubure, and we reluctantly lashed our cardboard boxes on top of our packs. We marched off to Aubure looking—and feeling—a bit like loaded beasts in a mule train.

The walk to Aubure is short but does not stint on the uphill aspect. To the Rocher du Koeningstuhl is a climb of some 667 meters (2,200 feet) through a forest of chestnut, beech, and fir, and past a touching shrine to a young man killed by lightning in 1887 at the col du Seelacker. At the Koenigstuhl (king's seat), René was already enthroned. We walked together to take in the fine view at the Rocher du Tétras. Clouds were moving in. René, a native Dutchman who sometimes confused his French and English in the Vosges, pronounced the weather "orageous," a neologism that should be in every walker's lexicon. He hurried on to find a tent site before the heavens opened.

After a few feeble drops, however, the rain ceased and the sun broke through. We entered Aubure in a blaze of sunshine and to wild applause. Our Vosges companions, forewarned by René about our Sherpa-like appearance, were gathered on the *terrasse* of a café waiting for us. They stood and cheered as we approached and waved us home, where the beers they had ordered for us tasted very good indeed.

We mailed the boxes the next morning. Both wine buckets arrived safely, but the glasses, alas, turned into millions of pieces on their way from Aubure to New York.

Day 8: Aubure to Lac Blanc
(ca. 25 km, 6-¼ hr)

This stage begins with less climbing than usual but makes up for it in the afternoon. The glacial Lac Blanc, where the stage ends, is part of a large hydroelectric plant in concert with its neighbor, Lac Noir, 100 meters lower down. At night, the pumps of Lac Blanc refill Lac Noir, so that it is ready to provide needed energy in the morning.

From Aubure, GR5 climbs gradually through a forest said to be under attack from acid rain and industrial pollutants. Literature we picked up at the Aubure town hall described the deadly effects of this pollution on the forest, lakes, drinking water, and vegetation. The brochure outlined some methods for dealing with the problem but lamented that "cette pollution n'a pas de frontière"—the pollution knows no frontier. . . . The problem is European, if not worldwide.

We were not unaware of it. The forests of Europe, and particularly the Bavarian woods in Germany, have been held up as an object lesson for Americans concerned about the devastation in our Eastern forests that is already spreading west. It made for a sobering departure from Aubure.

The trail climbs gradually and contours behind a big clinic, Centre de Cure Salem. Then it ascends to a crossroads of paths at Pierre des Trois Bans. From here, it is a brief nip up to the top for a view, then

back to GR5 to contour the hill of Rehberg toward Grand Brézouard.
GR5 does not attain the summit of Grand Brézouard, although the
megawalker can easily do so. This highest Vosgien peak north of the
valley of Kaysersberg offers a splendid view of the mountains. The trail
instead descends gently to the col between Rauenthal and Le Bonhomme
where there is a wonderfully situated refuge run by Amis de la Nature,
Refuge Haïcot, on a narrow ledge above Sainte-Marie-aux-Mines and
the wide valley below.

The route continues descending to the exciting and beautiful col des
Bagenelles. The village of Le Bonhomme nestles at the bottom of a wide,
green breast of meadow that slopes down from the col to the village.
Le Bonhomme is so agreeable a little mountain town that it is hard to
believe that it has been the scene of violent warfare three times in this
century. In World War I, more than half the village was destroyed;
in 1940 and again in 1944, fierce fighting raged here and along the ridges
and cols above.

Once down in Le Bonhomme, we joined Jan and Renske for *casse-
croute* (snack; literally, "breaking crust") on the terrace of a small hotel—
a last meal together. We watched them board the bus for Colmar where
they would catch a train back to Holland; then we set off uphill through
mountain pastures and into woods along a forest road. A privately
owned refuge, Étape de l'Étang du Devin, provided much-needed
refreshment after this sweaty climb. Then GR5 contours to the small
and marshy Devin lake, designated a *zone protegée* for its rare plant life.

From the lake, GR5 switchbacks interminably uphill to the ridge.
Just below the Roche du Corbeau at 1,130 meters (3,279 feet) is the
fenced-off entrance to a tunnel built by the Germans in World War
I. It once stretched 1,100 meters (3,630 feet) from Lapoutroie to the
fortification works atop the Tête des Faux, the summit toward which
we were aiming.

The summit is reached along a trail that passes stone-and-mortar
bunkers and clumps of rusted barbed wire—grim relics of past battles
that seem woefully at odds with the gloriously peaceful view from the
summit. It is said that in clear weather the Alps are visible from here;
we were not blessed with such clarity, but a Frenchwoman who had
joined us for the final push to the top said it was never that clear up
here anyway.

Less than an hour of gentle downhill walking along forest roads
brings the walker to the vicinity of Lac Blanc. A refuge on GR5 offers
lodging and food, and there are hotels with views of the lake some fifteen minutes further along, where the trail debouches onto highway.

Day 9: Lac Blanc
to Lac du Schiessrothried (ca. 20 km, 5 hr)

The Route of the Crests of the Vosges—*la Route des Crêtes*—was
built during World War I on order of France's military high command

to keep open the north-south communications and supply links along the Vosges front. Constructed just below the crest on the western side of the mountains where summer pastures slope gently downhill, the Route was built along what had been since 1871 the French-German border, the very thing under dispute from 1914 to 1918. The walker will see numerous bornes along the Vosges crest, marking that old border with F for France on one side and D for Deutschland on the other. At Roche du Tanet along today's trail, the walker will also see vestiges of the fighting that rearranged the border.

The Route des Crêtes today is a tourist highway, awarded a three-star Michelin rating, and GR5 runs parallel to it on the very edge of the crest. It is a top-of-the-world walk, but there are occasional abrupt meetings with the highway and with the tourists who frequent it, particularly at today's two high spots: col de la Schlucht and Le Grand Hohneck. GR5 here can also be a hiker highway, and on a summer weekend, the brightly colored packs are occasionally bumper to bumper.

The average elevation of the GR5 Route des Crêtes is around 1,250 meters (about 4,125 feet). It is a vantage from which you can see forever. To the west, high meadows, the famous *hautes chaumes* of the Vosges, slope gently downward to a valley beyond which more hills are ranged. To the east, the granite cliffs fall off sharply, with glacial steepness, to the Alsatian plain. Before you and, as you advance, behind you, is the undulating Route des Crêtes itself.

Shrunken, almost bonsai-like trees along the crest are testimony to the fierce wind and chill of these high corniches in winter. Even in mid-July, we saw patches of snow under the cliffs, and the Alpine flowers in the meadows and the patches of mules-ears were further evidence of recent snowmelt.

From the *calvaire* (cross) at the intersection of highways above Lac Blanc, follow toward the lake along D48 to find the right turn across the meadow. GR5 climbs gradually through woods, contouring above Lac Blanc, to reach the crest. Here it stays throughout the day, dipping to forested cols, but always rising back to the ridgeline before the final descent to Lac du Schiessrothried.

From Gazon du Faing (*gazon*, meadow or grass, is a very Haute-Vosgienne word), at 1,302 meters (4,297 feet), the view encompasses the Lac des Truites and the valleys of the Fecht and the Orbey to the east and the headwaters of the Meurthe to the west, while southward are Le Grand Hohneck and, well in the distance, the Grand Ballon, highest peak of the Vosges. GR5 continues along a corniche path through green meadows with views down to the shining Lac Vert, emerald-green, as advertised. At Roche du Tanet are the ruins of war works. Ahead along the trail, the walker can see the jagged, inimical cliffsides of the eastern flank of the Vosges before the trail drops down to col de la Schlucht.

At 1,139 meters (3,759 feet), col de la Schlucht is the highest highway intersection of the southern Vosges. It is also the most crowded, with

predictably overpriced restaurants, hotels, and souvenir shops. Step-
ping across it, you leave the department of Haut-Rhin and enter that
of Vosges. The trail climbs another spectacular corniche to achieve the
summit of Le Grand Hohneck at 1,362 meters (4,495 feet). Cars can
only get *to* the Grand Hohneck, not over it, but plenty of them make
the ascent. The view from here is staggering in all directions; the *table
d'orientation* on the summit even points your eye toward the Bernese
Alps, but they were lost in the afternoon haze.

A bewildering array of trails leads off Le Grand Hohneck. GR5
descends to the saddle between Le Grand and Le Petit Hohneck, then
contours around Le Petit, past a beautifully situated hillside ferme-
auberge, to drop quickly to the Lac du Schiessrothried, prettily nestled
under the steep escarpment of Le Hohneck.

The gardien of the refuge there joined us for a beer on the terrace
and told us to scan the escarpment for chamois brought here from the
Alps in hopes they would breed. We saw none.

Our accommodation in the refuge was a dortoir which we shared
with perhaps ten German boys, aged about sixteen to eighteen, all drinking sweet Vermouth. But they were kind enough to turn off their radio
when we asked; it seemed an odd place to find a ghetto-blaster.

Day 10 Lac du Schiessrothried to Le Markstein (ca. 23 km, 5-¾ hr)

The German boys were awakened early by their counsellor, who
had a moment of shock when he noticed two grown women in the
room. Perhaps he was embarrassed. In any event, as we were about
to trudge off with only a glass of water for breakfast, he offered us
coffee, bread, jam, butter, and a table to sit at. We accepted.

A good thing, too. Today's stage takes the walker downhill some
394 meters (1,300 feet) to the valley of the Fecht, then abruptly uphill
nearly twice that elevation to the Route des Crêtes before levelling out
to Markstein. The walk requires sustenance, and fortunately, there are
fermes-auberges aplenty as the day proceeds.

From Lac du Schiessrothried, GR5 drops down to the pond called
Lac du Fischboedle, a most picturesque spot. The Wormsa stream leads
down from here to the Fecht Valley, and GR5 follows it, a wooded,
cool walk. But on this summer Sunday morning, we felt as if we were
going the wrong way on a one-way street. A nonstop parade of ascending hikers passed us, many heading for the lakes, the more serious
among them—the knickers-and-alpenstock crowd—certainly heading
for Le Hohneck. This portion of our walk produced, hands down, the
greatest number of "bonjours" per day to date.

Arriving in the valley of the Fecht, GR5 heads for the town of Mitt-
lach, founded in the thirteenth century by woodcutters from the Tyrol.
Crossing the town toward the forest the woodcutters came for, we ran
into René, looking quite dapper in long pants and a real shirt. He was,

he told us, heading for a day of sightseeing in Colmar to avoid the hordes of Sunday hikers. We said our farewells and began the long, relentless climb to the col of Herrenberg—an elevation gain of some 600 meters (2,000 feet) in two hours. At the col, the walker is once again on the Route des Crêtes. The trail opens out into a wide meadow. On this Sunday afternoon, the ferme-auberge that sits in the meadow was jammed with lunchers both inside and out. We had only a snack—fresh Munster cheese, thick bread, wine, and for dessert, *fromage blanc* (soft white cheese drowned in kirsch). We lingered for quite a while, what with coffee, and conversation with fellow lunchers, and the view going way down and far out, and the hang-glider above, and the sailboat on the lake below, and the waves of gauze-soft mountains in the distance.

GR5 continues to follow the crest, darting over the highway Route des Crêtes from time to time, dipping to the col of Hahnenbrunnen before arriving at Markstein, a winter-sports center and summer tourist mecca with numerous hotels, refuges, and fermes-auberges.

Day 11: Le Markstein to Thann (ca. 29 km, 7-¼ hr)

Ballon is French for balloon, although in the Vosges, of course, a *ballon* is a rounded mountaintop. Nevertheless, we called le Grand Ballon, highest point in the Vosges, the Big Balloon, and GR5 achieves it today.

From Markstein along the Route des Crêtes, GR5 sticks close to the highway but routinely cuts its looping meanders. Then it contours around the peak of Storkenkopf and dips to the col du Haag before climbing head-on to the height of the Big Balloon—le Grand Ballon, also known as Ballon de Guebwiller. From the lofty summit at 1,424 meters (4,700 feet), the view extends over most of northeastern France, with mountains of Germany and Switzerland thrown in to the south and east. On a clear day, it is said, the range of the Alps, including Mont Blanc, is visible.

Visitors come in droves to see the view, and to visit the monument of the Diables Bleus, the Blue Devils, an elite corps of mountaineers and skiers whose exploits in the Vosges in World War I resulted in dreadful casualties—for both the Germans and the Diables Bleus corps. Just beyond and below the summit is the restaurant where most visitors have parked their cars, and yet further along is a ferme-auberge where we were unable to choose between fresh Munster and a freshly baked blueberry tart—so we had both.

GR5 gradually descends the crest, crisscrossing the highway and heading into forest to the col du Firstacker, where a military cemetery again evidences World War I. Still in woods, the route dips to col Amic. From here, a ten-minute detour will get you to a ferme-auberge for lunch. Or, continue past the *château-fort* of Freundstein, which served as an artillery observation post in the first World War; just below a loop in the Route des Crêtes highway is another ferme-auberge, also about ten minutes off the trail.

Of course, you might choose a *pique-nique sur l'herbe*. You will note, should you cross the highway anytime between 12:30 and 2:30 P.M., when traffic has virtually ceased because all of France is at lunch, that much of France is at lunch along the highway. When it is time for a meal, cars simply pull off to the side of the road. Families pile out of the cars. A card table and chairs are unfolded and set up directly on the roadside behind the car, and linen and flatware are produced. A meal of several courses lasting several hours then follows. All you do is call out "Bon Appetit" to these lunchers; you will be thanked, and, after a brief conversation during which your story will be much wondered at, you will be wished "Bonne Promenade" or "Bonne Route" or "Bon Courage." Then you will continue walking to Nice while they continue eating.

At the col du Silberloch (900 meters; 2,970 feet), a marked trail detours uphill for the half-hour's walk to the summit of Hartmannswillerkopf. The French call this place Vieil Armand; it is the site of one of the most celebrated battles of World War I. As an important strategic ridge on the eastern escarpment of the Vosges, Vieil Armand saw battle after battle, especially during 1915, when the summit changed hands time and again. A total of 30,000 French and German soldiers died here; in the French national cemetery at Vieil Armand are the remains of from 10,000 to 12,000 unknown soldiers—no one knows for sure how many.

From the col, it is a short walk west and uphill to Le Molkenrain. Here GR5 separates from the highway Route des Crêtes, which serpentines down to Cernay to meet the Route du Vin. Well to the west of the highway, GR5 follows the crest downhill in a southwesterly direction, ever lower on the rounded heights, to Thann. This is a particularly lovely town; hugged by mountains, it sits beside the River Thur amidst the last vineyards of the Route du Vin.

A saying goes, "The spire of Strasbourg is the highest, that of Fribourg-en-Brisgau the stoutest, that of Thann the most beautiful." A lacey spire of great delicacy, atop a roof inlaid with colored tiles, the *clocher* adorns the Gothic church of Saint-Thiébaut, considered by many the most beautiful example of Gothic architecture in all of Alsace.

The town is also well known for its wine, and it is a good place to stock up on trail food as well. The tourist office stocks maps, hotel lists, and even local topo-guides.

Day 12: Thann to Lac des Perches (ca. 21 km, 5-¼ hr)

A day of some spectacular climbing, so spectacular the GR5 walker may forget to watch the trail, which, at certain junctures, takes turns you might not expect.

From Thann, GR5 turns westward and climbs steadily to col du Staufen at 474 meters (1,564 feet), to the Plan Diebold Scherer at 625 meters (2,062 feet), to the col du Hundsrucken at 748 meters (2,468 feet). Hundsrucken marks the passage between the valley of the Thur and that of the Doller; there is a ferme-auberge visible here, and another is advertised at a walk of some twenty minutes away. Take care at this col. Many trails crisscross it, and the natural inclination is to head downhill. Be sure the direction you follow leads along the crest in a *northwest* direction; it doesn't seem much of a way to get from Holland to Nice, but it is the way GR5 takes.

Now you climb. GR5 moves uphill toward the height of Bourbach and on to the col du Rossberg at 1,100 meters (3,630 feet). A refuge at the col, and another ferme-auberge some 400 meters distant, may offer refreshment.

From col du Rossberg, GR5 bumps along the high spine of the Vosges through meadows and woods, past the high rocks of Vogelsteine (ferme-auberge off the trail here), on to the ferme-auberge of Belacker right on the trail, over the heights of Johanneskopf and Rimbachkopf, to the col du Lac des Perches. The lake is actually 300 feet down the slope, accessed by a fisherman's trail, and despite its name (Lake of Perch), most people, we were told, fish there for trout.

About 2 kilometers from this spot, along a blue-marked trail, is the Rouge Gazon—the Red Meadow—so called because of the soldiers' blood spilled there. But a detour along this trail leads to a ferme-auberge where the walker can find both lodging and meals. Ten minutes further downhill, there is another refuge, this one run by the Touring Club Français.

Day 13: Lac des Perches to Giromagny (ca. 24 km, 6 hr)

The end of the Vosges: a day of stiff but rewarding climbing before dipping down to Europe's continental divide.

The day begins by continuing westward, finishing off the loop taken to achieve the Grand Ballon and the valley of the Thur. It is rugged, steep walking up and down toward Ballon d'Alsace. To the south is the valley of the Doller with Lac d'Alfeld glistening at the head of the valley. To the north is the valley of Charbonniers (coal miners, or colliers). The valley's inhabitants are said to descend from Swedish and German coal miners hired by the Dukes of Lorraine in the eighteenth century. The megawalker has a particular link to the valley of Charbonniers: its streams feed the headwaters of the Moselle, a river with which the megawalker is well acquainted.

Across pastures framed by the mountains, GR5 climbs to the col des Charbonniers, continuing southwesterly along a now rocky trail. There is a low dip just before the final steep climb to the wide top of Ballon d'Alsace. This is the southernmost summit of the Vosges and, at 1,247 meters (4,115 feet), is one of the highest in the range. On a clear day, the walker can see north to Donon, where he entered the Vosges almost two weeks before. To the south is the Trouée de Belfort (the Belfort Gap), where the terrain dips and narrows between Vosges and Jura.

From the statue of the Virgin atop the Ballon, it is downhill through wooded slopes to Giromagny. In Giromagny, you have entered the department of the Territoire de Belfort, distinctive for being the only portion of Alsace which was not handed over to Germany in 1871 after the Franco-Prussian War. It is a quiet town. Despite the presence of some small industries, the noisiest sound while we were there was the gurgle of the stream that flows through the middle of the village.

14
The Spectacular Surprise of the Jura

There are many Juras. Two are polities: the French department of Jura and the fiercely independent Swiss canton of Jura. There is the great massif of the Jura plateau. There are the Jura Mountains, an extension of the Alps ranging in a southwest-to-northeast crescent between Rhone and Rhine. There is the geologic Jurassic, taking its name from these mountains and referring to the second stage of the Mesozoic era.

When the French speak of the Jura, they are referring to an area that today comprises all or part of the departments of Jura, Doubs, l'Ain, Haute-Saône, and the tiny Territoire de Belfort. (GR5 misses l'Ain and Haute-Saône.) It is the historic province of Franche-Comté, wedged between the gap at Belfort, just south of the Vosges, and the dip of Lake Geneva—Lac Léman—at the foot of the Alps.

This is the Jura the GR5 traverses, taking the walker south onto the plateau and then up and down along the grain of the Jura mountains, from ridge to ridge at an altitude never exceeding 1,500 meters—usually, at half that—but in a distinctly mountainous world.

The Jura was, for us, the great surprise of our journey. We had thought of it somehow as a vast, flat, dull plateau ringed around by industry. Nothing we heard from the French prior to our arrival there helped change this impression; the Jura is little enough known to Frenchmen of other regions, save for intrepid fishermen and, in winter, cross-country skiers.

Disappointment may be the megawalker's first reaction to this section of the journey, as he steps out of the distinctive region of Alsace into *la Trouée*—the breach known as the Belfort Gap—through which countless invaders have gotten at the soft underbelly of France. After the drama of the Vosges, after the considerable charm of Alsatian life, Belfort and the industrial plain of Montbéliard to which it leads can seem a letdown in more ways than just altitude. In fact, however, la Trouée is the gateway to a walker's paradise—a land of exquisite forests, meadows, waters in every possible configuration, hidden valleys and carved fortress ridges in whose villages and towns a distinctive montagnard life manages, vividly, to endure.

The mountains which give the Jura region its name—and its character—extend some 300 kilometers (ca. 190 miles) from the gorge of the Rhone River near Geneva to the Rhine near Basel. The mountains emerged first in the eponymous Jurassic period, when the oceans had advanced over large portions of the continents and dinosaurs roamed what was left high and dry. Later, in the Tertiary era, a counterpressure from the rising of the Alps caused the earth here to fold up. These folds, separated by hollows, ranged themselves west to east, but formed a crescent, abutting the Massif Central to the southwest and the Vosges to the northeast.

Folds. Not the needle peaks of the Alps nor the rounded ballons of the Vosges, but plateaus rising higher as they move east, turning into slopes, then into abrupt slopes—rocky escarpments forming the steep sides of gorges or of sudden, sharp valleys. That, at least, is what the GR5 walker sees—a varied and vigorous terrain. From the Swiss side, where the folds cease, the mountains seem an unbroken wall.

These mountains have a vocabulary all their own, the French terms making more subtle distinctions than the translated English equivalents seem to be able to manage. Here the *monts* separate parallel *vals*—vales or dales (as opposed to *vallée*—valley, or *vallon*—small valley). A *cluse* is a transverse valley, a notch between two *vals*. A *côte* is the slope of a hill; to get a bit more technical, it's the kind of a slope of a hill where one side is concave and a plateau inclines away from it. A *combe* (the dictionary translates this as "dell") hollows out the summit of a mountain; its steep edges are *crêts* (as opposed to *crête*, mountain ridge). *Crêt* is a distinctly jurassic word; the highest point in the Jura is the Crêt de la Neige, a rocky escarpment bordering a *combe*. At 1,718 meters, Crêt de la Neige climbs higher than anything in the Vosges, although GR5 misses it, turning east and south away from the crescent of hills to dip to Lac Léman.

We were told of these distinctions as we stood atop Mont d'Or, at 1,460 meters, and looked outward perhaps 80 kilometers (about 55 miles) for our first view of the Alps, forming a shining line of peaks that jutted up from a mass of morning clouds. Our instructor in this French lesson was Robert Ravaioli, one of only two other GR5 end-to-enders we met throughout our journey. (We met the other in the Jura, too.) For ten years, Robert had dreamed of hiking the GR5; he was hell-bent on the achievement and could hardly wait for the day when he would stroll in triumph into Nice, his home town. He first heard about "les deux Américaines" in Belgium, and he had been chasing us ever since. Unaccompanied on his walk, except by an occasional day hiker, Robert asked about us at hotels and cafés, computing and recomputing how fast he would need to walk to catch us (he didn't know about our detours and layover days). We had become, perhaps, a secondary goal of his walk, and our meeting in a mountain hut in the high Jura produced an instant and profound rapport among us chosen few who could speak with first-hand knowledge about such places as Renesse, Diest, Nessonvaux, and Berdorf. We walked together for two days, but Robert was eager to press on, to make time. Even on that sparkling morning atop Mont d'Or, he was impatient to lead us forward, away from the awesome sight of the Alps, but onward toward them among the forests, meadows, combes, and crêts of the Jura.

Low Jura plateaus face the Vosges across the Trouée de Belfort. The plateaus become higher to the east, but even the north-south walking along GR5 is not flat, although a ridge once attained may be a wide plain or a small flat-bottomed bowl. Here in the lower elevations are crops—potatoes, rye, barley, oats—but no berries and no fruit trees. Then fields give way to pastures and the Montbéliard cows, famous for their supreme cheeses.

The meadows of the Jura have distinctive qualities. There are the *prés*—small meadows of clayey soil deposited long ago by the glaciers; and there are the *chaux*—to which an ancient limestone base gives an almost barren appearance. From low to high, these meadows change in character, becoming increasingly forested as you climb.

The forests of the Jura once were one of the great natural wonders of France, and recent attempts at serious forest management would make them so again. In Roman times, as attested by Pliny, the entire region was covered with thick woods. Into this hostile environment came monks, and beginning in the sixth century, their axes made significant dents in the Jura forest. Around a farm or grange established in these clearings, small hamlets grew, although they remained few and very far between.

But by the seventeenth and eighteenth centuries, the forests no longer seemed hostile. As royal property, the trees were logged to build royal ships or to adorn churches and cathedrals. Agriculture grew apace in the denuded clearings. Forges were established—the remains of which GR5 passes—and used up great amounts of small brush. By the nineteenth century, the Jura forests were virtually destroyed.

They are coming back. Through a managed system of cutting and through considerable reforesting (often of farmland that is no longer profitable), the Jura region has again become almost 50 percent wooded. Vast tracts of the Jura today are again *forêt domaniale*, managed for limited cutting and protected by the National Office of Forests.

Also protected by the state is an animal, the chamois. Indigenous to the mountains of Europe, the antelope-like chamois have been all but wiped out by hunters; certainly, they have been forced upwards to the higher elevations—including, it is claimed, the high summits of the Jura massif. We saw none, neither in the Jura nor throughout our journey across Europe, but we spotted several roe deer in the Jura forests, and lynx are said to roam there as well. Owls, woodpeckers, and above all, le grand tétras—the grouse—also populate these woods.

The trees are mostly fir, pine, beech, and oak. The woods are carpeted by lichen, moss, and the mushrooms that figure so importantly in the cuisine of the region. The walker would do well to become familiar with the French names for some of the forest life. Among the trees, the *sapin* (fir), with its wide, almost flat top, drops soft needles on the ground, but its cones disintegrate, so you won't stumble on them underfoot. At elevations above 800 or 900 meters, and usually on the north faces of slopes, is the *épicèa* (spruce), with its pointed top, rounded needles, and hairy look. The *hêtre* (beech), stands particularly tall on its cylindrical trunk, dressed in beautiful oval leaves. It is long-lived, but does not grow at elevations much higher than the 1,500 meters or so the Jura mountains attain. Look for it on humid slopes.

Only the most ambitious student of French will attempt to learn any words for mushroom beyond the generic *champignon*; the variety is too great. In a restaurant in Vandoncourt, Susanna ordered a dish that comprised fourteen different kinds of mushroom, freshly picked that day.

As famed as the hills and forests of the Jura are the waterways that drain the region, the *eaux vives*, comprising rivers, lakes, ponds, and— concealed beneath the ridges and furrows of fossiliferous limestone— underground springs and caverns. With valleys oriented southwest to northeast, rivers heading west must meander between mountains until a *cluse* provides a passage from *val* to *val*. None meanders as crazily as the Doubs. (Pronounce it "dooh.")

From the source of the Doubs in the Jura mountains near Mouthe— GR5 walkers pass the source—to its confluence with the Saône is a distance of some 90 kilometers (55 miles), yet the Doubs in its course wanders for 430 kilometers (nearly 270 miles). It is the meanderingest river you've ever seen, forming an M as it heads first northeast, then swings back on itself at Saint Ursanne to turn west, then north again until, meeting yet another obstacle at Montbéliard, it turns south for the Saône. Along its course to the Saône, the Doubs becomes a large lake (Lac du Saint Point), cuts deep gorges, forms and crosses the Franco-Swiss border, and runs in a spectacular loop known as the Boucle du Doubs, thereby creating a setting of great beauty for the city of Besançon. The walker trying to follow the course of the Doubs on a map begins to wonder if this waterway does not finally refute Heraclitus's dictum that you cannot step twice into the same river. You begin to believe that, with careful planning and a fast car, you could start at the source of the Doubs and beat those very waters to Besançon. As GR5 moves upstream along the river, we had no opportunity to prove this, but somebody ought to.

Two full days of the walk through the Jura trace the gorge of the Doubs. It is a spectacular show of rapids and eddies, calm pools over a smooth riverbed alternating with shallows running noisily over rocks, jagged cliffs giving way to smooth slopes, meadow, woods, brush, moss—a microcosm of the Jura itself.

The Jura walk takes thirteen days and covers some 330 kilometers (just over 200 miles). Another day is added as a Lake Geneva layover at the end of the walk, although more than one day of rest might be desirable. The walk starts in lowland and rises up the plateaus to Saint Hippolyte, where the Doubs and the Dessoubre meet. The trail then climbs, attaining the ridge of mountains, and follows along the gorge of the Doubs to Villers-le-Lac. Here, where the Doubs Valley flattens out to Pontarlier, GR5 stays high, paralleling the Swiss border, along the crêts—and crests—to the high point of Morond/Mont d'Or with its view of the Alps. From here, GR5 heads west/southwest across forest to the valley of the Doubs and to its source, then east/southeast across forest to enter Switzerland and descend to Lac Léman at Nyon.

It is not surprising, given the area's bounty for *randonneurs*, that there are numerous trails here. Among the GR *sentiers* are the GR9 (Jura to Côte d'Azur), the GR59 (Franche-Comté), five variants of the GR59 exploring different *pays* within Franche-Comté, the GR559 (lakes and forests), and the GR-BL (the lake tour, Balcon du Lac Léman). Moreover, the GR5 route itself offers numerous variants; we have recommended taking some and rejecting others. Our aim in the selection process for this itinerary was to provide a sense of the diversity of the Jura's terrain—valley, plateau, summit, forest, and waterways—while ensuring a good look at the backcountry villages and at montagnard life. The walker who needs or wants to visit some of the larger cities of the area will find easy access by bus or hitchhike to Belfort, Montbéliard, and Besançon. But more than adequate provisioning is available in Pontarlier, about an hour's walk off the trail on Day 8.

The Franche-Comté has historically been known for a certain cantankerousness—and for a certain pride in that cantankerousness. The political shenanigans and bloodshed that long laid waste the area also nourished the spirit of resistance embodied in the ancient cry: "Rends-toi, Comtois! Nenni, ma foi!" Loosely translated, this is a call to the people of the Comté to yield, answered by a defiant "Not on your life!"

The harshness of life here may also have created the sort of earnest, vaguely primitive individual who is the stereotyped Comtois. While the western part of the region—where GR5 does *not* go—is called le Vignoble or le Bon Pays, that is not the primary Comté image. Of the Jura climate it is said that there are eight months of snow, two months of harsh wind, and for the rest of the time, unimaginably beautiful weather.

The winters gave rise to the kind of small, painstaking industries that can keep a person busy through cold indoor days and long cold nights—watchmaking and the manufacture of eyeglasses and precision instruments.

Woodworking was another mainstay of the region—all that wood and all that time to carve it. The tradition nearly died with the destruction of the forests and with the loss of much of the population (through wartime evacuation and urban migration), but it is now being revived, in factories and as a cottage industry.

The montagnard houses are distinctive. Built close to the earth, of thick stone, with tiny windows, they nearly disappear under the winter snow. Only their vast, low-sloping roofs remain above ground. The single roof covers all parts of the building—living quarters, stable, and grange—sheltering both humans and beasts. The arrangement ensures warmth and provides easy access to provisions, while the fodder stored in the attic serves as an extra layer of insulation.

Most distinctive of all is the chimney known as the *tué*. Made of wood, wide at the base and tapering slightly to fit under a hatlike wedge, the fame of the tué rests less in its appearance than in the fact that it smokes the famous sausages of the Jura.

Sausage and cheese—the quintessential hiker's lunch—reach what is perhaps their combined peak of perfection in the Jura. Buy great chunks of both wherever and whenever you can. Wrapped in plastic, they should stay tasty for quite a while, and there will be stretches of walking on this itinerary where the shops are few and far between. There is smoked sausage here that is hard to come by in other parts of France— even in Paris, much less abroad. Perhaps the most renowned are the *saucisse de Morteau* (also known as *saucisse à Jesus*) and the *saucisse de Montbéliard*.

Of the extraordinary cheeses of the region, the most famous is surely the Comté. This, the Mont d'Or (or Vacherin), and the famous Bleu have been made here for four centuries (some say for seven), so by now the art of doing it right has been pretty well perfected. We learned also to love Morbier, with its distinctive blue-black line, and we discovered Cancoillotte (or Colle), a base of curdled cream served either hot or cold, either alone or as a fondue-like sauce. It is a kind of smooth, superior, rich-tasting yoghurt with no pretensions to being a health food, although it probably is.

The wines of the Jura, from the vineyards to the west of the GR5 route, were known in the court of Henri IV and today come in red, rosé, white, and yellow versions. Most renowned of them all is the yellow Arbois, but other well-known wines come from Chateau-Chalon, Pupillin, Poligny, Frontenay, and Le Vernois.

Pierre Joseph Proudhon came from the Franche-Comté, as did Louis Pasteur. Victor Hugo was born here, but he was an army brat and never really counted as a Comtois. But Gustave Courbet, born in Ornans, certainly does count, and in his realistic depiction of landscape, the megawalker may recognize the woods and waters and hills he will come to know in this walk through the Jura.

Day 1: Giromagny to Châtenois-les-Forges (ca. 32 km, 8 hr)

Giromagny sits in a flattish bowl surrounded by low, rounded hills that obscure the sense of the high Vosges to the north or the Jura massif to the south. You are in the department known as the Territoire de Belfort—Belfort Territory—a small chunk of France that the Germans did not annex in 1871 and which has retained that distinction in its name. It is the breach in the wall of Vosges and Jura hills, and as GR5 starts off across it, now back to red and white markings, the terrain is tranquil, easygoing, and pastoral. The views the walker enjoys are of the soft curves of dwindling hills and the church steeples of the quiet country villages. It is a landscape dotted with ponds, a number of which GR5 passes as it follows narrow lanes among the fields.

Walk between two ponds to pass through La Chapelle-sous-Chaux (the name gives away something about the terrain; *chaux* means "limestone"), a pleasant, low village. Cross its bridge, then climb gently and dip again between the ponds of Malsaussis and Véronne before entering Bas-Evette, the resort town for the swimming, sailing, and sailboarding of Véronne lake.

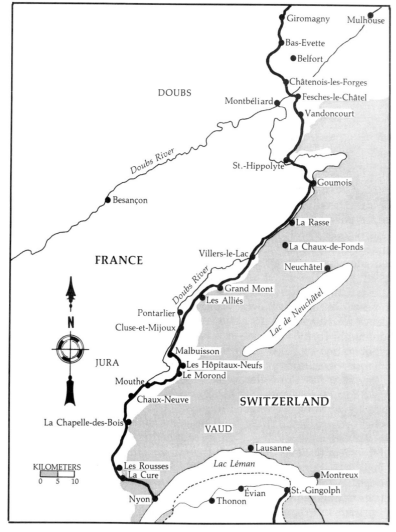

Jura

Jura

Day 1	Giromagny to Châtenois-les-Forges	32 km	8 hr
Day 2	Châtenois-les-Forges to Vandoncourt	16 km	4 hr
Day 3	Vandoncourt to Saint-Hippolyte	26 km	6-½ hr
Day 4	Saint-Hippolyte to Goumois	26 km	6-½ hr
Day 5	Goumois to La Rasse	21 km	5-¼ hr
Day 6	La Rasse to Villers-le-Lac	28 km	7 hr
Day 7	Villers-le-Lac to Grand Mont	28 km	7 hr
Day 8	Grand Mont to Cluse-et-Mijoux	25 km	6-¼ hr
Day 9	Cluse-et-Mijoux to Le Morond	28 km	7 hr
Day 10	Le Morond to Le Lernier/Chaux-Neuve	28 km	7 hr
Day 11	Chaux-Neuve/Le Lernier to La Chapelle-des-Bois	16 km	4 hr
Day 12	La Chapelle-des-Bois to Les Rousses	26 km	6-½ hr
Day 13	Les Rousses to Nyon (Switzerland)	26 km	6-½ hr
		326 km	81-½ hr

The GR5 makes an abrupt left turn just after the railroad crossing—there's a friendly café on the corner, if you require a break—and climbs gently, past the few houses of the village of Salbert and through deciduous woods, suddenly startling after the conifers of the Vosges. The climb ascends the slope of Salbert mountain, a hill that has been fortified since time immemorial, and whose fort was most recently the World War II key to the city of Belfort and the gap it controlled—an essential gateway, in fact, to Alsace and the Rhine. In November, 1944, French commandos slipped up here, walking, crawling, and rope-climbing in silence for five hours, to achieve a surprise attack on the Germans holding the fort. Their success was credited with clearing the way for the liberation of Belfort and the march to the Rhine.

From the summit of Salbert, actually a few steps off the trail, the GR5 walker has a fine view of Belfort, the Vosges, the Jura, and—on a fine day, so they say—the Black Forest and the Alps. It was a fairly fine day when we were there, if muggy, but we could see only as far as Belfort, which the GR5 now takes great pains to avoid. (Belfort, by the way, is an attractive town surrounded by unattractive outskirts which seem to cover the plain—the same plain over which Romans, Celts, barbarians, armies of the Holy Roman Empire, and German troops have marched and from which all were eventually repulsed. The city is dominated by the famous Lion of Belfort, a gigantic sculpture atop Vauban's ramparts, which was executed between 1875 and 1880 by Bartholdi, sculptor of the Statue of Liberty in New York harbor.)

Descending quickly, the route goes through woods and onto plain and fields, but it is mostly road walking here—not unpleasant—through the villages of Chalonvillar, Mandrevillars, and Echenans. Here the trail enters woods again, skirts a hill, and cuts over two highways before arriving at Brévilliers. It ascends a high meadow, offering views of some of the new towns of the increasingly industrial area edging the Pays de Montbéliard. The trail again enters woods and dubiously skirts the center of Châtenois-les-Forges. Much of the lodging available here is actually on the N437 highway. From the town center, some 300 meters off the route, you can also get a bus to Belfort or Montbéliard for a more urban—and urbane—night's stay.

We detoured to both in the course of scouting the countryside for this book—to Belfort to see the Vauban fortifications and to Montbéliard because by this time, one of us was mad to see a movie. The approach to Montbéliard is startling, as you zoom along highway through a world of automobile plants. But the city itself is a surprise. Despite the Detroit-like surroundings, it boasts a beautiful chateau and a delightful old quarter. Susanna caught a recent American feature, "À la poursuite du diamant vert" (*Romancing the Stone*) in a lushly comfortable four-theater film palace. It was dubbed into French, of course, but as she said, it wasn't one of those movies where it was essential to understand every word of dialogue.

Day 2: Châtenois-les-Forges
to Vandoncourt (ca. 16 km, 4 hr)

Here is a short day's walk after yesterday's long haul. It is a day that begins in a dispiriting manner, but take heart: by day's end, you are again in countryside—very lovely countryside, at that.

From the height of the town of Châtenois-les-Forges, the walker gets a good view of the industrial valley. To west and north in particular, you are looking at the Pays de Montbéliard, once a Roman *pagus*, or district, then an independent principality comprising a number of seigniories. More recently, the Montbéliard area became the site of the first automobile manufacturing in France. Today, the factories of Peugeot and others stretch across the landscape almost as far as the eye can see.

GR5 proceeds through the valley towards Nommay, paralleling the A36 autoroute, passing some unappealing ponds, gravel pits, and industrial installations of one sort or another. The area is busy as well as unpretty; lots of people camp beside and swim in the highway-edged lakes. Ginger dubbed this disheartening stint "walking intended just to get you from one place to another"—in this case, from Vosges to Jura.

GR5 proceeds on road, then crosses the A36 (and enters the department of Doubs) to find the tow path of the Haute-Saône Canal, part of the waterway linking the Rhone and Rhine rivers. The route crosses the Allan River to attain the wide Rhone-Rhine Canal, which it follows to Fesches-le-Châtel.

Here, too, the trail would miss the town, such as it is, but the walker can proceed along the D121 road for perhaps another kilometer into Fesches *centre* if provisions are needed.

Truly pretty countryside starts now, and the industrial drear of the Montbéliard area is left behind as GR5 proceeds through a wooded area that is ever so slightly hilly. The route edges the village of Dasle, where provisioning is possible, then crosses a wide, handsome plain into Vandoncourt, known as a garrison town for conscientious objectors. The walker will have arrived in good time to present himself at the *hôtel de ville/mairie*—the obviously official building in the town—for information about the private gîte. If the mairie is closed, a sign on the door offers instructions "aux randonners" about finding the gîte and obtaining the key.

In Vandoncourt, there is an exceptionally fine, not expensive, restaurant, the Auberge de Sarrazin, where the chef and his wife lean toward what might be called "nouvelle cuisine jurassienne." It was here that Susanna had the astonishing mushroom compilation, while Ginger ordered fish soup and smoked trout—all local delicacies.

Day 3: Vandoncourt to Saint-Hippolyte (ca. 26 km, 6-½ hr)

A day that alternates ascents up wooded hillsides with dips down to the village below, as GR5 follows, from a height, the valley of the Gland River, hugs the Swiss border, and finally descends into the valley of the Doubs River at the beautiful town of Saint-Hippolyte.

Leaving Vandoncourt, GR5 enters woods to find Le Pont Sarrazin, the Sarrazin bridge, a natural archway formed in the limestone rock. Legend has it that in the eighth century the villagers of Vandoncourt were inspired to resist the Saracen invader by one Vaddo, from whose name the village's name is derived. In any event, GR5 does not pass under the arch, but climbs into woods, then descends past the crossroads known as Six Chemins—Six Roads—to the village of Abbévillers.

Past the village, GR5 climbs again, then descends to cross and follow a stream, climbs yet again, and marches right along the Swiss border, marked by large stone bornes, to Villars-lès-Blamont.

Here, GR5 proceeds mostly on road, though it climbs at one point to cut a meander, offering fine views from the ruined fort on the rocky and wooded crest, before continuing on road into Chamesol. Be sure to note—and not take—the GR du Pays, which comes in to join GR5 from the top of the crest shortly before Chamesol.

Here GR5 is again in a bowl, sunk among suddenly dramatic ramparts of mountains that ring the shallow but rolling plain you now walk. Villages pop up in the distance across the expanse of green, and cars suddenly appear on the country roads, entering the plain through hidden lateral defiles in the crest.

GR5 crosses the plain, then descends into the striking valley of the Doubs to the town cemetery of Saint-Hippolyte. From here, you must detour about one kilometer, crossing the Doubs, to enter the town, which the GR du Pays also traverses.

Saint-Hippolyte is a town of formidable charm on the confluence of the Doubs and the Dessoubre. Hugged by wooded and rocky cliffs, it is a jumble of stone houses with steeply-pitched roofs. There is fine eating here, especially for fish lovers—the Doubs is renowned for its trout, perch, pike, and carp. Indeed, in the next few days along the Doubs, you may almost get sick of fresh trout, if such a thing is possible.

Day 4: Saint-Hippolyte to Goumois (ca. 26 km, 6-½ hr)

Today, the walker is confronted by a choice of GR5s. The official GR5 will take the high road along the gorge of the Doubs, coming down to it again at the place called Bief d'Etoz. The variant, which departs from GR5 near Fessevillers, enables the walker to walk *in* the gorge itself, and we unabashedly recommend it as the route of choice.

The walk of the Doubs gorge does not really begin until the next stage, Day 5, but the variant must be taken on Day 4, so it is today's decision and affects today's walk.

The walk begins with a climb back up out of Saint-Hippolyte, then a high walk above and along the Doubs to Soulce-Cernay. Up to this point, GR5 and GR du Pays have been the same route, but at Soulce-Cernay, the GR du Pays departs northward to complete its loop. GR5 goes down into the valley, crosses the Doubs, and begins to climb. This is mostly woods walking, but through the trees, you can find splendid views of the valley below and of the limestone cliffs beyond. It is a steady and fairly long climb—from 370 meters at Saint-Hippolyte to 770 meters at Courtefontaine. Courtefontaine has a *fromagerie* (cheese factory), and there is another at Fessevillers, so now is the time to begin buying some of the fine cheeses of the Jura.

From Courtefontaine, GR5 proceeds across the high plain. You begin to see the montagnard homes typical of the area—the sloping roofs that cover both house and barn, the tué chimneys under which fires are kept burning for smoking meat. On this wide, exposed plain, it is easy to imagine the harshness of winter and the comfort these houses must provide.

The trail makes a short, sharp climb to Fessevillers, passing beside the church, where a café and a gîte are available for the weary.

The official GR5 continues along the crest, through woods much of the time, and mostly on country road to Charmauvillers. The views are occasionally splendid, but more often the drama of the deep gorge below is obscured by woods and/or lower slopes.

The variant—the route of choice—drops down steeply into the gorge, departing the official GR5 just after Fessevillers at the place called Sur le Mont de Fessevillers. The variant's point of departure is well and clearly marked, and there is no change in the balisage: continue to follow red and white markers.

They lead you down to the river and the town of Goumois, half in Switzerland and half in France (well, rather more than half in France), with hotels and eateries in both countries. We chose to sleep in Switzerland but dine in France.

Day 5: Goumois to La Rasse (ca. 21 km, 5-¼ hr)

By the time we were ready to start our walk along the gorge of the Doubs, we had begun to suspect that we were in the throes of discovering one of France's best-kept secrets—the Jura. So far from being a letdown after the Vosges, as one Vosgien had described it, or a dull, flat plateau, as a Belgian had told us, the Jura was turning out to be a paradise of sharply scented woods, steep-but-not-high hills, secret valleys hugged by corniche cliffs, long valleys with field and meadow floors. It was, to an unusual extent, a water place, with water in every form: the meandering river, pools, streams, cascades.

This sort of surprise, we agreed, was one of the reasons the walk across Europe remained an adventure, even while it had become a way of life.

The walk along the gorge of the Doubs and the days that followed among the high meadows, woods, and crêts of the Jura, spectacularly confirmed the sense of discovery.

Day 4, our walk from Saint-Hippolyte to Goumois, had been a day of glorious sunshine, and we were looking forward to more of the same for our walk along the river on Day 5. We anticipated a languid lunch on the riverbank and refreshing dips in limpid pools when the heat became unbearable.

Of course, Day 5 began with fog and rain which, by afternoon, had slowed to a thick mist. Despite this, the walk to La Rasse was a beautiful one, and the high limestone cliffs, thickly covered with sapins, were lovely in the mist.

You are deep in a gorge that allows little access except at either end and via a very few transverse roads. The trail is quiet and sparsely populated. Fly-fishermen disperse themselves in the water and cast their lines, and an occasional camper or walker may pass you by as you wind with the river's course, climbing a bit when the Doubs meanders.

At Bief d'Etoz, the official GR5 comes down from Fessevillers. Join it to climb to the Ferme de la Charbonnière, where another variant presents itself. This one goes back to the riverbank and follows along it; it enables the vertiginous walker to avoid the Échelles de la Mort, the Ladders of Death. These metal staircases down a very steep cliff are reached by following the official GR5 through lovely woods. Though the ladders' name is rather overly dramatic, they are indeed steep and narrow, and there are three of them, with sharp switchbacks in between.

The walker who is not happy with such steep, exposed means of descent will do well to follow the variant. It meets GR5 again at the foot of the ladders, where you proceed along the gorge to the Barrage du Refrain, a large dam forming an artificial lake.

GR5 goes around the lake, passing a bridge crossing (and customs control) to the Swiss hamlet of Biaufond. Stay on the French side of the river until another auto bridge is reached at La Rasse. Cross this second bridge, then walk south along the road for about a kilometer to Maison Monsieur, one of the more elegant of the mountain *refuges* on our journey across Europe.

It was on this day that we suffered the only major catastrophe of our journey—Susanna was bitten by a dog. It happened just as we were leaving Goumois, following a road past some houses to head into the woods. A boxer dog emerged from one of the houses, barking loudly to establish his territorial rights. Suddenly, he darted toward us, still barking. A car was coming along the road behind us, and we stopped between dog and car. Susanna spoke soothingly to the dog, who seemed to grow calm; then the car screeched to a halt, and its driver, a young woman, began screaming out the window at the dog and at us. At this, the dog panicked and nipped Susanna's leg, instantly drawing blood. She put her arms up in a reflex of self-protection, and the woman leaped out of the car and began yelling at Susanna.

"You idiot!" she began, "Don't you know you must never show fear before a dog. It's all your fault, you moron, you fool!"

Still hurling insults, and without a word of concern for a thoroughly stunned hiker, the woman hauled the dog into the house, then emerged to retrieve her car.

She continued screaming at Susanna, but Susanna, over her surprise and equally enraged, began yelling back. In the end, her French was unequal to her anger, so with a final sputter, she blurted out: "Go to hell, lady!"—in perfect English. As we walked away, however, the woman had the last word. "Go back to Switzerland!" she called after us. "Go back to Switzerland where you belong!"

In situations like this, as every hiker knows, the sensible thing to do is to seek immediate medical attention, just to be on the safe side. Look for officialdom. At Goumois, we reasoned, there were customs officers and a small tourist office (quasi-official). Neither was necessary, as it turned out. We hitched—very easy and very safe in Switzerland—to the sleek modern hospital at Chaux-de-Fonds. Here, Susanna received a medical examination, a tetanus booster shot, and a prescription for an antibiotic—just in case.

The consultation and tetanus injection were extremely cheap, and the hospital accepted credit cards. The prescription was problematic. Being from a Swiss hospital, it could not be filled by a French pharmacist, and we carried no Swiss francs. Fortunately, Susanna was able to make it to a bank just before closing while Ginger begged the pharmacy to stay open "pour quelques moments." All ended well, but the incident reconfirmed the importance of having Swiss currency along the Swiss border and of carrying credit cards.

Day 6: La Rasse to Villers-le-Lac
(ca. 28 km, 7 hr)

Variants upon variants today, choice upon choice. This stage of the route offers several opportunities to climb up from the gorge and, once on the high plateau, several other opportunities for reconnecting with the riverbank GR5. Some of these variants were built for those occasions when dam operations may make the waters of the Doubs too high for comfort; others simply offer the up-or-down choice; some are reroutings. But the walker may always remain along the bank of the Doubs, and since it is difficult, anywhere in the world, to find a river walk like this one, not bounded by roads or noisy with motorboats or crowded with people, staying low is a good choice.

For much of this day, the widening river runs more slowly than it did downstream. The walker moves more slowly, too. The trail is somewhat crumbly with limestone gravel underfoot, and the river meanders in broad, lazy loops. But there is no compulsion to hurry, especially since the last 7 kilometers of this stage may be achieved by boat.

For us, this day was the most beautiful we had seen since arriving in Europe—sunny, hot, clear, and dry. One fisherman we met opined that it was even *trop beau*—too beautiful—to go fishing. He was possibly missing a bet, because we saw schools of large, shiny trout cruising along with relaxed impunity in the shallow pools of the Doubs.

You begin by retracing your route to the bridge of La Rasse to cross back into France. The trail then continues upstream along the left bank of the river. Look here for lavender campanula, which has accompanied the walker since Belgium and will remain with him to the bottom of Europe.

The trail soon presents you with a choice: climb the Sentier Bonaparte—Bonaparte Trail—and follow the gorge from the high plateau, or stay along the river. The Sentier Bonaparte is a steep climb of short switchbacks, from some 600 meters on the riverbank to nearly 1,000 meters at Grand'Combe-des-Bois, a small village, complete with café-restaurant, at the top of the plateau.

It is a beautiful ascent through woods and a good work-out for those who like uphill walking. At the top of the plateau, along a road, this variant offers exciting views of the gorge below. But be sure to take the trail returning to the riverbank at the farm called Les Planots. This descends somewhat steeply at first, but then contours to meet the riverbank GR5 at Chez Némorin.

Those who do not climb the Sentier Bonaparte will continue among thickening vegetation, through which you see the high cliffs of the gorge, carpeted with trees, and the tortured curvings of the Doubs. The *usine* of Châtelot is a hydroelectric plant and a startling amalgam of wires; a funicular steeply climbs the Swiss bank of the river, opposite. The trail passes the former iron works of the Forges du Pissoux and begins to ascend. The cliffs on either side of the gorge become castellated walls.

The place called Chez Némorin is a wooden house in a clearing offering a stupendous view across the gorge. Seeing no one around, we walked to the edge of the clearing to look over the cliff—the spot is so situated on a bend of the river that the view is wide open and vast. Three people emerged from the house carrying platters of food to a picnic table in the middle of the clearing. Greetings were exchanged, we explained ourselves, and the host offered us a beer.

Three hours later—after beer, steak grilled outdoors over a brick oven, red wine, fresh salad, cheese, coffee, and kirsch—we reluctantly departed. Our lunch companions, all Swiss, consisted of Ben Schüpbach, who rents the house of Némorin for weekends and vacations, and a young couple who were his guests. Schüpbach showed us the house, which has changed little since Némorin died in 1933, and which Schüpbach hopes to maintain unchanged, even going so far as to sleep on a pallet of straw on the floor.

This is Némorin's story, as Ben told it to us:

The youngest of eight children from nearby Pissoux, Némorin, whose name means "man of the forest," became a recluse who chose this spot for his solitary life. He had once served in the army, and later he married, but, unable to forget his mountain aerie and his solitude, he left his wife and moved back. Long before it was as fashionably prevalent as it later became, Némorin made a point of living off the land. He drank only water and ate mostly fish. He kept himself to himself, except for occasional forays into Pissoux to pick up his army pension and, it is said, go on brief benders. The locals respected Némorin's ways, and at the end of his life, when he was quite ill, they persuaded the authorities to release him from the hospital so that he could die in his chosen place in his chosen way.

From Chez Némorin, it is a short walk to the dam of Châtelot, a tourist attraction equipped with a parking lot and metal staircase leading down to the water. The dam holds back the Lac du Moron, which GR5 now edges until it reaches the Saut de Doubs—the Doubs waterfall. The waterfall, a *site national* (national site), draws numbers of visitors; it is a worthwhile sight, 27 meters high. Just beyond the overlook are a number of restaurants, hotels, and souvenir stands. Here the walker can board one of several riverboats heading upstream to Villers-le-Lac. The ride is pleasant and a nice change of pace.

The walk, if you choose to make it, is entirely on road.

Day 7: Villers-le-Lac to Grand Mont
(ca. 28 km, 7 hr)

This stage of walking takes you up and away from the Doubs to the côte of the high plateau and the crête of the Jura summits. It is a day that alternates woods and pasture, up and down, ending with a variant route that brings the walker to one of the nicest gîtes d'étape of the journey, owned and managed by a true Jura mountain man.

In fact, this day's stage brings the walker past a number of rustic gîtes, which, if the gardien is there, can be pleasant stops for refreshment and conversation.

The walk starts with a good climb from Villers to the Fermes du Prélot, bringing the walker onto the plateau and over it—the crest of it is called Creusys and offers fine views—to the road at Sur la Roche, where there is a gîte.

The trail climbs again, and the walker begins to notice a distinct change in the landscape. The woods here are conifers—and not planted conifers, either. In the fields that alternate with the woods, the walker notes scattered farmhouses—not villages where farmers go out to their fields, but self-contained and widely dispersed farms with house and barn under one roof. There are small ski facilities here as well, and a number of signs for *ski à fond*—cross-country skiing. In fact, the Jura is the cross-country capital of France—some say, of Europe. Its famed Grande Traversée du Jura is a 150-kilometer, avalanche-free course over the very landscape GR5 now tracks.

The trail achieves the top of the crest at a place called Haut des Roussottes. Here, at 1,188 meters (3,920 feet), GR5 veers to the right, marching along the Franco-Swiss border, which follows the line of the crest. It isn't for another 7 kilometers, however, at the road at le Gros Gardot, that a customs control point really marks the border—that and the attendant restaurant/café that seems de rigueur at frontier crossings. At le Gros Gardot, you are on the high Swiss plain of the Jura, between and above two valleys. The site is exceptional, anywhere you look.

Onto road now, then again through woods and pasture to the tiny, charming hamlet of Les Cernoniers with its tiny, charming chapel. The GR5 proceeds along a road among pastures to the gîte-ferme-hôtel of Vieux Châteleu. We stopped here for a beer and met Owen Jones, a young Welshman who, like us, was walking the entire GR5. There was much excitement at our meeting—an instant camaraderie of megawalkers. Owen said he had heard about us from a Frenchman he had walked with for a while, a fellow named Robert Ravaioli, who was also walking the GR5. "He's chasing you," Owen told us; "he's asking everyone about you because he wants to catch up with you."

The trail climbs again, dips into a valley, crosses a ravine (on a bridge), then climbs the summit called Des Ages to come down to the separated clusters of houses known as Meix Bosson and Le Rozet. From here the walker can look out onto the town of Les Gras and the walk ahead.

Les Gras is a delightful town, with a rushing fountain in its central square. From the square, find the GR5 variant that leads to Théverot via le Grand Mont; it is a forest climb of less than an hour to the top of Grand Mont—1,034 meters (3,412 feet)—and to the wonderful gîte there.

The gîte is run by Pierre Jouille and his wife, who together spent several years reconstructing the building. It's a handsome place, the interior finished in smooth blond wood, the roof with a tué chimney, which the Jouilles put to its appropriate use smoking meats. Pierre Jouille is the coauthor of a book on Jura hikes, *Les Monts du Jura, 81 Randonnées Pedestres* (published in 1980 by Editions S.A.E.P.), and he knows the Jura by foot and on skis. The Jouilles know other mountains as well, having hiked in Alaska, the Canadian Rockies, and the American West. Dusk, nightfall, and morning in this spot will convince even the most hard-nosed purists that the Jura are real mountains.

Day 8: Grand Mont to Cluse-et-Mijoux (ca. 25 km, 6-¼ hr; variant 36 km, 9 hr)

The start of this day's walk is downhill, completing the loop from Grand Mont. At Théverot, you are again in a dip between côtes, where you meet the official GR5, abandoned yesterday at Les Gras.

A teeth-gnashing choice now confronts the walker: whether to go on the GR5 or take the variant past Montbenoît, where, among tué-topped farmhouses, the lovely Montbenoît abbey is located. The only comfort about this difficult decision is that you can't go wrong either way.

The variant climbs up and over the opposite côte, les Roches du Cerf—the rocks of the stag—back into the Doubs Valley and over the river to see the Montbenoît abbey. For historical interest, perfection of regional architectural style, and beauty of setting, the abbey has few peers in the Jura. It sits on a rock cliff overlooking the Doubs, running swiftly below. The abbey was founded in 1150 by the then Sire de Joux (Lord of Joux), the power in this area, who thought he could use a little divine cooperation to mitigate his sins, particularly the sins of extortion and outright thievery, which the house of Joux committed fairly routinely against wealthy merchants. The sire offered the site to the archbishop of Besançon, who called in Augustine monks from Valais. They in turn solicited the aid of Swiss compatriots, the Saugets. The valley came to be called the val du Saugeais, and the inhabitants of it are called Saugets (Saugettes, fem.) to this day. Their patois is still reputedly spoken in the twelve villages around the abbey, and the Saugets are said to maintain a fierce individuality which they manifest, particularly at festival times, in song, costume, architecture, and sarcastic joking. Our favorite Sauget dictum is the one which advises that "it is better to tell a lie than to sit there with your mouth hanging open."

The Montbenoît variant crisscrosses the Doubs and winds along its valley before reascending the côte and coming back down to meet official GR5 at the hamlet of Les Alliés. In all, the variant is an 18-kilometer walk, almost five hours of walking—plus time to visit the abbey.

Official GR5 takes less than half that time to reach Les Alliés. Unhappily for the walker who has trouble making up his mind, this shorter walk is also a splendid one; it parallels the Roches du Cerf, so that the walker has views of both côtes at all times.

It is a difficult choice, perhaps best decided by the walker's inclination at the moment. If time and distance are issues, the walker of the Montbenoît variant might consider that it is an easy hitch from the abbey to Pontarlier, returning the next day to complete the stage to la Cluse-et-Mijoux. Indeed, as some map study shows, there are all sorts of possibilities for walking or hitching to Pontarlier at various points along this stage for variant walkers and for those who stick to GR5.

Pontarlier represents a detour from the route. It is a major center for excursions and offers many of the facilities of a large town, including post office, hotels, restaurants, and many kinds of shops. It is a pleasant, busy place. Since ancient times, Pontarlier has served as a pit stop along the passageway from east to west (and vice versa). It's the gateway to the Jura. Cars with license plates from a great variety of European countries whizz through, a fair indication that the ancient tradition still persists.

So the walker can easily make the stage from Grand Mont to la Cluse-et-Mijoux a two-day stage. We did, detouring into Pontarlier to mail off packages, shop, and enjoy what Susanna persisted in calling the "fleshpots," meaning any café in a town big enough to boast a traffic light.

But be sure to return the next day to Les Alliés, a charming hamlet with a fromagerie. From here, an exquisite walk leads down the pastured gully between côtes to the Passage d'Entreportes, where another choice presents itself. The left-turn variant up the Rochers du Larmont is a decidedly steep climb and 2 kilometers longer than the GR5, but from the summit, the famous Grand Taureau (Great Bull), it offers splendid views of the notch in the ridge called the Passage d'Entreportes, and of Pontarlier and the Jura plateaus to the west. The Grand Taureau, not surprisingly, is a major winter sports area.

GR5, by contrast to the variant, hugs the flank of the hill and offers views of the Rochers du Larmont.

Both trails meet at Grange des Jantets. From here, GR5 proceeds across pastures, then makes a good, stiff climb up to the Fort du Larmont Inférieur. Here is another choice of routes, but the walker should stick to the official GR5, both in order to see the Fort of Joux and because it's the way to the night's lodging.

The belvedere of the Larmont fort offers a striking view of the cluse, a transverse gash in the Larmont mountain, just big enough for the autoroute and the railroad—a true passageway between France and Switzerland. Head down the steps to the highway, N67, cross it, then follow the balisage up to the Fort of Joux. (Or, you might just head along the highway for a hotel and save the visit to the fort for the following morning.) It's the place where Pierre Dominique Toussaint L'Ouverture, the liberator of Haiti, was imprisoned by Napoleon, and it's where he died.

Head down to the N67 to find a hotel in the small hamlet of Tuilerie. If, in this much-traveled area, no lodgings are available, you are only about 5 kilometers, by foot or by thumb, from Pontarlier.

Day 9: Cluse-et-Mijoux to Le Morond
(ca. 28 km, 7 hr)

This is a walk of the kind we came to think of as the usual Jura combination—wooded crests alternating with high pastures and flower-filled meadows where cowbells clanged. A beautiful walk, ending with a triumphant climb up Morond mountain, the highest point GR5 reaches in the Jura.

From the storybook Fort of Joux, GR5 moseys among the few houses near the hamlet of Tuilerie, then climbs the wooded crest of Le Crossart, locally called *le bois noir* (the black woods), with views through the trees down to the Côte des Rasses to the east.

Emerging from woods, the walker has a view of the Lac du Saint Point, the lake the Doubs forms, although legend offers another origin. On the banks of the Doubs at this spot, so the legend goes, was a town that rivalled Sodom and Gomorrah in the inhumanity of its inhabitants. One stormy winter night, a woman sought refuge in the town for herself and her little son, but every door was slammed in their faces. Resigned to her fate, the woman pressed on with her child, and along the way, ran into the monk, later Saint Point, who gave them shelter and hospitality. In the morning, there was a lake where the town had been, its cruelty destroyed with finality by an angry divinity.

The lake is 6.3 kilometers long and 800 meters across. It is said to freeze over entirely in winter. With a dam at its northern edge, it serves to regulate the wandering waters of the Doubs. From Chaon, which GR5 now traverses, the view of the lake is exceptional. Then a quick uphill walk brings the walker to Montperreux, with more good views of the lake.

GR5 stays high, continuing through woods. Take the small detour, marked in bright blue disks, along a trail dubbed a sentier escarpé (steep trail, but it isn't very) to the Source Bleue (the Blue Spring).

At least two legends are connected with this spring. One says that the water took the color of the pale-blue eyes of a young woman who threw herself into it. The more interesting legend, since it concerns real people, tells of Berthe, the wife of another charming Sire of Joux named Amaury. Returning after five years' fighting in the Crusades to discover that Berthe had been unfaithful, Amaury threw her into a dungeon. From her cell, undoubtedly by Amaury's design, Berthe could see the gallows on which her lover was hanged. She wept so much that her tears flowed into the spring, coloring the water blue.

Equally likely is the explanation that the blue color is the natural hue of this very pure water seen in shallow depth. It *is* blue, transparent, limpid, and worthy of whichever legend you choose.

After the detour to Source Bleue, GR5 climbs again, then descends to Malbuisson, a lively resort town on the lake, and a good stopping point for lunch or for buying picnic provisions; there's a well-stocked fromagerie here. It was, of course, raining the day we were there, so we asked a small café to build us some sandwiches, which we munched indoors. Nevertheless, we visited the fromagerie. Susanna had taken to stockpiling cheese as if she feared a coming famine, an unlikely eventuality in the lush Jura.

GR5 climbs out of Malbuisson to another wooded crest taking the walker eastward, away from the lake. This crest turns into pasture—the cowbells announce the fact before the trail actually debouches into open meadow—with numerous stiles to go through or over, and finally, with wide views forward to the basin where several towns nestle.

The trail heads down, turning south, and takes the walker along abandoned railroad track. There are a number of ski chalets here, and a wide plain separating the small towns of Métabief and Hôpitaux-Neufs.

The trail enters Hôpitaux-Neufs, where the GR5 walker should proceed at once to the Syndicat de Tourisme. There are two gîtes on Morond, but both require phone calls; the gardien may not have been planning to come up that day, or a gîte may have been given over to a group, or you may want to arrange for a meal. (The gîte of Gros Morond, run by the Club Alpin Français, does not officially serve meals, but you can ask to have the gardien prepare dinner and breakfast for you—for extra money.) The syndicat staff will make the phone call and arrangements for you, following which you should check your food supply and stock up, even if you have arranged for a meal. From here to Mouthe, 25 kilometers away, there is no chance for provisioning.

The climb up Morond is steep but obvious. Up there is the ski station on the summit—to which some people are heading via lift, passing almost over your head and pointing to you with obvious interest—and down there are your legs trudging uphill toward the summit. Once on top, you can celebrate with refreshment at the ski station. Outside is a table d'orientation directing your eyes south across hills and east across plain to discern, if the weather permits it, the slopes and peaks of the Alps rising beyond it.

The weather did not permit us that view, although, of course, the sun came out by the time we reached the gîte we had reserved (the CAF gîte of Gros Morond). This, in any event, allowed us to enjoy the dwindling afternoon on warm rocks in front of the gîte, with lovely views westward to the Jura plateau.

There we sat. One of us was trying to darn a pair of shorts, if such a thing is possible; the other held a book but was really just soaking up sunshine. A hiker arrived, a jolly fellow who began chatting animatedly with the gardien. We heard the gardien tell the hiker that we were "deux Américaines," and the hiker promptly went berserk with excitement. Well he might, for this at last was Robert Ravaioli, who had been chasing us for thirty-four days, since he first learned of our existence at the refuge of the Amis de la Nature in Hockai, Belgium. (Walking a minimum of 30 kilometers a day, Robert was bound to catch us eventually, even if we hadn't made detours and taken layover days.) For thirty-four days along the GR5 (which he trekked alone), at every hotel, refuge, and café, Robert had asked if "les deux Américaines" had been there, and if so, when. He knew almost as much about us as we did ourselves—names and addresses, that one of us was dark and one fair, that one carried a green pack decorated with a GR5 legend and one carried a blue pack with a U.S. flag made of colored tape, that one of us knew French and that the other understood it. He simply wasn't sure which of us was which.

He had met many of the people we had met, and had shared a meal with our dear Henri and Monique, who had filled him in further about many of our eccentricities.

Robert told us that everytime he saw two hikers ahead, he stopped, cupped his hands to his mouth, and shouted "Gin-gaire! Su-sannn-a!" But no one ever answered.

The excitement of our meeting was infectious. There was a group of ten hikers from Marseilles in the gîte, as well as a lone German named Gerhard. A family of three from a nearby vacation home came by for a visit to their friend, the gardien. We all moved indoors, where wine was produced and where the gardien managed to cook us a meal despite official policy. The evening turned into a party. Robert recounted the story of his pursuit of us, we three compared notes on inadequate balisage at various points along the route, and everyone drank wine. It all went down very well.

Day 10: Le Morond to
Le Lernier/Chaux-Neuve (ca. 28 km, 7 hr)

The ongoing beauty of the Jura does not pale with familiarity, but on this stage of the walk, a couple of highlights add to the walker's pleasure. First, the day provides a dramatic view of the Alps to come. Second, it takes the walker to the source of the Doubs River—a pretty, bubbling stream, set in a valley of great beauty where the big, flat river begins its extraordinary wandering. The walker of GR5 may well come to feel a great fondness for the Doubs, for its beauty, variety, and certainly its many twists and turns—and saying goodbye to it, at its source, can be a sentimental moment.

From the top of Morond, GR5 dips down into the combe of Mont d'Or, with its ski lifts silenced for the summer and its splendid view of the Alps. You stand on the edge of the corniche of Mont d'Or for the panorama of the massive white bulk of Mont Blanc flanked by needle peaks in the distance, while forested limestone hills stretch down and away from you toward an undulating plain below.

It was our first view of the Alps. The weather was sparklingly clear that morning and the distant mountains just shone in the sun. It was strange—and exciting—to contemplate that we would be there in perhaps ten days.

For the moment, though, GR5 heads down, away from the crest and the view, following an electric line through woods—thick now with ash trees (*fresnes*, in French) out into the open meadows, past chalets, granges, lazy cows. Signs on trees and posts announce that this is the route of the GTJ—Grande Traversée du Jura—the famed cross-country ski trail that takes skiers from gîte to gîte along the Jura plateau. Imagine this as a white world—the wildflowers and pastures covered with snow, snow on the branches of trees, snow drifting up against the fences that mark the fields and against the low walls of the houses. The cows would be gone, the smoke from the tués would look inviting, and it would all be very quiet.

We, on the other hand, were a noisy foursome, talking in three languages. In a mixture of German, English, and French, Gerhard instructed us in the best way to get through a herd of cows (we also applied the lesson to sheep and goats in the Alps):

First, look the nearest cow in the eye. Really. Then, clap your hands together sharply and, in a voice ringing with command, shout "Allez! Allez! Allez!" (It is a given that, in France, cows understand French.) We grew quite adept at this method; indeed, the GR5 walker finds it necessary to have some method for dealing with herds in the path. But some caution should be exercised. Robert told us that, so far from being completely benign animals, a cow once hind-kicked him halfway across a field. We took comfort from the fact that this happened in the Pyrenees, and that the offending beast probably understood only Spanish.

A very short detour, clearly marked, leads the walker to the source of the Doubs—a bubbling, crystal-clear stream emerging at 937 meters

Hiker atop Mont d'Or where there is a view of distant Mt. Blanc and the Alps ahead. In the Jura Mountains of France. Photo by Ginger Harmon.

from the base of an abrupt cliff of the Noirmont forest. The trail then proceeds into Mouthe, which typically registers the coldest weather anywhere in France during the winter months. In the summer, the flat, wide valley in which Mouthe is situated is lush and green, but one can picture how desolate it must look when it is leafless, with wind whipping across its vast openness. Little wonder it is called the Siberia of the upper Doubs. In Mouthe, even on a hot day, the megawalker can easily imagine the isolation of Jura winters—at least in the past—and can understand why humans and beasts huddled together for warmth, and why the former got to be so good at watchmaking.

From Mouthe and the low valley, GR5 enters cool woods that rise slightly until the trail debouches into a lovely open plain where storybook villages stand on their separate hillocks just a few paces from one another—Chaux-Neuve, Petite-Chaux, Châtelblanc. Head from Le Lernier to Chaux-Neuve to find lodging and food for the night.

Day 11: Chaux-Neuve/Le Lernier to La Chapelle-des-Bois (ca. 16 km, 4 hr)

A very short day today—again, because of the capricious availability of lodgings. Take advantage of the leisure as we did, by visiting the fromagerie in Chaux-Neuve before you leave.

Robert had gone on ahead; with a deadline hanging over his return to Nice (and to his family and his work), he wanted to make 40 kilometers that day. We made plans to meet in Nice, and we waved him on his way; he had caught and passed us at last.

To visit the fromagerie, we simply asked the *fromager* and *fromagère*—a handsome young couple, sinewy with manual labor—if we might. They assented, and we watched them making authentic Comté cheese. In each mechanized copper-lined vat two thousand liters of milk swirled. The fromager then netted the cheese from the vat in a cheesecloth, which was lifted out by the fromagère using a hook on a pulley. The fromager set the cheese in its rack, smoothed it, tightened a press around it, and left it. In the *cave*, cheeses were ageing. The legal minimum is eighty days, although some cheeses are aged for as much as six months; in the fromagerie of Chaux-Neuve, the usual length of time is two and a half months. Each day, the fromager turns each cheese in the cave, alternating treatment: one day, he sprinkles the cheeses with water, the next day with salt. Big sacks of *sel de mer*—sea salt— sat on the floor. The fromager also let us see and smell some cheese that had been ageing for six months.

Back to the trail, which takes the walker lazily out of town up a rise, then into woods and across pasture and again into woods—the usual Jura combination. The trail climbs a road to the clearing known as Chez l'Officier at 1,276 meters. This is a forestry area, and the trail traverses clear-cut areas, thick woods, and logging roads until it debouches onto the plain and heads into the town of La Chapelle-des-Bois.

This town charmed us. It's hardly a town at all, but rather a cluster of houses huddled near the church with isolated farmhouses spread out across the plain. It is a high plain—1,080 meters—and wide, and rolling. The fields are rimmed with walls of field stones—piled up somewhat sloppily and sometimes held by barbed wire. East of the town, and serving as a backdrop for the church and central square, is the formidable calceous-and-forest cliff that blocks Switzerland from La Chapelle-des-Bois and La Chapelle-des-Bois from the Swiss.

With the clangor of cow bells going on nonstop, it isn't surprising that La Chapelle-des-Bois would have a fromagerie. What is a bit surprising is that this one is *biologique*, all organic. Happily, the Morbier we purchased there tasted just as good as cheese from cows who had eaten polluted grass.

Day 12: La Chapelle-des-Bois to Les Rousses (ca. 26 km, 6-½ hr)

A day of forested crêts, and a day of some unexpected turns along GR5.

The walk starts with a choice. The official GR5 climbs very steeply up the cliff on a limestone path that can prove slick and slippery in moist weather. (You're going *up*, however, not down, so it isn't really treacherous—just sweaty.) The variant follows the road out of La Chapelle-des-Bois and climbs very steeply to meet GR5 at La Roche Bernard. The difference is fifteen minutes in favor of the variant.

Another difference is that the official GR5 edges the Swiss border, which is marked by wonderful bornes, many of them old, with F on one side, S on the other. Where the border angles east, an old, low stone wall proclaims the fact; a dolmen-like borne, dated 1649, wears incised coats of arms. GR5 sticks with the fleur-de-lys of France, and continues south/southwest to La Roche Bernard to cross the departmental border into French Jura.

La Roche Bernard affords what is, in fact, the walker's last real panorama over the Jura massif, and it proves a microcosmic view of the region: forested hillocks, brown and white dots of cows (whose bells are still audible at La Roche Bernard's 1,289 meters), green parcelled fields, the line of hills pointing north. And all the big tin-roofed farmhouses and clustered villages and the network of narrow roads uniting them. And water: the lovely lake of Bellefontaine, with low bogs beside it.

The trail plunges into deep forest, where it will stay for the rest of this stage. This, too, is a forestry area, and *abris forestiers*—small woodsmen's shelters—occur at frequent intervals. Much of the trail follows forestry road and induces a smooth, rhythmic pace that lulls the walker into inattention, but the trail frequently departs from the road onto path, so some caution is advised. You are walking a long south/southwest line along Crêt des Arêtes and Crêt des Sauges, until finally you follow the contour of the Gros Crétet, with its radio tower.

Pick up a last *route forestière* (forest road), and debouch to meadow, road, and the busy ski resort of Les Rousses.

Day 13: Les Rousses to Nyon (Switzerland) (ca. 26 km, 6-½ hr)

It is less than a two-hour walk from Les Rousses to the Swiss border at La Cure. In Switzerland, the red and white GR5 balisage gives way to yellow *tourisme pédestre* markers. Surprisingly for a country known for its hiking paths, Switzerland has not identified the GR5 well at all. Markers are few, far between, and easily confused with other markers on the same sign. The best advice is to study carefully the maps and descriptions in your topo-guide. If that doesn't help, then, as Ginger put it, just "blast on downhill to Nyon," more or less via Saint-Cergue and Trelex.

In leaving Les Rousses, GR5 climbs over pasture and through woods to the youth hostel of Bief de la Chaille. Here GR5 and GR9 are one walk as far as the D29 highway.

In La Cure, you can take refreshment in a restaurant that has a front door in France and a back door in Switzerland—though which is front and which is back may depend on your point of view.

The trail stays high as far as Saint-Cergue, where another trans-European trail is met, the E4. GR5 then begins to head downhill to the now visible lake with the Alps of Savoie behind it.

From Saint-Cergue, GR5 follows the ancient stones of the Roman road that once linked Lac Léman with Paris. An engineering marvel, it cuts the switchbacks that today's highway requires.

From Trelex, the route heads across fields, along vineyards (!), through suburbs, and into the town of Nyon. Keep going, down through the old town, past the towered chateau, over the ancient ramparts to the flower-decked quays beside the lake.

Nyon, a town of great charm, comes at about the one-thousand-mile mark of the walk across Europe from top to bottom. Though this is about two-thirds of the way, Nyon had always loomed for us as a kind of halfway point—an ineluctable, ineffable milestone on our journey.

We had now done the Europe of cold coast and pastoral plain. We had done the round hills of the Vosges and the folds of the Jura. Before us lay an extraordinary rampart of steep summits, a huge wall between us and the sea.

In the dip of Lac Léman, we planned to regear ourselves to attempt this wall. Our lightweight boots had stood up well, but both of us had arranged to change to sturdier footwear for the Alps. Most clothing was still in good shape, but not all, and we were bored with what we had to wear—bored with wearing it, and bored with looking at the same thing on one another. And we had learned some lessons in the two months we had been walking that would enable us to further reduce the weight of our packs yet make some useful additions to our baggage.

The pleasant, temperate shores of Lake Geneva provide any number of choices for the walker's layover day or days—Nyon itself, Geneva, Lausanne. Towns and cities along the lake are linked by train and boat for easy access one to the other.

A layover day here does not properly belong to the Jura alone; rather, it is a long sigh of achievement after the Europe crossed thus far and a new intake of breath before beginning what the French call, with justifiable pride, La Grande Traversée des Alpes.

15
The Great Crossing of the French Alps

*"Mirari se quinam pectora semper
impavida repens terror invaserit . . . quid
Alpes aliud esse credentes quam
montium altitudines?"*
— *Livy*

"What is this wondrous panic that has suddenly seized the hearts of men who have never felt fear before? . . . What do you suppose these Alps *are*?—other than high mountains—"

Thus Hannibal, at least in the words Livy gave him, exhorted his reluctant troops, paraded before him in the valley at the foot of the Alps. The twentieth-century megawalker might do well to keep the words in mind, especially as his boat brings him across Lake Geneva to the little town of Saint-Gingolph, just barely squeezed between the waterfront and the massive heights visible above the rooftops. That is when the walker, craning his neck up, up, up to see only a wall of mountains that clearly cannot be gone through or around, may experience a slight *frisson*; may even inquire of himself, "What am I doing? And why?"

Hannibal's urgings were ultimately persuasive, and his arguments are as meaningful to the GR5 walker today as they were to the Carthaginian soldiers in 218 B.C. The general reminded his troops of all they had overcome—the rivers they had forded, the plains they had crossed, the foreign nations they had successfully passed through. The Alps, he assured them, were only higher versions of mountains they themselves had crossed in the past. Nor would they be the first to attempt the Alps; many others had done so, many times. People *lived* there, tilled the earth, herded animals. (Hannibal was to rue this statement; the Carthaginian army that crossed the Alps was decimated, not by the climb, but by the armed resistance of hostile tribes.) Finally, Hannibal recalled to his troops that the greater part of their campaign was behind them; these Alps were not a barrier, but the very "walls of Rome." Jump this one last hurdle, he seemed to be saying, and we've got what we came for.

The Alps are the most famous mountains on earth—so famous that the name has become an adjective for everything mountainous. Ironically, that is a misnomer, since an alp is a high summer pasture for herds, not an ice-bound peak. At least, local usage of the word makes it a pasture; some linguists hold that Latin *Alpes* actually derives from Celtic *alb*, "white" or "height." Whichever theory you accept, alpine, alpinist, and all the rest are words that bring to mind high mountains—mountains like the definitive ones, the Alps.

For the megawalker, the Great Crossing of the French Alps along GR5 is one of the supreme experiences of hiking anywhere on earth. All the clichés of Alpine beauty come dramatically to life in the great spectacle of this high world: the broad plains, the river basins, the sudden hidden valleys, flower-filled meadows, rushing streams, towering peaks, glacial cirques, scree slopes, jagged rock faces—all of it. It is true that the air is as heady as champagne, that first light turns the ice peaks blue, that sunset makes the world orange-pink and leaves a rosy alpenglow, that nights are jet-black, and that the stars, huge and brilliant, seem very close.

It is also true that the clichés of classic mountain hiking come dramatically to life here: the relentlessly steep, sweat-soaked ascents; the equally steep, tiptoeing descents; the delicious taste all food seems to have (although in the Alps, the food often is remarkable); the dog-tired physical weariness at the end of each day; the thrill, nevertheless, of starting out again each morning; the importance of being in shape, equipped, prepared.

The megawalker who has followed GR5 from Holland is by this time certainly in excellent shape for the Grande Traversée des Alpes. Still, you are about to spend a *long* time doing strenuous mountain hiking—every day—and this can have its effects. When we began the crossing of the Alps, our collective walking experience included serious hiking and backpacking in the Sierra, Appalachians, Rockies (of the United States and Canada), Himalaya, Scottish peaks, and scattered Alps of Switzerland, Austria, and Italy. The Grande Traversée was like all that walking, only more so. As Ginger wrote in a letter home, "We knock off four to five thousand vertical feet before lunch—every day." Every day for nearly thirty days: it is a demanding walk.

No one who goes up into the Alps should even attempt the walk without being outfitted for every possible eventuality. This is, of course, canon law for mountain hiking anywhere, but it bears repeating here. In the month we spent in the Alps, we fried, froze, scrambled over rocks, slid down scree, sloshed through mud, slipped on ice and snow, and were pelted by rain, hail, and sleet. You need the proverbial sturdy, warm, weather-resistant boots; the layers of wool and/or polypropylene for warmth; the top-to-bottom rain and wind gear against the weather. You need a hat with a brim and sunscreen and sunglasses and a long-sleeved cotton shirt. You need to carry food—one of the delights of this walk—and to be sure, every morning, that you have plenty of water.

You should have a good, basic, first aid kit, and you should know—or learn—the universally recognized Alpine distress signal: A series of six visual or audible signals—one every ten seconds, pause for one minute, repeat. And the reply to the distress signal: A series of three visual or audible signals—one every *twenty* seconds, pause for one minute, repeat. If you have given the distress signal, and you hear a reply, answer back; then continue giving periodic single signals till you are found. Obviously, to be able to give the signal, you should carry a whistle, flashlight (with extra batteries), and mirror you can flash in the sun.

Clouds move in quickly in the Alps. Photo taken from Col du Brévent above Chamonix. Photo by Ginger Harmon.

The best protection against distress is, of course, adequate precaution. Be prepared, stay on the trails, exercise good sense in the face of bad weather, know where you are and where the nearest refuge or town is—all the things that good hikers do as a matter of course. Our worst disaster in the Alps was a long day of such soaking rain that virtually everything we owned was wet, and a scrunched-up, soggy sock caused a blister on one of our four feet. We headed for the valley, took a hotel room, strung it with clothesline till it looked like a tenement, and dried ourselves and our gear. If we lost a day of walking, we gained a day in the lovely town of Samoëns, famous for its Alpine garden. Besides, we were in no hurry. The Great Crossing of the Alps is far too beautiful to rush.

You will use four topo-guides in the Grande Traversée. The step-by-step information they provide, coupled with the overwhelming size of the mountains and the strenuousness of walking them, often make you lose sight of the bigger picture of where you are. This is part of the joy of hiking here, of course; you're concentrating on getting up the next col, then looking down into the next surprise valley, or you've suddenly walked into a high meadow in the bowl of a mountain and, entranced, you convince yourself that this is all there is to the world—at least for the moment. But it is also good, at the top of the pass or at the end of a day, to consider the path you've trudged as a part of something, to get a longer view than the usual one, which is mostly of your feet.

One of the things that is most helpful for this is another set of maps—specifically, the IGN (Institut Géographique National) 1:100,000 topographic maps or, even better, the Didier Richard 1:50,000 maps (also published by IGN, by the way). These maps show the GR5 and other walking routes, are perfectly beautiful, and cost a pretty penny. They are readily available in most towns along the way.

In reading these maps, the walker will need to add to his vocabulary a number of words with which French makes subtle distinctions among mountain features. *Pic, crête, tête, dent, cime,* and *sommet* all mean mountaintop. *Pic* also means pickax, which may give an idea of its true sense; a *crête* is a ridge or crest; *tête* means head; *dent,* tooth, is a jagged peak; *cime* and *sommet* each mean the top of something—in this case, a mountain. Other words that may prove useful are *pente,* the slope or incline or pitch of a mountain, and the two ways a *pente* is typically described—either *douce* (gentle), or *raide* (steep). The most useful word is *col*; it means collar or neck in daily use, but in the mountains, it is a pass. A col is sometimes referred to as a *collet* or a *pas,* but it's a high pass nevertheless. There are a lot of them; we stopped counting at forty, but be prepared for at least one a day. *Alpage* is another key word; it refers to the high mountain meadows that are the gentle lulls of this Alpine crossing. *Bergeries* are the sheep pens you often see in *alpages; vacheries* are the cow sheds.

One other language tip: the French for "to climb" is *grimper.* As you meet fellow hikers, you will hear and eventually use a phrase so common and so appropriate it becomes almost a hiker's greeting: "Ça grimpe, hein?!" The inexact English equivalent would be, "Some climb, huh?!"

One hundred and thirty million years ago, according to most geologists, the great sea of Tethys covered what is today Europe—and a good deal more. Molten rock emerging from within the earth caused the ocean floor to spread; as it spread, it carried the continents along. Two sliding continents, the African and Eurasian plates, were squeezed together. The Eurasian plate tipped down as the African rose over it. Islands emerged. Compression created interfingerings of sediment and crust; these thickened. It all took a long time. Then, about five million years ago, strong uplift pushed all this up in the form of mile-high mountains. Over time, these heights were eroded—are still being eroded—into the Alps we know today, a crescent-shaped range on a southwest-to-northeast path extending for 300 kilometers (186 miles) in length and some 150 kilometers (93 miles) in width.

These are very young mountains in geologic terms; that translates into very steep mountains in hiking terms. The steepness and the repeated glaciation of the recent (geologic) past make for instability and accelerate the erosion process. Harsh weather slows the nutrient cycling, and soil is constantly sliding downhill, so there is less and less organic material for things to grow in. There's just nothing to grab onto up there, as the GR5 walker discovers at first hand.

The fact is that these mountains are still "happening," and some of the man-made influences are speeding their destruction. We saw places where badly managed human incursions have wreaked such damage that eventually, as Ginger put it, "there won't be anything to hike here." Four human industries in particular have had an effect on the Alps: war; herding and the over-grazing it has led to; the creation of hydro-electric power facilities; and tourism. The first two, at least, have been going on for a very long time.

There is no real wilderness here; as Livy had Hannibal point out, people have been living in these mountains for years—thousands of years by now. Hannibal also proved, in the most dramatic possible way, that the Alps are not an impassable barrier, although they are generally considered to be the great cultural dividing line between cool, gloomy, rational Nordic Europe and the mercurial, sensuous, warm south. In fact, well before Hannibal and as recently as World War II, getting at an enemy over the Alps has been a persistent military occupation.

Tribes of Allemanni and Goths and Huns under Attila poured over the Alpine ramparts to sack Rome. Lombards, Ostrogoths, and Franks surged downward over the high passes, and then surged back up again. Charlemagne sent armies here, as did the dukes of Bavaria, the Swiss, the Austrians, the French, and the Russians. Napoleon's stunningly swift—and successful—invasion of Italy over the Saint Bernard pass convinced him that top priority must be given to creating military roads over the Alps—roads passable for artillery. They are today the great transalpine automobile highways.

World Wars I and II saw mountain troops manning positions on ridges and resistance fighters holed up in hidden valleys. The GR5 walker will pass some of the debris of these wars and will see in small montagnard villages the plaques bearing the names of local boys who died in the fighting. The ultimate effects of the wars on the mountains themselves were redrawings of the frontier lines, once in World War I, then back again after World War II. The French-Italian border often follows the ridgeline at the top of a crest; putting a border in such a spot would seem to be meaningless even to the mountaineer who achieves the summit. In what we have called the Middle Alps section of the walk, some two weeks into the Grande Traversée, the walker enters the Vallée Étroite, the Narrow Valley, and heads for a cluster of refuges to spend the night. This is France, officially speaking, and the refuges certainly accept French currency. But there is no question in anybody's mind—the people who put up the signs in Italian, the folks from Bardonecchia a few miles away who have driven up for a day-walk, the gardiens running the refuges, and the cooks who prepare the meals there—that this is Italy. Some political or cartographic fluke makes this valley French, but the GR5 walker will know for sure that he has spent a night in Italy.

The most picturesque industries in the Alps are cattle and sheep raising. Cows are pretty much everywhere, but you see more sheep the further south you go. The latter are raised for slaughter, the former for cheese. Many of these cheeses are sold through *fruitières*—cheese cooperatives—found in most villages along the way, but the walker may also be able to purchase cheese right from the chalet in a high meadow, and he should certainly ask. (If you see goats around, be sure to ask for *chèvre*, goat cheese.) The most famous cheese-producing cows are the Abondance of the northern Alps and the Tarine, originally from the Tarentaise region. (Note: For tips on getting through herds that block the path, see instructions in Chapter 14 on the Jura.)

The chalets along the GR5 are hardly the charming, flower-bedecked, balconied houses advertised in sleek brochures about quaint Swiss villages. They are rude herdsman's huts—piles of stone for the most part, with overhanging roofs of wood or slate or whatever was at hand, the roofs often held down by rocks. In fact, they are similar to the outbuildings around them, where the herds might be sheltered at night—utilitarian, and nothing more.

And in fact, most of the chalets are abandoned—evidence of the dying of montagnard life, as young people head for the cities, not the hills, and villages that no longer need to be self-sufficient turn themselves into ski resorts or hotel stops along the Alpine tourist highways.

The harnessing of water power—and the industries it has spawned—is a fairly recent development in the French Alps. Most of its effects are well out of view of the walker, except in the valleys of the Isère and Arc rivers and particularly at Modane, a busy industrial city, where much of the industry is obscured by the even busier aspect of Modane's role as a transportation center and tunnel crossing. Nevertheless, "hydro," on most of the great rivers draining the Alps, has had an effect on the environment itself and has helped to urbanize many of the Alpine valleys.

Tourism, however, has had the most visible effect, with mountaineers, skiers, jet-setters, and anyone who can drive a car or take a tour seeking beauty and a variety of pleasures in the Alps.

Coming here for fun used to be a very esoteric, indeed elitist, pastime. In 1786, two Chamonix locals, Michel-Gabriel Paccard and Jacques Balmat, made the first ascent of Mont Blanc, thus proving that it could be done. They were followed shortly by the Swiss scholar, Horace Benedict de Saussure, and for a while, mountaineering was the province of naturalists and mineralogists. The nineteenth century saw the golden age of Alpinism, when most of the great climbers seemed to be British "gentlemen." Often they were aided by local guides, who formed themselves into *compagnies*, such as those of Oisans, Pralognan, Grenoble, and—still the most famous of all—Chamonix, rich in lore and ritual. In 1855, a man named Alfred Wills, whose legacy the GR5 walker will find in Sixt and at the Collet d'Anterne, wrote a book suggesting that climbing around in the Alps was actually fun. The notion may have helped bring a new kind of tourist to the Alps—hardy families who made long journeys from all over Europe to spend summers in high Alpine retreats, breathing fresh air, taking long walks, and eating the fresh dairy foods.

But around the turn of the century, what had once been practiced in Scandinavia as an essential mode of transportation began to catch on as a sport. Skiing—and later a host of other snow sports—turned the Alps into a winter paradise, while advances in transportation made the mountains easily accessible.

Today, the tourist's problem in the Alps is the availabilty of hotel rooms, and numerous small villages, virtually isolated for centuries, are rushing to get a piece of the holiday action. The development of the Alps as a playground has been rapid, mostly unplanned, and in many cases destructive of the very mountains that make the area a playground to begin with. This the GR5 walker will see in unhappy abundance, but, at least in the summer of 1984, we also saw evidence of local—and national—resistance to the free-for-all developing that has gone on in the past.

Hannibal, his troops, and all their elephants crossed the Alps from west to east, from what is today France into Italy, there to reap victory. Not final victory, of course, or the entire western world might today be speaking Punic and worshiping cruel if endearingly fat-bellied gods. Hannibal was eventually defeated by the power of Rome, which some years later spread its empire northward in another famous crossing of the Alps—slower, more deliberate, and with longer-lasting implications.

With those two exceptions, most Alpine crossings have been from north to south. That is the direction GR5 takes, though it does not so much cross the French Alps as follow them, up and down, up and down, up and down, to what is really their beginning at the Mediterranean.

The French Alps are the first northward thrust of these mountains, before they turn east at Lake Geneva to Switzerland, Italy, Liechtenstein (entirely in the Alps), Germany, Austria, and Yugoslavia.

The Grande Traversée des Alpes, from the south shore of Lake Geneva at Saint-Gingolph to the north shore of the Mediterranean Sea at Nice, is a walk of some 720 kilometers (a little more than 445 miles). Our itinerary calls for covering that distance in thirty-one days—twenty-nine of them afoot. If you like averages, the walking comes to just about 25 kilometers or 16 miles a day. Here in the Alps, time means more than distance—time and the number of cols to be crossed—and most of the daily stages are about six and a half hours in length.

The walk goes through five departments of France (and actually dips into Switzerland and Italy on a couple of occasions). These departments roughly correspond to five separate groups of Alps, north to south.

From Lake Geneva more or less to the Isère River, the walker traverses the great massif of Mont Blanc in the department of Haute-Savoie. These mountains are an extension of the Pennine range of Alps to the east, where the Matterhorn rises—the range the Rhone River separates from the parallel Bernese Alps to the north.

Between the Isère and Arc rivers are the Graian Alps and the Vanoise massif—the department of Savoie. The two great river valleys, the Tarentaise (Isère River) to the north and the Maurienne (Arc River) to the south, are regions rich in vestiges of montagnard life. Between them is the Parc National de la Vanoise, France's first national park, a refuge for Alpine flora and fauna and a paradise for the hiker.

The Cottian Alps rise up from the valley of the Durance to include the craggy region of Queyras in the department of Hautes-Alpes. It is here, according to the latest accepted theory, that Hannibal made his crossing, well to the east of GR5, through the col de la Traversette above Italy's Mount Viso.

Across the Ubaye River are the Alps of Haute-Provence in the department of the same name. This group of Alps is given shortest shrift by GR5, and soon you are up the Pas de la Cavale to look down onto the Tinée Valley and enter the Maritime Alps and the department of Alpes-Maritimes. Here the walker touches another national park, that of Mercantour, in the final trudge toward the sea.

Despite the numbers of mountain groups, and the even greater diversity of *pays*, or regions, through which the walker passes, the Grande Traversée falls naturally into three sections, each constituting a distinctive whole.

First is the North Alps section, the unequivocally upward thrust onto the massif of Mont Blanc. In ten days here, the walker crosses some of the most famous Alpine passes. In fact, it is here that the GR5 walker will most likely meet the greatest number of other Alpine hikers—walkers on the nine-day, three-country Tour de Mont Blanc, which loops from Chamonix through Italy and Switzerland around the massif via a series of high refuges, right back to Chamonix.

This North Alps region is quite evidently a world away from the South

Alps, which the GR5 picks up after Briançon and follows for eleven days to Nice. Where the north is cool, moist, and lush with dense conifers, the South Alps are dry, brown, a land of larch trees and gray olive. Here, the vegetation seems brittle, the walker kicks up clouds of dust, the air is full of the chirping of crickets and the smell of wild herbs.

Between these two vastly different regions, in the section we have called, simply, Middle Alps, the walker crosses the loftiest heights along the entire Grande Traversée while also coming to know its most important valleys. In an eight-day walk from the Tarentaise over the Vanoise massif to the Maurienne, then up into the high Alps to Briançon, Europe's highest city, the GR5 walker gets a unique look at the village life of the high Alpine valleys. It is often a look into a remarkable past, and into the changes that are occurring to that way of life, virtually under the walker's footsteps.

Our itinerary calls for two detours, one into Chamonix—simply because it is such a famous shrine of mountain views and mountaineering and also possibly the best place in Europe to find hiking gear—and another detour along a variant of GR5 that takes the walker down the valley of the Arc River. This variant provides a break from the bird's-eye view of valleys that GR5 usually provides, and it enables the walker to wander through a variety of charming and intriguing towns, some of them almost living museums of that fading montagnard life.

In the national parks and in the regional nature parks and nature preserves, ibex (*bouquetin*), chamois, marmot, weasel (*hermine*), badgers, martens, foxes, and all the other classic Alpine fauna are protected by law. So are such birds as the grouse. We saw—and heard—plenty of marmot, lots of grouse, and one hermine, but we never caught a glimpse of ibex or chamois, despite careful searching through field glasses along the most likely crags in the Vanoise.

Wildflowers, on the other hand, we saw aplenty. They were everywhere—and in profusion. Homespun flowers: garden-variety daisies, violas, forget-me-nots, columbine, azalea, and dandelions. Then the special flora of this lofty world: varieties of gentian, aster, anemone, primula, rhododendron, saxifrage, cinquefoil, campion, lily, and the gem of the Alps, edelweiss. Flowers peek out from under rocks, line the streams in high meadows, and sometimes occur so directly underfoot that you must quickly step aside to avoid destroying them. Perhaps most moving of all was the sight of the ever-present campanula, with us since Belgium.

The forests of the Alps continue to feature the majestic épicéa and sapin, but a new tree, the larch (*mélèze*), becomes evident as you head south into the valley of the Isère. It is a long while before you see your first olive tree, but when you do, you know that you are in a very different environment, and that the end of your walk, if not in sight, is at least a reality.

The most common plant along the way, however, is the meadow grass being munched by the most common wildlife, the Alpine cow.

Which brings us to cheese in particular and to food in general. The cheeses and cheese dishes—such as fondue—of the Savoyard region are well known and should all be tried. Remember these names: Beaufort, Tomme de Savoie, Chévre, Reblochon.

Reblochon has a particularly nice history, being born of the time-honored human habit of cheating the government. In the Middle Ages, the lords of the region imposed a tax payable in the form of milk, so much per cow. To be sure they'd have something left over for themselves—and perhaps also just to get back at the tax man—local farmers took to milking their cows only partially. After the tax collector had come by for the liege lord's portion, the farmers secretly went back to the cows to finish the milking. This extrarich milk was then made into cheese; in the local dialect, its name was *reblochon*, second milking.

But the truly wonderful fact about eating your way down the Alps is the change that occurs, well along in the walk, when you cross the great demarcation we dubbed the olive oil line. Somewhere you will notice that you have shifted from the thick, hearty, sometimes heavy fare of the north to garlic, pasta, and the sun-drenched tomatoes of the south. The Hoek van Holland and the gray North Sea will seem a long way away when you can taste saffron in your evening meal.

At 2,764 meters (9,068 feet), col d'Iseran is the highest point along the entire GR5 (and the second highest col in all the French Alps). We crossed it at about the midpoint of the Grande Traversée. Standing at the top of the col, wearing everything she owned against the chill, Susanna shouted through the wind, "From now on, it's downhill to Nice." It isn't, although she repeated the phrase at the top of every col thereafter. In fact, the second and third highest points on the GR5 are still to come. Indeed, Susanna wasn't right until the last hour of the last day, when we topped a rise and looked down on a city, which we then proceeded to walk through until we could go no further.

The Great Crossing of the French Alps is a great achievement for any walker, and it is an inimitable experience. When you look back on it as a whole, you gather the richness of it—the passage from mountains of dense forests and glacial torrents, through valleys higher than most hills, to mountains parched and craggy, finally to the smell and sight of a bright blue sea. It is an experience of high mountain huts and the camaraderie of people who, like you, have chosen to come there. It is a close look—the closest, one step at at time—at the extraordinary natural beauty of these mountains and at the chalets and villages of people whose way of life is fast fading from view.

16
The North Alps—Up and At 'Em

Right from the start, the walking in the North Alps sets the pattern for virtually all of the Grande Traversée des Alpes: the relentless steepness; the frequently poor condition of trails due to overgrazing (and overwalking: people have simply created their own paths, which is pretty logical, since the general direction is invariably either up or down); the spectacular views from the col; the sudden surprise of valleys; the clanging of cowbells; the refuges with their bread-and-cheese offerings.

The walk begins in the Chablais region, crossing the pre-Alps of the Haute-Savoie, a region the French call *moyenne montagne*, though it will probably not seem very "middling" to the walker's leg muscles. At the first col, col de Bise, the walker is atop the great limestone mass that is the Franco-Swiss border. Indeed, after crossing the valley of Abondance and a few more cols, GR5 dips into Switzerland at the col de Chésery, then heads back into France over the col de Coux.

At col de Golèse, the walker heads into the Haut-Giffre region and begins to sense a subtle change in the landscape. The almost pastoral quality of Chablais gives way now to the more rugged, crystalline Faucigny. Here are the great rock faces of higher summits, waterfalls and lofty lakes, permanent snowfields, and, despite the presence of other hikers as the GR5 nears Mont Blanc, a somehow more remote feeling to the environment.

The walker feels this remoteness on the long walk up to the col d'Anterne, past waterfalls, the exquisite lake, and the rocks of Fis, until Mont Blanc itself heaves into view. Then it is down into the gorges of the Diose and another long walk up the ice-bound rock of the col de Brévent before the descent into the Chamonix valley.

Mont Blanc still dominates as GR5 takes the walker over col de Voza into the Montjoie valley, then follows the ancient Roman road of Rochassets up the famous col de la Croix du Bonhomme. Here GR5 takes its leave of Haute-Savoie—and of the much-frequented Tour de Mont Blanc—and enters Savoie, the Beaufortain region, ascending the rocky and spectacular col de Bresson, some 214 kilometers from Lac Léman.

In the North Alps even more than in the Alps further south, the instability of the weather is a fact of life. The classic pattern of mountain weather tends to prevail—sharp, clear mornings offering the best views of surrounding peaks, with mountain storms and thunder-boomer clouds coming along in the afternoon. But here in the North Alps, the

Heading for Col d'Anterne in the North Alps. Photo by Ginger Harmon.

pattern tends to go to extremes. The sun glinting off snow and ice can be fierce, and the sudden storms—often *very* sudden—can be frightening. The wise walker will keep a sun hat handy at all times and will pack foul-weather gear close to the opening of his backpack, where it can be retrieved quickly.

Day 1: Nyon/Saint-Gingolph to Novel (ca. 7 km, 1-¾ hr)

The Compagnie Générale de Navigation offers a variety of steamer tours of Lake Geneva; these present the walker with several choices

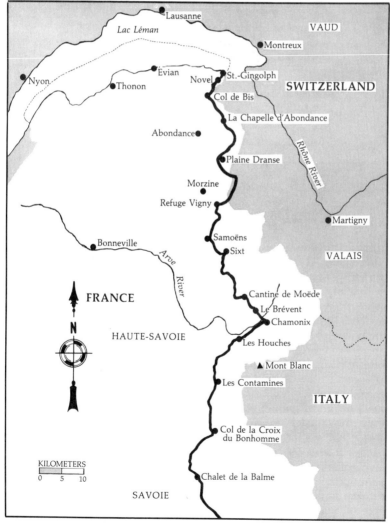

North Alps

North Alps

Day 1	Nyon/Saint-Gingolph to Novel	7 km	1-¾ hr
Day 2	Novel to La Chapelle d'Abondance	26 km	6-½ hr
Day 3	La Chapelle d'Abondance to Plaine Dranse	26 km	6-½ hr
Day 4	Plaine Dranse to Refuge Vigny	26 km	6-½ hr
Day 5	Refuge Vigny to Sixt	24 km	6 hr
Day 6	Sixt to Cantine de Moëde	24 km	6 hr
Day 7	Cantine de Moëde to Le Brévent/Chamonix	16 km	4 hr
Day 8	Chamonix to Les Houches	6 km	1-½ hr
	Via télépherique to Bellevue Bellevue to Les Contamines	14 km	3-½ hr
		20 km	5 hr
Day 9	Les Contamines to Col de la Croix du Bonhomme	22 km	5-½ hr
Day 10	Col de la Croix du Bonhomme to Chalet de la Balme	23 km	5-¾ hr
		214 km	53-½ hr

for getting over to Saint-Gingolph—depending on what stops, if any, you wish to make along the way. It is also possible to travel by bus or train to several of the other boat landings. This was our choice. We took the train from Nyon to Lausanne and the next day caught a mid-morning ferry that crossed to Évian before pulling in at Saint-Gingolph.

Saint-Gingolph is a curious place, being split down the middle by the torrent of the Morge into a Swiss sector and a French sector, complete with a lively customs station on the main street. As a result, the town has two of everything, except for the church, which is in France. It may have been our imagination, but we both thought that the Swiss side of Saint-Gingolph was neat, spotlessly clean, highly organized; its waterfront, however, was given over to private homes and allowed no access to the casual tourist. The French side, on the other hand, seemed chaotic, undisciplined, and a little messy; along its lakefront was a delightful public walkway where townsfolk and tourists alike could enjoy the views outward across the water and upward to the Alps.

Saint-Gingolph is a fine place for last-minute provisionings: food, maps, guidebooks, banking, post office—keeping in mind, of course, the cardinal rules about lunchtime closings and possible half-days in the shops. You will need French francs, of course, but it may be useful to carry some Swiss money as well for the coming foray into a tiny piece of Switzerland.

Novel is only about a two-hour walk away, so Saint-Gingolph makes a nice place to enjoy a leisurely lakefront lunch, weather permitting. This will be your last experience of this sort of thing for a long time to come; the next time you sit in a café beside a large body of water, it will be along the Promenade des Anglais of Nice, and the body of water will be the Mediterranean.

This, at least, was in our minds as we enjoyed a post-chore glass of wine on a sun-drenched terrasse near the boat landing, with the water of the lake lapping up against the rocks, swans aswimming on the tide, a blue sailboarder tacking up and down persistently, flowers in abundance, and the high wall of the Alps at our back.

GR5 departs Saint-Gingolph along the D30 highway but leaves it at once to climb smoothly along the ancient mountain road that lines the

The boat pulls into Saint-Gingolph at the foot of the Alps. Photo by Ginger Harmon.

Morge. It is a thickly green, mossy, moist walk to Novel, a town nearly 600 meters (about 2,000 feet) above the lake. A variant of the Balcon du Léman trail also passes through Novel; this may occasion confusion tomorrow when you're looking for the GR5 on the way out of town.

For the moment, however, look north to the Pic de Blanchard, southwest to the Dent d'Oche, southeast to Mont Gardy and la Chaumeny. You are surely *in* the Alps at last—and for the rest of your walk across Europe.

Day 2: Novel to La Chapelle d'Abondance (ca. 26 km, 6-½ hr)

Two cols today, for a total of some 4,000 feet of climbing, in a walk that serves as a brilliant introduction to the Grande Traversée des Alpes at its best.

From Novel, GR5 continues to parallel the Swiss border in the little valley of the Morge, couping the meanders of the road to reach the cluster of chalets called La Planche.

As we began to cross our first Alpine meadow, our progress was very nearly halted altogether by a stubborn cow who refused to move from in front of a stile. The New Yorker among us stepped forward, exhibiting the same defiance she routinely uses when jaywalking through oncoming traffic on a busy avenue in Manhattan. For a moment, it looked like a classic standoff: the cud-chewing cow warily sizing up the New Yorker as she stood what was, after all, *her* ground; the New Yorker glaring at the animal with a withering stare. After a few moments, the cow turned with a single jangle of her heavy bell and stepped aside, allowing the hikers to proceed over the stile—proof, once again, that walking Europe from top to bottom requires a variety of resources and skills.

From La Planche, GR5 crosses the Morge and debouches into a wide meadow. Here is picture-postcard Alpine scenery: the flower-strewn meadow backed by a high, jagged cliff. The trail climbs now among rocks and boulders along a pebbly, zigzag path up the ravine of the Vez—a steep climb through conifers. Topping the rise, we looked down on a snow bridge, a cascade tumbling into it noisily. Ahead on the trail we could see the derelict chalets of Neuteu.

Rain began to fall, turning quickly to hail in a sudden, fierce storm. We hurried along the trail, now white and stumbly with large hailstones, toward the deserted chalets. In the doorway of one of them, like ghosts, stood two men, a woman visible behind them. "Entrez," they said.

Inside, provisions and tools were neatly stacked on shelves, and a wood fire was burning nicely in a blackened stove. The three were using this derelict chalet as a camp while they rebuilt and restored one of the others to serve as a ski lodge. While hail clattered on the tin roof, we sat out the storm drinking hot chocolate and getting warm near the fire. The storm ended as suddenly as it began; our hosts went back to work, and we set off through the rain-freshened meadows.

From this height, GR5 offers views back to Lake Geneva to the north. Shortly after passing the chalets, a large boulder marks the spot where GR5 meets a variant coming up from the lake. This variant, which starts at Thonon-les-Bains, offers a more gently pastoral route up the ridge before meeting GR5 for the final steep push up to col de Bise. The trail to the col twists and turns a good deal, and its exact meanderings are often obscured by rocks, low shrubs, and animal trails. Watch carefully here for the red and white balisage, although you cannot really get lost; the general direction is up, toward the large, wooden cross visible in the dip of the col.

Another breathtaking view awaits the walker at the top of the col: on your right, the Dent d'Oche; on your left, the ridge of the Tête de Charousse; ahead, the snow-creased formation of the Cornettes de Bise; below, a green amphitheater of a meadow, with paths crisscrossing, chalets clustered in the center of the bowl, cows lazily grazing.

Down steeply to the chalets, one of which is a gîte of the Club Alpin Français (CAF), one a restaurant. Both sell cheese, including the chèvre produced by the goats sheltered at the chalets.

GR5 climbs again immediately, a quick, sharp ascent of some 300 meters (1,000 feet) up a goat path (marked as such) to the pas de la Bosse. From here, there are views across the valley of Abondance to tomorrow's ridges, and beyond to the snow-covered crest of the Dents du Midi. The goat path continues upward, but GR5 starts the long descent to La Chapelle d'Abondance.

This is a popular winter ski resort, and a popular stopping-off point for summer Alpine tourists. In the summer of 1984, two of the hotels on its main street were being enlarged, and several small chalet-guesthouses were clearly brand-new. The *chapelle* of the town's name dates from 1661, however, and the inhabitants seem concerned to keep at least the look of the town's ancient rustic charm.

We dined on a quintessentially Savoyard meal in La Chapelle d'Abondance, a meal we were often to repeat. First came *salade Savoyarde*, made with escarole, *lardon* (a thick bacon), walnuts, croutons, and tomatoes, dressed with oil and vinegar, and topped with a poached egg. The juxtaposition and eventual mixture of the hot egg and the cool salad make this dish special. We followed it with *fondue Savoyarde*, about which poems have rightfully been written. The true fondue of Savoie, we were told, mixes Emmenthal, Gruyère (Comté), and Beaufort cheese, adds white wine, and flavors it all with kirsch.

We slept well that night.

Day 3: La Chapelle d'Abondance to Plaine Dranse (ca. 26 km, 6-½ hr)

This day sees an occasional difficulty in following the trail, which makes some sharp turns when you least expect it. You will want to pay close attention.

It is a good idea to stockpile some food before leaving La Chapelle. Provisions are hard to come by until Samoëns, three days away.

GR5 leaves La Chapelle d'Abondance along the road, then turns right sharply to cross the river and head steeply up the Mattes torrent. A side trip of a few minutes takes you to the cascade itself and is certainly worth the detour. Follow the Mattes to the open meadow where the chalets of Sur Bayard are found, then track along the fence before finding a sharp right turn heading steeply uphill to the Chalets des Crottes. In the summer of 1984, these abandoned chalets were in fact a construction site, but we could not determine what was being constructed.

Continuing up, GR5 debouches into the fabulous meadow of La Torrens. Here is a rude chalet, with a water supply, and here the sound of automobiles from below gives way to the incessant clanging of cowbells from the herds high up the slopes.

Cross behind the chalet and start up to the col de Mattes on a marshy, sometimes hard-to-follow path—dotted with snow the day we were there. Again, the general direction is up, so it is not easy to lose your way.

From the top of the col, the trail leads down a marshy path, crossing a couple of streams, to the *alpage* and farm of l'Etrye. There is a choice of paths here; be sure to take what looks least like a walking trail and most like a farm road.

This leads up and then down to the farmhouses of Lenlevay, where we were able to buy delicious chèvre. GR5 then moseys easily along a flat road until it comes to an intersection, where a sign points to Grands Plans. Detour here, following the road to Grands Plans. You will climb up to the highway; then turn left to find a cluster of buildings at the bottom of a ski lift. Refuge Plaine Dranse is here, and here is your best bet for a night's lodging.

Day 4: Plaine Dranse to Refuge Vigny (ca. 26 km, 6-½ hr)

A multi-col day, part of which is spent in Switzerland.

Follow the road from the Refuge Plaine Dranse to col de Bassachaux. Then hook left, walking level for a time, then climbing across meadows to the col de Chésery. You'll be in Switzerland here, and the time is one hour earlier.

Head for a cross in the distance, past some abandoned buildings which may be useful shelter in bad weather. They were for us.

The trail goes around the Lac Vert, limpid in its bowl of a col, then climbs the col itself, called Porte du Lac Verte or Porte de l'Hiver. Dip left at once and follow the trail down to Champalin in Switzerland, where refreshment is available at a canteen.

GR5 continues under various ski lifts to pass a series of chalets— Pas, Pisaz, and Poya, which hangs from a rock—before heading up toward col de Coux.

For us, this entire day was a wet one, and as we started up the col de Coux, the rain was pouring down on us and on the cows lining the path (who, however, seemed unconcerned), while fog rolled in in great waves, then rolled out to create a sudden clearing through which we could see great snowy slopes, peaks, cascades, the rock strewn in the valley below.

The col is marked by a wind meter and weather station—both closed tight when we arrived in a very soggy state.

The top of the col marks the re-entry into France; readjust your sense of time to one hour later. GR5 heads down leftward from the col, across *prairie* (grassland), offering views deep into the valley crowded with cows. Then it heads into conifer forest, across streams—swollen and fast when we were there—along the flank of the Morzine Valley, back into pine forest to a road, which looked newly cut (and was very muddy) in the summer of 1984. A sign points downhill to the right toward Refuge de Vigny, the stop for the night.

We were overjoyed to arrive at the refuge after this long and thoroughly soaking day. Only a few other adult hikers were in attendance, but there was a group of some fifteen ten-year-olds—mostly Parisian kids who were summering at a nearby camp and had come as a group into the mountains. Overcoming their disbelief and disappointment that, although native Americans, we did not personally know Michael Jackson, they fell madly in love with us and set out to learn English— right now! The cozy refuge soon echoed with the insistent question "Comment dit-on . . . ?"

When they were in bed, the adults sat down to eat beside the stove. We had only meager provisions left, so everyone chipped in to share their meals with us. The gardien of the refuge made something he called *pain Canadien*—a loaf of bread baked with cheese in the middle, and three climbers offered us wine and promised us coffee for the morning. How nice, after such a wet, cold day, to find such warm shelter and friendship.

Day 5: Refuge Vigny to Sixt (ca. 24 km, 6 hr)

This is an easy day after yesterday's long haul and provides time and resources for reprovisioning as well.

Follow back up the road from the refuge of Vigny to meet GR5, then head up to the col de la Golèse—a climb of some twenty to thirty minutes only. The col is a particularly busy point of passage for birds, and ornithologists come here each autumn to track various migratory cycles, clocking black titmice who pass through every two years en route to Italy, Spain and Egypt; blue titmice on yearly flights; and siskins from as far afield as Russia.

Just after the top of the pass, a left-turning path, with local markers, heads down from the road to the refuge of Tornay. Shortly thereafter, another left heads across meadow toward some chalets visible from the trail. This was, unbeknownst to us, the GR5 of the summer of 1984, but the markers were very confusing, and the way was decidedly unclear. The fact is, it doesn't matter. All the trails that strike off leftwards from the road here eventually meet at the tiny hamlet of Les Allamands. If you make a mistake and find yourself at the refuge, if you strike out across the meadow and the forest of Bossetan, or even if you follow the road past les Chavonnes, you eventually come down to Les Allamands and the paved road.

At Les Allamands, GR5 follows the road down to the bridge over the Torrent d'Oddaz, then turns left toward Latay. It parallels the road and the Clévieux stream into les Moulins; from here, detour into Samoëns; you should be in good time for lunch, but be sure to reprovision first, before the shops close up tight for the sacred midday meal.

Here in Samoëns, the walker is in the heart of the valley of the Giffre, one of the biggest tributaries of the Arve, which drains the high limestone mountains of the Faucigny region. The town itself is nestled in what seems a bowl cut out of this limestone, at the foot of the sharp rock outcrop of Criou. Samoëns is a lively winter resort, and is lively enough in the summer as well, with tourists and mountaineers—and shops catering to all.

Here too is the Jaysinia alpine garden, a beautiful exhibit of Alpine—and alpine—flora from all over the world.

GR5 leaves Samoëns at the point where the Giffre and the Clévieux stream meet; the trail follows the river along a wooded, shrubberied path before debouching onto the N507 highway at Pont Perret.

The trail then climbs a narrow gorge that was once the riverbed of the Giffre. It is a beautiful and exciting walk along here, through deep declivities in the limestone, and the walker is often aided by ladders. Through the trees, there are occasional views of tomorrow's climb and of the Gorge des Tines.

The trail crosses the noisy torrent at the quiet hamlet of Le Fay; detour from here into Sixt to spend the night.

Sixt was founded by monks in 1144; its abbey is today a hotel, once slept in by such luminaries as Prince William II of Prussia and King Albert I of Belgium. The town is actually an important tourism center, despite its small size; it serves as a point of departure for trips to various sights—among them, the famous Fer-à-Cheval, a limestone mountain cut by glaciers and washed by waterfalls.

But as the walker will see in the fountained square of this minute village, Sixt is also a hiking center. A sign in the square lists a number of hiking destinations, with the estimated times for getting there; Chamonix is last on the list. There is another reminder of Chamonix—and climbing—in the inscription which reads, "À la mémoire de Jacques Balmat, vainquer du Mont Blanc, décédé accidentellement au glacier du Ruan en septembre 1834" (To the memory of Jacques Balmat, conquerer of Mont Blanc, accidentally killed on the glacier of Ruan in September, 1834).

Sixt is set within a Réserve Naturelle, which includes the Fer-à-

Cheval, and a small museum in the town is dedicated to the area. Here the walker can see exhibits on montagnard life of the last century, the Compagnie des Guides de Sixt, and Alfred Wills. Wills was a British climber who explored this area in depth, as two of his books, *Wandering the High Alps* and *Eagle's Nest in the Valley of Sixt*, clearly attest. Wills's devotion to the area (he built a house here which is now the refuge near col d'Anterne) was also reflected in his desire to preserve the natural features of the mountains and the way of life of the inhabitants. In this sense, Wills, who lived from 1828 to 1912, was a benign eco-freak ahead of his time.

Day 6: Sixt to Cantine de Moëde (ca. 24 km, 6 hr)

Today's walk is a great hike—demanding (5,000 vertical feet all told) and beautiful, giving the walker the sense of being deep in the world of high mountains.

Walk back to Le Fay and follow along the torrent toward the highway above. In 1984, the trail at this point moved through a gravel dump and was somewhat problematic; remember to keep the stream on your right. (You can also follow road from Le Fay or Sixt, picking up GR5 at the bridge crossing, Pont de Sales.)

GR5 crosses the stream and achieves the road near Pont de Sales, then climbs, couping the road's meanders, and attains the Cascade de Rouget—a giant, hurtling waterfall of the Torrent de Sales, with a nearby *buvette* (refreshment bar). The trail continues to climb till it strikes out across meadow at Chalets du Fardelet, then passes the Chalets de Lignon, all the time more or less paralleling the Torrent de Sales. The climb steepens, still following the torrent, which grows smaller and narrower as you climb, to the intersection with GR96, the walk of the pre-Alps of Haute-Savoie and the tour of the Lac d'Annecy. This intersection is just above the exquisite Cascades de la Pleureuse et de la Sauffla and is a popular—and obvious—lunch spot.

We had seen more hikers already this day than on our entire journey so far, and we were joined in our picnic on the rocks by a group of British hikers who were spending a week in Sixt and striking out for day hikes. It was nice to speak English again.

GR5 splits sharply left here and climbs, contouring the face of the Faucilles (sickles) de Chantet and offering views back down to the valley of the Giffre, and Sixt, and the patchwork of fields and hamlets below. An astonishing series of power lines dips across the valley here and, slung from towers on the ridges, rides high over the *faucilles*. How anyone managed to construct such a power line may well occupy the walker's thoughts as he trudges upward to the collet d'Anterne, a wide meadow, decorated—the day we passed through—with resting hikers.

Soon you turn the corner to a view of the col d'Anterne across a scrubby Alpine meadow filled with azalea, surrounded by rocky and snow-covered slopes down which cascades tumble—silently, at this distance. GR5 crosses the spongy meadow, following the stream, to the Refuge Wills.

Susanna was the first to arrive at the refuge; she made straight for the terrasse, nodded to the other hikers already lounging there, and ordered a beer. The friendly young gardienne brought the beer and seemed disposed to chat; the Usual Conversation ensued: Yes, all the way from Holland. Yes, all the way to the Mediterranean. Two of us. American.

"Les deux Américaines!" The gardienne was on her feet. "Mais, j'ai une lettre pour vous!" She disappeared into the refuge.

Susanna was incredulous, to say the least. To think that in this isolated point on earth, nearly 6,000 feet high, a letter might find her. . . . To the American hiker, it is unbelievable enough to think of having a beer 6,000 feet up, but a letter!

She could only imagine that it was a note from Robert Ravaioli, our co-GR5er, who had promised to leave word for us at huts and stopping places along the route. But in fact, it was from our friends from the Vosges, Henri and Monique, now returned to Paris, who had hoped that by chance the gardiens would go into town for mail, and that by chance we would pass that way, and that by chance we would stop at the refuge Wills, and that by chance the gardiens would take us for Americans . . . and so on.

For Ginger, arriving after a 4,000-foot climb, it was enough to see her companion sitting in a café drinking a beer—for all the wonders of California, this is not one of them. It was even more of a shock for her to see said companion waving something in the air and to hear her call out, "Hey, Ginger! We got mail!"

The gardienne and her husband and the other hikers assembled on the terrasse gathered around as Susanna read aloud, editing as she went:

Dear Susanna and Ginger,
This is like putting a bottle in the ocean. The gardiens of this refuge are very nice, [edited portion: but last year they made us a boeuf bourguignon that was just terrible].
Have you met Robert Ravaioli yet? Do you have sun hats? They are essential, even though it is true that you have very hard heads anyway if you're walking from Holland to Nice.
We miss your company. Give our regards to the marmots and jackdaws along the way. If the Los Angeles Olympics had a walking event, you would have won the gold medal by now. We send you our friendliest thoughts and hope to see you in Paris in September.
Henri and Monique

The letter produced great excitement all around—and for us, an added fillip. Now we were not only the two Americans who were walking from Holland to Nice, we were the two Americans who were walking from Holland to Nice and got mail along the way.

Thus rejuvenated—with additional help from beer and hot *citron pressé*—we pushed on.

GR5 climbs from the refuge along a trail that, near the lip of the ridge, becomes crumbly, muddy, and hard to follow. Do what everyone else has done here—just head *up!*

The trail then dips for a stream, rises gently, and stands the walker on the crest of the well in which sits the lac d'Anterne. South and west are the astonishing rocks of the Tête à l'Ane. In the meadow are wild forget-me-nots, violas, gentian, alyssum. The lake just sits there—green, glassy, still. It has no outlet but loses its water in a limestone fissure. Several people were hiking across this lake-meadow with us; we all moved slowly, trying hard to engrave the image of the place on our brains, reluctant to leave this bit of paradise.

The trail climbs up from the lake until the backward look at it is lost, then crosses a snowfield meadow to reach the col d'Anterne. Here are splendid views, weather permitting, of the white face of the opposing massif—Mont Blanc sticking its head up above it. Head down from the col to the Cantine de Moëde. It was lively with hikers and alpinists and professional guides the night we were there—a busy place, with hearty food, plenty to drink, and lots of good cheer.

You sleep this night in the shadow of Mont Blanc, Europe's highest peak. It is, if you think about it, a long way from the dikes of Holland.

A leisurely breakfast at Cantine de Moëde. Photo by Ginger Harmon.

Day 7: Cantine de Moëde to Le Brévent/Chamonix (ca. 16 km, 4 hr)

The morning at Cantine de Moëde rewards you, if the weather is fair, with a superb look at the Aiguilles Rouges—the ridge cut by the col de Brévent—and beyond to Mont Blanc. On a good day, such as we had, the sun glints brilliantly off the great mountain's white vastness. The transient inhabitants of the chalet-hotel scrunched together at windows for the view or gathered on the terrasse for picture-taking and general staring.

Official GR5 skips Chamonix, but it would seem a shame for most hikers, and especially for Americans who have already traveled a great distance to get here, to miss this shrine of mountain walking. Our itinerary therefore calls for a detour down to the valley and the town—a detour that may be negotiated by téléphérique or on foot.

From Cantine de Moëde, the route heads downhill to the abandoned Chalets de Moëde, then continues descending across spongy ground to the seasonal Pont d'Arlevé over the Diose (or Diosaz). A seasonal bridge is a bridge that is put down each summer and picked up each autumn. Under it, the Diose runs swiftly on its way to the deep gorges it cuts before falling into the Arve near Servoz.

Shortly before we arrived at the bridge, we saw something we had never before seen anywhere along GR5 and were never to see again: a trail maintenance crew. At the time we passed them, they were sprawled on a rock eating a tempting breakfast of huge hunks of cheese on huger hunks of bread, but it was evident that they had been trimming back the branches along the flower-lined trail. Later, climbing the much-used trail up to the col de Brévent, there would be further evidence of real trail construction—a good gradient, sensibly switchbacked, with water bars and rock treadway against erosion. Trail maintenance of the GR5, we were later to learn, is a local responsibility which the "Paris office" has no authority to command. Trail work is carried out according to the inclination and available manpower of each local club. In the Mont Blanc area, where hiking is both a way of life and an important part of the total tourism picture, local trail maintenance is an ongoing function and one that is well performed.

From the Diose, the trail begins to climb in pleasant switchbacks, crossing little mountain brooks that stream from the higher snowfields, and affording the walker a look back at the col d'Anterne crossed yesterday, and forward to the famous col de Brévent looming high above.

Some forty-five minutes of this gets you to the stone ruins of the Chalets d'Arlevé, a good spot for a break before the long climb to the col. This begins gently enough across a wide plain, then assumes a more earnest steepness—an ascent of about an hour or more to the snow-carpeted col.

Here, clear as crystal in good weather, is the storied postcard view of the great mountain opposite and all its chain: the aptly named Aiguilles (needles) d'Aigle, du Géant, and the landmark du Midi like a shining spire above Chamonix; the Grandes Jorasses, the Mer de Glace glacier that flows from their ridge, the famous Grand and Petit Dru. Even in sunshine clarity, the massif does not wear a hospitable face; in fog-clouds that soon obscured it from our view, it becomes downright inimical.

On the ice-and-rock col, GR5 joins with the trail of the Tour de Mont Blanc; it will continue to meet the TMB for the next three days. Now it slabs and scrambles its way over the north slope to Le Brévent and the téléphérique station. A snack bar here enables the walker to ponder the choice before him—walk or ride—over a cup of hot chocolate or coffee or the ever-reliable cold beer.

The téléphérique is itself an essential part of Mont Blanc lore. Built in an era when such constructions were the height of grandstanding engineering audacity (some people still feel that way, especially when they're inside the cable car and sense that their stomachs are outside), the téléphérique at Brévent is one of a network of cable railways around the Chamonix valley. These téléphériques enable nonmountaineers to ascend the Mont Blanc massif without moving a muscle. Indeed, one of the great tourist attractions of Chamonix is the traverse, by a series of téléphérique rides, of the Mont Blanc chain.

The Brévent-to-Chamonix run is in two stages: first to Plan Praz, then by *télécabine* down to Chamonix. Follow the street down from the station to the very center of town.

The walk to Chamonix from Brévent begins by following GR5, continuing over scree along the southwest arête of the ridge to the ruined Cantine de Bellachat. A trail heading left from here heads steeply down to the valley and the town—a walk of about two and a half hours.

Chamonix has long held a reputation as the world capital of mountain climbing and as a major center of year-round skiing. (Take the téléphérique up the Aiguille du Midi for summer skiing in the glacial combe of the Vallée Blanche.) Since 1965, it has also been famed for the 12-kilometer Mont Blanc tunnel, which puts Chamonix just 20 kilometers away from Italy's Courmayeur. This was, until 1978, the longest car tunnel in the world, but the completion in that year of Austria's Arlberg tunnel, at 14 kilometers, broke the record. The Mont Blanc tunnel, however, still holds the record for the highest "cover": cars pass under the Aiguille du Midi—at 2,480 meters, a substantial ceiling.

Construction of the tunnel began in 1959 at both sides of the massif, and when the teams met four years later at the center of the mountain's core, they were only 5.3 inches apart in axis. Dynamite was used to smash the last stone barrier to what one observer described as a "symbolic reunion of two great Latin peoples." Seventeen workmen were killed on the project.

The town of Chamonix has everything—and everything is crowded: restaurants, shops, discos, post office, tennis courts, train station, cafés, hotels. The streets will seem mob scenes to the walker whose idea of a crowd has been a group of school children hiking the same trail. The

New Yorker among us found the town "as crowded as an IRT subway platform at rush hour, but not as interesting, and not as congenial."

The lack of congeniality indeed struck us with some force after the hospitable welcomes we had grown accustomed to. It confirmed for us both Ginger's Law of the Inverse Relation of Pleasantness and Tourism, to wit, "The closer you come to an area frequented by tourists, the surlier people are."

There are few sights to see in Chamonix, apart from the surrounding mountains, a formidable sight indeed, but the GR5 walker will certainly be interested in the Musée Alpin, with fascinating exhibits of documents, photos, and equipment of early mountaineering. In the little square not far from the casino is a statue of De Saussure. It was erected by a group of mountain clubs from around the world, including, as U.S. contributor, The Appalachian Mountain Club of Boston.

For the rest, Chamonix offers everything the walker needs—gear, food, maps, fleshpots, English-language books, American newspapers and magazines.

We had the good fortune to arrive on the eve of the Assumption, a major holiday throughout France and particularly in Chamonix, where it is the date of the famous *fête des guides*. Among the activities routinely scheduled for the event are the laying of wreaths on monuments to Balmat and other guides who died in pursuit of mountainous heights; the "call of the guides to the church"; an exhibition of *escalade* (climbing); the blessing of the *piolets* (ice axes). Most of these events were held on the day of the fête itself, but the night before saw a street dance and a band concert enlivened by the presence of some ten *cors de chasseurs* (or *trompes de chasseurs*)—hunting horns. After the concert had officially ended, the horn players moved together and jammed a series of flourishes for aficionados.

In Chamonix, it is pronounced "chamoneexe."

Day 8: Chamonix to Les Contamines (ca. 20 km, 5 hr; without téléphérique, 28 km, 7 hr)

Today again offers the chance to climb a hill via téléphérique—a saving of about two hours of walking. This day's stage also brings the walker into what is surely one of the most beautiful valleys of the GR5 journey—the valley of Montjoie.

From the post office, head out of Chamonix along the main street toward Les Houches. You pass Les Gaillands, the famous practice cliffs for the climbing schools of Chamonix. Even on Assumption morning, the cliffs were already decorated with climbers of various skill levels in various positions.

Just beyond Les Gaillands, a sign directs you to the Promenade de la Rue Droite of the Arve, toward Les Bossons and Les Houches. This trail allows you to get off the road and walk above the big, fast river, white with glacial milk. Theoretically, the path stretches right into Les

Houches, but in the summer of 1984, we were forced back onto the road at Les Bossons. A sign on a barrier at that point claimed that the path from here forward had been rendered *impracticable* by an avalanche earlier in the year.

From what we could see of the area from the road, impracticable was a mild term. The hillside looked stripped, bald, as if a huge piece of adhesive tape had been ripped off the slope, pulling off trees, rocks, grass, everything underneath it.

At Les Houches, where you will again meet the GR5, you must decide whether to walk or ride to the col de Voza. Fortunately, Les Houches offers plenty of places where you can ponder the decision over refreshment.

The téléphérique ride in fact takes the walker to Bellevue. From here, a plainly marked, pleasant road leads over a wide plain to the col.

The walk up to Voza from Les Houches takes a left-turning road some 50 meters past the téléphérique station. This leads to the Schuss Battendier, considered one of the most difficult points along the downhill slope on which the 1960 world skiing championships were run.

From Schuss Battendier, GR5 continues past several sets of chalets, crosses a stream, then takes a steeply switchbacking trail through woods to the hotel at the col de Voza.

At the col, GR5 heads south, downhill along a wide road, past a number of squat, weathered wood buildings with slate shingle roofs that are characteristic of the area. The walker has entered the Beaufor-

Alpine chalet with lauzes *for a roof and a* tué *chimney. Photo by Ginger Harmon.*

tain region, where rock slide and scree are easier to come by than wood, and where it is easy enough to pile these *lauzes* (shingles) one on top of the other. But in the structures along the route from col de Voza, some creativity has been let loose; we saw many roofs on which flat-edged shingles alternated with round-edged shingles for a scalloped effect that is quite pretty.

The route leads into Bionnassay, a cluster of wooden chalets with a most agreeable gîte d'étape. Here the walker can find refeshment in the shadow of the Bionnassay glacier and the Dôme de Goûter on the Mont Blanc massif above. Then it is downhill to cross the Bionnassay torrent, up stiffly to a road, and turn right for Champel, another charming hamlet with another chance for refreshment.

GR5 drops down swiftly now to the valley—delightfully pastoral and tranquil after the sleekness and frenetic pace of Chamonix. At the two-trough fountain at the far end of La Villette, be sure to turn left, contouring among chalets to cross the torrent of Miage before coming back down the slope to Tresse. The route crosses the highway to the left bank of the Bon Nant River and passes along it through a series of little hamlets on various levels of the valley.

The walker will see Contamines clearly from the riverbank, although the GR5 does not actually enter it. Do what we did: head for it as best you can; this will probably require some road walking. Be aware that the center of Contamines is further along than you think, but it is a lively town, filled with ski shops, climbing shops, and elegant alimentation shops.

(Note: It is also possible to reach Contamines from the col de Voza along a high route, a TMB variant that goes over the col de Tricot and along the flank of Mont Blanc.)

Day 9: Les Contamines to Col de la Croix du Bonhomme (ca. 22 km, 5-½ hr)

For years, since first hearing the name *Col de la Croix du Bonhomme*, Ginger had been fascinated by the thought of the place. Why it exerted this fascination she could not say. Perhaps it was the almost poetic scansion of the phrase. Perhaps it was just a promise of exotic intrigue she heard in the sound, ranking it with names like Namche Bazar and Kilimanjaro for their power to capture the imagination. Col de la Croix du Bonhomme is the destination of today's stage of the walk across Europe.

But before you leave Contamines, stock up. Between here and Landry, two days hence, there is little or no provisioning available, although gîtes and refuges provide some meals.

The route out of Contamines stays on the right bank (east side) of the Nant. A gravel road along here, marked GR5, is also described as the *vieille route* (former highway); its place has been taken by a new highway on the other side of the river.

The trail stays flat to Notre Dame de la Gorge, a church that marks a major pilgrimage site, as the registry signatures of Lord Byron, Chateaubriand, and Victor Hugo attest. Here GR5 starts to climb, and so do the numerous TMBers, as we began to call the walkers of the Tour de Mont Blanc, heading for Italy. The chalet-hôtellerie du Nant-Borrant, at the top of a wide meadow, is a good place to stop for refreshment.

The trail crosses the torrent of Lancher and levels off across a wide *alpage*. At the end of the alpage, ringed by the high aiguilles of Penaz and the Roches Franches, is the Refuge de la Balme—a spectacular place for a lunch stop, as was evidenced, when we were there, by the crowds of TMBers sprawled on rocks and sitting at tables on the terrasse.

From the refuge, GR5 climbs, then levels off across an alpage, climbs again, flattens out to traverse a snowfield, and heads steeply up to the col du Bonhomme. A small hut sits atop this col. We were glad of it as harsh weather rolled in and we sought some protection from the wind, at least long enough to put on some more clothing. Apart from the hut there is nothing up here but a view—north to the long thread of the Montjoie valley, northeast to the massif of Tré-la-Tête, south to the valley of Chapieux and the hills of Beaufortain, southeast toward the Tarentaise.

The trail climbs again, following the contours of the slope that flanks the col, then crosses a torrent before arriving at the false col de la Croix du Bonhomme. The real col is half a kilometer further along, just beyond the refuge. No less an authority than Michelin made this mistake and set up a marker here after World War II; the mistake has proven a difficult habit to break.

Step forward and you cross from Haute-Savoie to Savoie. Head down to the refuge at the real col; this refuge, run by the Touring Club de France, is heavily frequented by TMBers and can be very lively. The night we were there, the dortoir for twenty-four held thirty-three people, but just as you wouldn't want to be turned away from a hut on these cold heights, you wouldn't want to see anyone else turned away either, so you learn to sleep in a crowd.

Day 10: Col de la Croix du Bonhomme to Chalet de la Balme (ca. 23 km, 5-¾ hr)

Bid farewell to the TMBers; they will be heading down the valley of Chapieux before turning east to loop around their mountain. GR5 will take you south up to the col de Bresson, on the high ridge overlooking the valley of the Isère in the Tarentaise region.

From the refuge, GR5 veers slightly southwest for the Crête des Gittes, winding back and forth from one flank of its knife-edge to the other, while wide panoramas stretch down the green and rocky slopes all around you. The trail drops down to col de la Sauce, which we traversed without noticing, then descends to some ruined chalets before debouching onto the road. Refreshment is available here at the refuge of Plan de la Lai.

A sign opposite proclaims the Roseland (!) dam area. GR5 turns into it, passes a couple of chalets, then turns sharply left across pasture, although the inclination is to go straight. The trail moves up steeply to the chalet of Petite-Berge, then follows a long contour above the dammed Roseland lake until it turns a corner to the Treicol Valley. The trail descends sharply here, then contours just above the scattered buildings of the tiny hamlet in this narrow valley. The slope here is quite steep, and numerous paths crisscross it, so be sure to stay fairly low on GR5.

Near the end of the valley, the trail starts to climb, going through the waterfall of Treicol and up the steep cliffs of the torrent of Treicol to reach high alpage and the derelict Chalet de Presset. A trail leads right, almost due south to the col du Coin, but GR5 turns left, up steeply in a southeasterly direction, climbing over rocky slope as a pastoral landscape unfolds below. It is an exciting climb, although a bit tricky to follow; as in many places in the Alps, numerous trails have been created and are interwoven. Try to stay with the main one, the one that seems biggest and clearest, and remember that the general direction is up.

Col de Bresson is a dramatic spot, with a beauty that differs from that of the scenery hitherto. Its aspect is dolomitic, with spiky, monster-shaped arêtes and aiguilles guarding the pass. The great monolith to the south (on your right as you achieve the col) is La Pierra Menta; further to the southwest is Mont Pourri in the Tarentaise. Just to the northeast (look left) is the dramatically situated Refuge de Presset, a refuge built by the Club Alpin Français in a spot sheltered from avalanches. The refuge is not staffed by a gardien, but there are sleeping and cooking facilities in it.

The way down from the col along the torrent of the Ormente is a walk of exceptional beauty. It is a rocky walk, and a slow one, as you move through what might be a great playground onto which the mountains above have gleefully hurled down pink boulders the way mere mortals toss pebbles—and left them there in disarray. Clear streams of meltwater giggle their way downhill too, and the whole gully seems to be laughing.

This splendid walk is capped by your arrival at the charming chalet-refuge de la Balme. The refuge has places for twenty-four, but there were only six people staying the night we were there—further evidence that we had left behind the crowds of the TMB. Two of the six were climbers planning to ascend the Pointe de Gargan to the north the next day; two were overnighters from the valley of the Isère; we were the only ones there that night who had started in Holland and were making for Nice. But we were not the only GR5ers the refuge had ever seen; a note from Robert awaited us there.

17
The Middle Alps: Mountain Valleys and Villages

Tarentaise, Vanoise, Maurienne. A mountainous massif, the Vanoise, bracketed by two valleys—this is the world of the Middle Alps.

The Isère River and the Arc River both rise in glaciers just east of the col d'Iseran, and both flow generally westward. The Isère, however, loops northward and progresses to the Rhone, while the Arc splits off in a southerly direction, then curves upward to fall, eventually, into the Isère itself at Miolans. The hunk of mountainous land these rivers encircle is the Vanoise massif, with 82 square kilometers of glaciers and numerous peaks above 3,500 meters. In the Vanoise is the highest col along GR5, col d'Iseran, at 2,770 meters.

Tarentaise is the name given to the valley of the Isère. This curving valley was once most famous for the cheeses created from the milk of the famous Tarine cows. Today, however, it owes its repute to "white oil," the hydroelectric power produced by its waters, and to skiing. Jean-Claude Killy put Val d'Isère on the sporting map; if these were the slopes *he* learned on, they must be pretty good.

For the megawalker, the dip down into the Isère valley is particularly significant; here, suddenly, is a distinct change in the air and vegetation. You notice it at once as you head downhill toward the river; in fact, this slope is called *le versant du soleil*, the hillside of the sun, and it produces an immediate—and somewhat false, or at least premature—impression of being *in* the South. It is here, too, that the walker first sees larch.

The National Park of the Vanoise was the first national park of France, created in 1963 for the express purpose of saving the ibex. The story is that, long before, on a royal hunt, Italy's "hunter-king," Victor Emmanuel II, personally saved the very last of this breed from complete extermination. To create a permanent refuge for this distinctly Alpine mountain goat, the Italian government in 1922 created a national park in the massif of Gran Paradiso, the Italian extension of the Vanoise. It took the French forty years to catch up with the idea, but the 53,000 hectares of the Vanoise are now secure from further exploitation, and Alpine flora and fauna here find protection. What is good for ibex, chamois, marmots, weasels, edelweiss, and the like is also good for hikers. The walk across the Vanoise is a gem, although some of the development that *has* been allowed to take place here throws into serious question the French talent for resources management and, harder to believe, French aesthetic standards.

GR5 follows a circuitous route across the Vanoise. From the Isère crossing, the trail marches southeast uphill to the gateway of the national park, then moves almost due south between the flank of Mont Pourri and the range of Bellecôte. At the col du Palet, however, GR5 makes a sharp left turn, heading eastward downhill to Tignes and Val d'Isère. It continues southeast as it climbs col d'Iseran, then dips straight south to the Arc valley before turning westward again to follow the river. In fact, in its walk along the Arc, GR5 makes another wild leap, this time north to loop deep gorges—a leaping loop our itinerary eschews in favor of the variant trail along the valley and through the villages of the Maurienne. GR5 thus curves around the eastern flank of the Vanoise massif, rather than striking due south across it. (Another Grande Randonnée, GR55, *does* cut over the massif; this is the *haute montagne* route that stretches from Tignes to Modane, crossing the 2,796-meter col de Chavière, the highest col crossed by any GR trail.)

The Maurienne, along the narrow valley of the Arc, is a world away from the Tarentaise. Though only about 35 kilometers apart, the two regions are separated by the mountainous hulk of the Vanoise and have thus remained isolated from one another—as well as from much of the rest of the world, at least until fairly recently.

In this dry, straitened valley, farmers were said to make hay till the last blade of grass was used, provisioning themselves for the long winter when each village in the narrow defile of the valley might be cut off from contact with its neighbor by deep snow. During those winters, the villagers huddled in their fortlike houses and set themselves to woodworking and other crafts, by which they adorned their churches and chapels and made protective talismans against the Devil. Moving westward along the valley, the walker will sense the potential for danger here, imagining the kind of destruction that might be wreaked by a winter avalanche in this narrow space.

In time, these villages—and a few resident families in particular—became known for their artisanship, and today the churches, sculptures, woodworking, and painting found here are seen, collectively, as a masterful example of early Baroque art in France.

To see these villages, and to make a change of pace, the walk across Europe detours along the GR5E variant, also known as the Sentier du Bonheur (path of happiness), to wander along the floor of the valley from village to village.

It is worth noting that the Middle Alps section of our walk—in the Graian Alps—is all within the department of Savoie. This region was late in becoming part of France—the last of the departments, in 1860. The area has long been known for the tough, sometimes abrasive personality of its people. It is a personality fashioned by the ruggedness of the terrain, the isolation of life here, and the haphazard and transient nature of contact with other people—armies on the march since Roman times (heading back and forth to Italy over the col du Mont Cenis); pilgrims relieved not to have killed themselves among the glaciers and summits along the route; and today hikers, tourists, skiers—people, for the most part, heading someplace else.

It is a walk of 216 kilometers in eight days—a couple of them very long, and one, at least, extremely short.

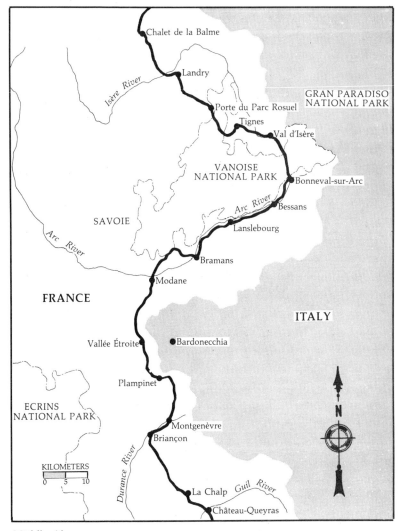

Middle Alps

Middle Alps

Day 1	Chalet de la Balme to Porte du Parc Rosuel	26 km	6-½ hr
Day 2	Porte du Parc Rosuel to Val d'Isère	32 km	8 hr
Day 3	Val d'Isère to Bonneval-sur-Arc	22 km	5-½ hr
Day 4	Bonneval-sur-Arc to Bramans	32 km	8 hr
Day 5	Bramans to Modane	27 km	6-¾ hr
Day 6	Modane to Vallée Étroite	28 km	7 hr
Day 7	Vallée Étroite to Plampinet	16 km	4 hr
Day 8	Plampinet to Briançon	33 km	8-¼ hr
		216 km	54 hr

Day 1: Chalet de la Balme to Porte du Parc Rosuel (ca. 26 km, 6-½ hr)

Like so much Alpine walking, today's stage proves the reverse of the law of gravity: what goes down must come up. The walker goes down to the Isère River, then straight up the massif to the gateway to Parc National Vanoise (PNV).

We were reluctant to leave the charming chalet de la Balme and the almost secret world under the col de Bresson. All six of us spent an inordinately long time gathering and packing gear. Susanna chatted with the two climbers and learned that after their climb this day they would be heading home.

"Where is home?" she asked.

"Samoëns."

"Samoëns?" The delight of recognition entered her voice. "We were there about—" she counted in her mind—"six days ago."

One of the climbers nodded. "And it will take us two hours to drive there," he said.

Moments like this can sometimes be disheartening to the walker.

From the chalet, GR5 proceeds down a jeep trail along the left bank of the Ormente. The valley opens a bit at the Chalets de Laval, where a troop of French scouts were hunting stones the day we passed by. Here GR5 moves up slightly over the flank of the hill along a pipe-ridden irrigation canal (it feeds the town of Valezan), then passes the picturesque Chalets des Fours—some of which were inhabited by vacationers. From here, the walker is treated to a wide-open view of the Isère valley, which, as you descend, grows longer and longer in your view.

Valezan is a steep and intriguing village; its houses climb the hillside, and its main street, which is GR5, follows the steepest possible line straight downhill. You can brake your forward motion at an épicerie off the trail, or at either (or both) of two gîtes d'étape. We chose the first one we came to—it advertised *boissons fraiches* (cold drinks)—and enjoyed casse-croûte on its sunny terrace, with a magnificent view over the valley to the climb awaiting us.

Boissons fraiches may prove particularly welcome because at this point the walker has clearly entered a different climate—the air is drier here, the foliage has gone to fruit trees and vines as well as the familiar cool conifers, and there is a dry crackle in the browning grass, which is noisy with crickets and thick with ankle-high butterflies. The occasional cool woods that break up the downhill walk across grass and through orchards to the river are a comfort on a sunny day.

The walk passes the tiny hamlets of Rocheray and Le Crey, where another refuge advertises boissons fraiches, and heads into Bellentre—plenty of boissons fraiches here, and other provisioning as well. Continue down toward the river to the bridge, cross it, and follow the left bank of the Isère into Landry.

It is a long and fairly steep climb through thick deciduous woods from Landry, crossing and slicing the D87 road that switchbacks uphill quite wildly. The trail crosses the Ponturin and follows along its course to the village of Le Moulin—a stone's throw from Peisey-Nancroix, with its numerous shops and lodgings. GR5 then recrosses the Ponturin, stretches past a long, heavily inhabited campground, and follows a forest road to Les Lanches, a cluster of chalets. Again the Ponturin is crossed, and yet again at the hamlet of Bettières. From here, the dis-

The Vanoise valley. Photo by Ginger Harmon.

tinctive roof of the Refuge de Rosuel becomes a welcome objective, which is soon reached.

There is method to the apparent madness of the refuge's waving sod roof: a snow slide can trundle right onto it and keep going, without destroying the building. The refuge itself is a well outfitted and busy place, although much of the crowd, having arrived by car for the day, will leave by nightfall. You cannot blame people for coming here in droves—the setting is so spectacular. Here you are on a high, wide plain of a high, wide valley of picturesque hamlets. Up-valley, where it narrows toward the ridge, you look across green fields to a waterfall, above which are snowfields, glaciers, jagged peaks. We were at dinner when an avalanche boomed off one of the peaks; the noise was fierce and echoed for a long while.

Day 2: Porte du Parc Rosuel to Val d'Isère (ca. 32 km, 8 hr)

Today's very long stage might serve as a rubric for the Grande Traversée des Alpes; it certainly provides a vivid example of the striking contrast between the protected environment of the national park and the encroachments of unplanned development.

GR5 winds uphill gently from the Refuge de Rosuel, along a trail clearly built and maintained for walking. Indeed, as we set off on the day's walk, we were part of a long line of hikers—most of them heading for the Lac de Plagne, the destination of a popular day-walk in the area.

The trail is still following the line of the Ponturin, moving between the great hulk of the Dôme de Platières across the valley and the tapered Aliet, whose flank GR5 here contours. This part of the walk edges a lovely forest of larch, but as the trail rises, views of the narrowing end of the valley continue to open, and the three stupendous cascades on the wall opposite are always visible.

Heading now up a field of slickly polished rocks, moving with the milling crowd and watching your feet as you step carefully, there is a good chance you might miss the split-off of GR5 from the Lac de Plagne trail. Be sure to keep to the left of the Ponturin stream (that is, on its right bank). Another reason the trail is easy to overlook is that the wooden PNV trail signs are nicely unobtrusive—environmentally sound, but beware you don't miss them altogether.

Forking left, GR5 crosses a bridge at a place called Les Pertes du Ponturin, then turns a bend to arrive at the Chalet du Berthoud, a hut for PNV rangers. Here the trail strikes out across a wide, flat meadow stretching along the Ponturin. The abandoned Chalets de la Plagne mark the end of this plain, and GR5 begins to climb, windingly, to reach a rock-bound height from which the blue Lac de Plagne is visible below, backed by high gravelly slopes.

On and upward from here, to yet another striking meadow, ringed by mountains limned with snow and carpeted with primula, gentian, yellow anemone, and globeflower—*boule d'or* in French. From this meadow, the walker needs to make one more push up to the sudden Lac de Grattaleu, then a quick nip to the refuge of the col du Palet. As everyone does, we stopped here for refreshment. Our route to this point had been along the best maintained trail we had yet seen in the Alps, excellently marked with GR5 balisage so clear it looked as if it had been formed with a template, and equally well marked with the tricolor that denotes the limits of the PNV. It had also been one of the most beautiful walks of our journey—a meander inside the mountains, into a place accessible only on foot, though some of the feet belong to cows and sheep.

From the refuge, the trail pops up to the col du Palet for a top-of-the-world view—high and wide in all directions. But as GR5 begins to descend, moving almost due east now, the view of the valley below becomes clearer, and it is not a pretty sight. What you see are denuded hillsides scarred by ski routes and service roads, burdened by clumsy lifts seeming to go every which way, cut with potholes where the sedimentary rock has slid downhill, while outsized man-made fences try to catch the man-made erosion. Finally, in the well of the valley, you see the towns of Tignes-le-Lac and Val Claret, hastily thrown-up highrise towns for the lodging, feeding, and entertainment of the year-round skiers on whose behalf these mountains have been raped.

It would be hard to describe this view as anything other than ugly, but in fact the striking juxtaposition between the Tignes valley and the one you left on the other side of the col makes it downright grotesque.

In the Hôtel du Refuge in the town of Tignes-le-Lac, a hotel run by a former mountain guide, the walker can see some documentation of the changes wrought to this valley. Two photographs hang on the wall. One, in black and white, shows the valley in 1928, when the refuge that became Hôtel du Refuge was the only building in the valley; the second photograph, in color and dated 1956, shows the first construction of the lackluster buildings that were to become this world-famous year-round resort. The former guide himself said that the valley used to be *beaucoup plus agréable*; however, he seemed to have no regrets about reaping a comfortable retirement income from the hotel's success.

GR5 hurries across Tignes, skirting the tennis courts to contour the hill, then climbing gradually away from the town to reach the plateau of Pas de la Tovière. The plateau is green and broad, dotted with stone chalets, but also strung with ski lifts on every surrounding slope.

Once across the plateau, GR5 heads down through woods to Val d'Isère. If it is less ugly than Tignes, it is nevertheless not particularly pretty, but its abundant lodgings and shops make it a welcome stop after this long and perplexing day.

Day 3: Val d'Isère to Bonneval-sur-Arc (ca. 22 km, 5-½ hr)

This stage takes you to the highest point along the GR5, col d'Iseran, into the region of Maurienne, and to its highest village, Bonneval-sur-Arc.

The day begins with a climb—what else is new? Find GR5 shortly after Val d'Isère's main intersection, on the right. It contours at first, paralleling the highway, then heads uphill steeply, quickly, relentlessly. At first, you are in cool larch forest. Then the trail heads across and up a field gorgeous with wildflowers. Down the slope, however, is the highway, and across it is another mountain denuded for skiing.

GR5 meets and crosses the meandering N202, then pushes on upward along the Iseran torrent among bleak hills, with a network of ski lifts overhead. The trail cuts the meanders of the highway heading to the col, then tops the col at last—a climb of some three hours from the valley.

The col (2,764 meters, 9,121 feet) is marked by a monument, a lot of cars and picture-taking tourists, and a busy restaurant-cum-gift shop. It was here that Susanna made her ill fated proclamation, "From here on, it's downhill to Nice."

No, but it *is* downhill quite steeply—almost perilously—into the high Maurienne region. The trail arives at the road near the snow bridge called, fittingly, Pont de la Neige. Then it fords, if possible, the swift feeder stream of the Lenta. It was not possible the day we were there— the stream was far too fast and high—so we were forced to walk the road for about half a kilometer before finding a red and white marker that brought us steeply down to the Lenta gorge. (Official GR5, after fording the stream, winds along the opposite bank of the Lenta, under the overhanging rock wall of the Ouille de la Jave, and crosses the torrent on a feeble wooden bridge. But the stream is impassable often enough that the alternative along the road is well marked.)

The trail winds delicately down to the left bank of the swiftly rushing Lenta, moves away from it toward the highway at a road-workers' hut, the *maison cantonnière de Pied-Montet*, then edges the riverbank again. Across the water are travel-poster chalets; one uses a conveniently situated huge boulder as a wall.

GR5 comes to the bridge, known simply as the "second bridge" in the valley of the Lenta. Here, where the highway makes an enormous curve, is the intersection of GR5 and GR5E—the variant to Bonneval and the walk through the Maurienne villages. Follow GR5E: stay on the Lenta's left bank, walking along the road as far as a turning marked with GR balisage; head downhill to Bonneval.

The highest village in the Maurienne at 1,835 meters (6,055 feet), Bonneval is also the most distinctive—and surely one of the most beautiful. It is distinctive because, since the Middle Ages, Bonneval has escaped both avalanche and war—even World War II, which hit other parts of the Arc valley quite hard. It thus presents to the visitor an appearance that has been caught in time. (The modern upper town is where you find most of the hotels, built to type quite tastefully.) Bonneval's old-quarter buildings are of stone, some with rough-hewn wooden balconies and struts, and covered by rust-colored slate roofs. Although cows are still herded through the narrow, auto-free streets (cars park outside the town), some of Bonneval's buildings have been gentrified behind their restored façades into shops and services—a café, a fromagerie, a gallery-gift shop—for the tourists who flock here.

So it was all the more surprising to us to learn that unique, attractive little Bonneval is threatened. The first inkling we had was a poster-cum-petition on a shop in the upper town: "Those who love this village as it is, help us to make all its inhabitants understand that it is in *danger*. Sign the petition."

During a conversation with some townspeople over a glass of wine— a good way to listen—we learned that the fight was over a decision by the mayor and some other *commune* leaders to link Bonneval to Val d'Isère by téléphérique and pick up some of the overflow resort action. It was interesting to us that the resistance to this move involved not just locals and tourists who cherished Bonneval (and its valley) for the history of the place, and not just conservationists, but a good many of the town's merchants and shopkeepers as well.

One knowledgeable source told us that France had no powerful, national conservation organizations—"no equivalent of the Sierra Club," he said—but pockets of activism were beginning to pop up in opposition to various government or development proposals: a group in Névache opposed to a new autoroute; an anti-power-plant organization further down the Arc; and so on.

After a pleasant afternoon and evening wandering through Bonneval, visiting its church (the steeple is typical of these villages—a stone-and-mortar dunce cap, with a dovecote hole in it and four wings at the corners), and availing ourselves of its fromagerie, we too began to feel a certain possessiveness toward it, and we could already anticipate the sense of loss we would know if it were turned into Val d'Isère or Tignes.

"Village for Sale!" another poster shouted. "Apply at the mayor's office." It went on: "Friends, our village today faces a bankruptcy which has been *contrived* for the express purpose of selling the village—irrevocably—to developers. If you want to help stave off the prostitution of this beautiful village . . . sign the petition of protest."

For Bonneval, a showpiece of French history and French montagnard life, there ought to be better ways to make a buck.

Something else about Bonneval: flies. We noticed many *mouches* here—quite a change from any place we had been through so far. Flies in great numbers—*too* great numbers—pester the villages all along the Arc Valley. Afterwards, although they return to a normal-sized population, they remain with the walker all the way to Nice.

Day 4: Bonneval-sur-Arc to Bramans (ca. 32 km, 8 hr)

The choice of the valley trail over the official GR5 is more than just a high-versus-low decision; rather, the choice of road affords the walker a unique look at a unique way of life. Official GR5 *does* stay high; it is called here the Sentier Balcon de la Maurienne, offering a mezzanine view of the valley as it re-enters PNV and serpentines at an altitude of some 2,000 meters. It is mountain walking to be sure, with long stretches between refuges, and a long loop around the Doron Gorge and under the Pointe de la Réchasse—mountain walking not unlike what the walker has been doing for some time and will do again. Peak-baggers in particular—col-baggers in this case—will regret missing it.

The GR5E valley route, Villages de Haute-Maurienne, takes the walker along the Arc, through old (and in some cases threatened) villages. This route will provide a still vivid picture of montagnard life in this narrow, difficult valley with its single pass, the col du Mont Cenis, leading to Italy, just on the other side of the ridge. There is much to see here, and there is plenty of provisioning along the way—and it *is* nice to walk low after two weeks of Alps.

Study the topo-guide maps and make your own route, as we did, staying on the right bank of the river (north of the highway) as far as Bessans, then crossing to the left bank. The 30-kilometer Sentier du Bonheur stretches along the Arc to Bramans, the end of the day's stage, but do not neglect going into the villages along the way: Villaron, Bessans, Lanslevillard, Lanslebourg, Termignon, Sollières, Le Verney, and Bramans. It makes for a long day; you *must* get an early start and you will be glad to have a guidebook like *Guide Michelin*, although most of the villages have tiny tourist offices where you can find local information.

From Bonneval, follow the course of the old road (beware of bees, as the signs warn you) past the deserted hamlet of Évasset, through pink crocuses and among rocks and boulders fallen from the steep slopes above. Cross a stream to arrive at the Rocher du Château, said to hold prehistoric paintings of deer. We searched as best we could, but saw only the detritus of rock climbs and a few graffiti; one was very legibly signed "Jérôme Séverin" and was dated 1939.

In among larch trees now, and across meadows and fields offering views of the cascades on the opposite side of the valley—to Villaron. Be sure to see its church, and find, if you can (you can), the handsome sculpted beam on the third house after the church. A pleasant gîte d'étape follows, where you might be able to find refreshment.

GR5E stays above the village, meets GR5, which has dropped down temporarily to the valley, then crosses a bridge over the Arc into Bessans. Despite having been destroyed in 1944—the town is mostly reconstructed—Bessans is the *chef-lieu* of the Haute-Maurienne villages, so you will want to take some time here.

Since the Renaissance, Bessans has been a major center of Alpine folk art, particularly of religious sculpture, whose apex was attained in the sixteenth century by the Clappier family. Also notable are the *diables de Bessans* (the devils of Bessans), one of which grimaces down at you from a pole in the square. Look beyond the devil to the close walls of the valley and the avalanche corridors that surround Bessans and you may better understand the town's historic preoccupation with protection from evil—and its well-known cynicism.

The story behind the original *diable* tells of a young man who sold his soul to the devil in exchange for supernatural powers. Toward the end of his life, a life filled with supernatural fun, he began to regret the bargain and applied to the Pope for pardon. This the Holy Father granted, on the grounds (there are always grounds) that the Bessanais assist at three masses in three towns widely distant from one another. The fellow managed the deed by using the last of his devil-gotten powers to show up in all three towns at once.

The main sights of Bessans are its church and chapel, and the Michelin people (and others) urge you to see the interiors of both. Here are the statues and paintings that have brought Bessans its fame. To enter, you must apply to the *curé*, who, on the day we were there, had left a note on the door saying that he had been obliged to be absent all day. We had to content ourselves with looking at the interesting remains of the paintings on the exterior wall of the chapel—the Vices, chained together, heading for the gaping mouth of hell, and followed by the Virtues.

In the cemetery beside the chapel, we saw something else of interest: the fresh grave of Jérôme Séverin, 1924–1984, the man who had painted his signature onto the Rocher de Château in 1939, at the age of fifteen.

Bessans has another reputation, which travellers to Paris might keep in mind. Since the valley has never been able to ensure a living for all of its inhabitants, emigration has long been a tradition. After the annexation of Savoie to France in 1860, most of the movement has been toward Paris, and particularly to Levallois-Perret, where the Bessanais have taken up taxi driving. So if you find yourself there after walking Europe from top to bottom, and if you should happen to take a taxi . . .

Just west of Bessans, GR5E crosses the Ribon torrent over Pont de Charriondaz, cuts over the highway, and heads up into forest, passing the chalets of Chantelouve d'en Bas, which offers superb valley views. Down from here to Lanslevillard, also destroyed by the Germans during World War II, and also containing a chapel, Saint-Sébastien, dating from 1446, well known for its interior murals—considered among the best in all of southeastern France. At Lanslevillard, the French-speaking walker will also come upon the curious usage of *l'adroit* and *l'envers* for the right-bank and left-bank sides of the town. In fact, these have turned into the names of actual hamlets, as the walker will note again at Sollières.

It is a quick walk from Lanslevillard to Lanslebourg, and you must cross the river to enter the town. Lanslebourg was almost entirely destroyed during World War II, except for the ancient church. The destruction is not surprising as Lanslebourg sits at the bottom of the col du Mont Cenis, a passageway to Italy. With trucks and cars still heading over the mountain via Lanslebourg, it continues to wear the aspect of a military frontier town. For the walker, however, it is an excellent provisioning stop—and a good place for lunch.

Recross the river to find a forest road and head for Termignon. Just above the town, the walker has a good view across it to the ancient communal field system lying below the Dent Parrachée. Caught in a looping meander of the Arc, Termignon is a jumble of thick stone houses. In its church, which seems planted on a rock, are four remarkable altarpieces, most dating from the seventeenth century. The main altar, fashioned between 1675 and 1678 by Claude Rey and his son, Jean, boasts of being the greatest in all of Savoie; art historians point out that the simple, almost folksy tranquillity of these sculptures differs markedly from the exuberant baroque style of Italian artists, just a few miles away over the hill.

From Termignon, stay on the river's left bank. In Sollières (l'Envers), there is an interesting archaeological exhibit devoted to the finds from the grotto of Balme. Here are numerous Bronze Age objects testifying to the mineral richness of the Maurienne from as long ago as 2,000 B.C.

Continue above the valley, past a small airfield, then past the settlement of Le Châtel. Be sure to head down into Le Verney to see the houses with their little bridges along the main street; this again meets GR5E to enter Bramans.

Bramans, whose gîte can accommodate fifty people, is something of a hiking center for all the many walks of the Arc Valley and the narrow side valleys which the walk across Europe—alas!—does not allow time for.

The gîte d'étape in Bramans sells tee-shirts featuring a portrait (sic!) of Hannibal. Col du Mont Cenis was once a candidate for the Carthaginians' route over the Alps, with the further claim that Hannibal came through the valley of the Arc and thus past what is now Bramans. Although there is general agreement today that the honors of Punic passage go to col de la Traversette further south, the Bramans locals are not about to give up so easily. Why should they? It is likely that we will never know for certain exactly where Hannibal made the crossing. Mark Twain's comment on the incertitude is apt. "The researches of antiquarians," Twain wrote, "have already thrown much darkness on this subject, and if they continue it is probable we shall soon know nothing at all."

However, since each col seems to have its day as the antiquarians' favorite, maybe Bramans should just hold out until its turn comes around again.

Day 5: Bramans to Modane
(ca. 27 km, 6-¾ hr)

You will notice it again today: dry-looking hillsides with scrubby, thorny vegetation and insects that keep hopping over your feet. You're getting there—that much is becoming clear. But there is still a long way to go, and a lot of climbing along the route.

From Bramans, head down to the N6 highway, turn left, then cross a bridge on the right—marked GR5—and start some of the climbing. A dirt road leads you to Aussois, yet another vacation center, which the walker enters through an archery range.

The day we arrived, our trail up to Aussois had been littered with broken pine cones, evidence that squirrels had begun laying in nuts for the winter. Now as we crossed through the town, we saw posters announcing end-of-season dances. It was after August 15, and these were two sure signs that summer, particularly the Alpine summer, was on the wane.

GR5 leads to the top of Aussois to the beautiful, minute chapel, then leaves the village along a ski *piste* (route of a ski run) beside the base lodge, just left of the tourism office.

Ça grimpe! A stiff upward march. But here we met a couple we dubbed the Cutest Pair seen thus far (they retained the title, as it turns out): two elderly Parisians, stalwart in their thick-soled shoes and carrying walking sticks and field glasses. He wore a hack's cap, and she sported a sturdy, wide-hemmed dress, sensible for walking. They were a delightful and very classy pair, full of admiration for us. And of course they wished us "Bon Courage."

We needed it. The way continues steeply upward toward the dam of Plan d'Aval. Just below the dam, the trail keeps to the left—it may be hard to find—then goes up and up in endless switchbacks to the desolate col du Barbier.

Desolate the walk continues to be, well above tree line, contouring the flank of the mountain, past ruined chalets like piles of flat stones, with the valley and its hydro works far below, and spikey mountains across it.

The trail begins to slope down through a cool forest strewn with gray, lichen-patched boulders. Down and down you go, then suddenly and fiercely the trail turns briefly up again to find the chalets of Orgère and, in the loop of the gully, the rather snazzy Porte du Parc refuge.

From here, there are two choices: GR5 follows and parallels the D108 highway to meet GR55; the two then head downhill to Modane together. Another trail, labeled *pente douce* on a wooden PNV sign, descends to the east of GR5 but meets it at the top of Modane at Loutraz. We chose this trail—actually, we did not *choose* it; we thought it *was* GR5—and if it was *pente douce*, we would hate to imagine *pente raide*. It is a steep descent.

Arriving at Loutraz, the trail crosses the river into the old quarter of Modane. From here, you will probably want to hoof along the highway to Modane-Gare, where there is a greater abundance of lodgings and shops. There is yet a third part to Modane, Fourneaux, from which you will depart on tomorrow's stage.

Modane is a busy industrial and transportation center, an international city because of its car and railroad tunnels into Italy, a customs port, and a military outpost. This makes it a lively place, full of shops where the walker can purchase maps, books, and food. It has a cosmopolitan air about it, a buzz of excitement that is not unwelcome after the Arc Valley walk with its sense of another era.

Day 6: Modane to Vallée Étroite (ca. 28 km, 7 hr)

A day of lunar landscapes, a spectacular hidden valley, and a walk into Italy—although you never set foot out of France.

Head to the far end of Fourneaux to find the railroad overpass leading left. The ensuing climb is steep and steady, more or less following a ski piste and revealing, now and again through gaps in the trees, ruined ski lift pylons.

You emerge to cross the Charmaix torrent and enter, if you need refreshment, the new development of Charmaix. In the summer of 1984, construction was proceeding on all fronts in this hoped-for ski resort of the Val Fréjus, and it struck us that Charmaix, without hotels in 1984, might be able to replace Modane as a night's stop before too long.

Signs for the GTA (Grande Traversée des Alpes) lead the walker up the valley of the torrent, over the Pont Traversier and the Pont de la Glaire, past ruined gun emplacements and military barracks. In the nineteenth century, the Modane portion of the Arc Valley was widely fortified by the king of Piémont-Sardaigne against possible French attack. Near Aussois, one of the forts has been renovated as a tourist attraction; the installations near Pont de la Glaire are part of that older fortification, but were also used in more recent wars.

The trail now contours past a pumping station to Chalets le Lavoir, switchbacks up, and contours again to the Chalets la Losa, locked tight. Still along the mountain's flank, but moving gently upward past stone piles (former chalets), GR5 climbs the col de la Vallée Étroite, once the border between France and Italy. Bear left just before the top; the right fork leads to the Refuge de Mont Thabor across the wide combe, and you can see walkers proceeding to and from this popular hiking destination on both sides of the basin.

GR5 starts down from the col. We had met a storm on the way up, but now the weather cleared as we entered a plain described by the topo-guide as *largement ouvert* between the summit of La Planette and the rock of Cheval Blanc. *Largement ouvert* indeed. The clanging of bells alerted us to the cows we soon saw grazing in the meadow. The torrent rushed along. Wisps of cloud hung in the spikey, jagged peaks atop ruggedly rocky slopes striated russet, brown, and gray. Cross the torrent after the first sharp descent; you are on spongy plain now, with splendid views of the lush valley opening before you.

Down the slope, GR5 crosses the torrent of the valley at Pont de la Fonderie, then takes a dirt road. It is, however, a motorable road, busy the day we were there with cars with Italian license plates. Groups of Italian-speaking day-trippers walking up the road greeted us with "Buon Giorno." Susanna finally asked, in French, "Are we in Italy or France?"

"France," came the answer—in Italian.

There are a few refuges clustered together near the granges of the Vallée Étroite; we stayed at the one run by the Club Alpino Italiano, which was happy to recognize our American Alpine Club affiliation in the form of a discount. The sign on the refuge called it the Rifugio della Valle Stretta, and for dinner we had roast veal flavored with wine and rosemary, peppers roasted in olive oil, and polenta. After dinner, we had jet-black Italian coffee.

The road we had walked on to the refuge leads on into Bardonecchia, only about 12 kilometers away. Everyone in the refuge—the staff and the few overnighters—was Italian, except us, and Susanna had a little trouble keeping her French and Italian quite separate. We paid for the night's meal and lodging in French francs, but to this day we swear we were in Italy.

Day 7: Vallée Étroite to Plampinet (ca. 16 km, 4 hr)

This is necessarily a very short day, so relax over a leisurely breakfast and drink as much Italian coffee as you like.

From the gully behind the refuge, GR5 turns left into the forest, climbing easily up gentle switchbacks, each turn of which offers a new view down over the valley. The trail emerges from woods to cross the Combe la Mille, with more wonderful views south and east.

Past a ruined grange, up over a lip of the ridge, the trail leads gently down to the small lake of Thures (also called Chavillon). This is a wide alpage, with a broad breast of slope to the west, seemingly carpeted, the day we passed through, with a large flock of scurrying, bleating sheep.

The col des Thures is marked by a wooden sign and a board inscribed with a prayer of Saint Francis beginning "Altissimu deo . . . " We decided it was either very early Italian or very late Latin or a mixture of the two.

Along the right bank of the Thures stream, GR5 proceeds to the Chalets des Thures and to the marked fork of GR5B and GR5. The former is a variant that loops around the massif over the Bardonnecchia valley to meet GR5 on the ridge above Plampinet. Fork right for the GR5 and head down through a resinous forest filled with strange formations of yellow rock. The area is badly eroded; the torrent of Robiou has carried off much of the hillside, leaving red sedimentary earth in great gashes.

GR5 crosses the Robiou at a small forestry cabin on a wooden bridge and proceeds along a forest road to the resort settlement of Chapelle des Ames. Provisioning and refreshment are possible here, and the construction of more facilities was underway in 1984.

GR5 follows the N94 briefly, then turns right onto a dirt road to cross the Robiou—again—and the Clarée. The rather pleasant walk that follows parallels the Clarée and the N94, then meets both again at Plampinet.

The walker can enjoy a good, and probably much-needed, rest in Plampinet. It is quaintly picturesque, and a walk around it takes no more than five minutes. Be sure to see the sixteenth-century church with lovely frescoes and wooden appointments painted to look like marble. Ask at the gîte about touring the church.

Since crossing the col de la Vallée Étroite, the walker has been in the Briançonnais region, a country known, as Vauban described it, for "mountains which touch the high clouds and valleys which descend to the abyss." In fact, these valleys—Guisane, Clarée (where Plampinet sits), Vallée Étroite, Cerveyrette, and Durance—all converge in the center of the Briançonnais, more or less at Briançon itself. This has made the region, and particularly the city, a great crossroads of the Alps. This, plus a fairly benign climate influenced by Mediterranean sun, have meant that the region has always known prosperity and a certain cosmopolitan sophistication. Commerce has been a standby here for centuries, not a substitute for agriculture, and when the region's lively textile industry was closed in 1933, the Briançonnais took up tourism with enthusiasm and no small measure of success.

Day 8: Plampinet to Briançon (ca. 33 km, 8-¼ hr)

Looking at the map the morning we began this stage, Ginger wondered aloud and complainingly why GR5 insisted on taking us up over two cols to land us just a few kilometers along the valley of the Clarée River, in Briançon. The answer came as the day progressed, a spectacular day of high, high walking—but a strenuous day, and a long one, requiring an early start.

The first climb out of Plampinet is gentle enough, taking the walker along the former military road that lines the torrent of Acles, which pours noisily down its narrow gorge. GR5 crosses the Acles at a meadow where a cluster of chalets sits, forking to the right and crossing almost immediately the Opon stream, whose ravine the trail now climbs.

The top of the ravine debouches into meadow, then into a wide well formed by surrounding scree slopes, which GR5 crosses to climb the col de Dormillouse. At the col, the walker can see—seemingly forever—over the well beneath the Crête de la Lauze and to the trail ahead. It was at this point that Ginger forgave the trail designers.

GR5 scurries around the shoulder of the crête to climb the col de la Lauze, hidden from view around a corner until you're almost atop it. The view from here is of a wide, wooded, rock-bedecked, rolling meadow, which the GR5 now descends, meeting the N94 into Montgenèvre.

The armies of Caesar, Charlemagne, and Napoleon—among others—passed this way, and it was Napoleon who built the road the N94 has replaced. Montgenèvre is therefore a good place for the megawalker to stop for refreshment and contemplation of the many illustrious footsteps he follows.

The refreshment will serve the walker well. It is a long way downhill to the Durance valley and Briançon. GR5 stays above the highway, in the woods, emerging to meet the village of La Vachette in the valley. From here, it turns back into the trees to follow a canal bed, then cuts across the top of the hamlet of Envers-du-Fontenil. Bear right, still above the Durance, to contour the valley.

The entrance into town is a dramatic once. At 1,321 meters (4,360 feet), Briançon claims to be the highest real city in Europe (the resort of Davos, Switzerland beats it by about 236 meters), and the first view of this rock-top place is striking, taking in the massive ramparts of Vauban with the statue of La France and the citadel rising above the walls. As if the view itself weren't enough, GR5 enters the town across the famous Pont d'Asfeld, a stone bridge built in 1754, arching its way across the Durance at a height of 56 meters.

You will want to walk your way through the high city, especially along the Grande Rue (or Grande Gargouille) with its ancient houses, shops, fountains, cafés, and the water gutters down the middle of the street. A tour among the winding streets, past the citadel, and along the wide ramparts with their fabulous views takes as much time as you want to give it. You can then walk down to the new town outside the walls, where hotels and all modern conveniences are readily available.

18
The South Alps: Home to the Mediterranean

It is probably at this point in the megawalker's journey across Europe that he begins to feel some sense of the excitement of arrival. Nice is only eleven days away; after three months on the trail, that does not seem like very much.

In fact, however, there is a good deal of walking ahead, including some of the most ruggedly beautiful and some of the highest. The second and third highest cols along GR5—after col d'Iseran—are still to be achieved. The walker must traverse three groups of Alps (and three departments of the same names): the aptly labeled High Alps (the department of Hautes-Alpes is the only department of France which is entirely in the mountains), the Alps of Haute-Provence, and the Maritime Alps. He will dip down into, cross, and climb back up from several major river valleys: the Guil, the Ubaye, the Ubayette, and the Tinée.

The sense of being in high mountains does not really lessen until the last days of these eleven. And the somewhat lower crests and ridges of the final days still require frequent nips up and down; there truly is no such thing as "downhill to Nice" until the very last walk from the city's park down through its streets.

Still, you *are* getting there. One step at a time.

The GR5 of the South Alps heads in a more or less southeasterly direction, although there are glitches in its course, as always.

The valley of the Ayes torrent, which GR5 climbs on leaving Briançon, is the gateway to the Queyras region, an area known for the wealth of its Alpine flora.

At col Girardin, second highest on GR5, the walker leaves the Hautes-Alpes for the Alpes de Haute-Provence and enters the high valley of the Ubaye River. This the GR5 crosses on the extraordinary bridge of Châtelet before ascending among needlelike crags toward the valley of the Ubayette and the col de Larche.

Along the little valley of Lauzanier, GR5 climbs to Pas de la Cavale, third highest col of the journey. This is the entry into the last group of Alps, Alpes Maritimes, and it is the portal into the Tinée Valley.

GR5 follows the Tinée Valley, then crosses it eastward toward the valley of the Vésubie, eventually dipping into the gorge of the Vésubie and crossing it. (Both the Tinée and the Vésubie merge with the Var and flow with it into the Mediterranean.) Once the Vésubie is crossed, the walker is in among the hills behind Nice; from here, it is *almost—* but not quite—downhill to Nice.

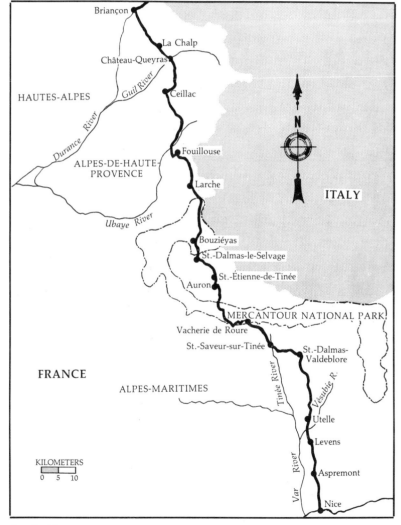

South Alps

South Alps

Day 1	Detour from Briançon to Sachas	2 km	½ hr
	Sachas to La Chalp	23 km	5-¾ hr
		25 km	6-¼ hr
Day 2	La Chalp to Ceillac	30 km	7-½ hr
Day 3	Ceillac to Fouillouse	27 km	6-¾ hr
Day 4	Fouillouse to Larche	21 km	5-¼ hr
Day 5	Larche to Bouziéyas	25 km	6-¼ hr
Day 6	Bouziéyas to Auron	26 km	6-½ hr
Day 7	Auron to Vacherie de Roure	34 km	8-½ hr
Day 8	Vacherie de Roure to Saint-Dalmas-de-Valdeblore	31 km	7-¾ hr
Day 9	Saint-Dalmas-de-Valdeblore to Utelle	33 km	8-¼ hr
Day 10	Utelle to Aspremont	26 km	6-½ hr
Day 11	Aspremont to Nice	12 km	3 hr
		290 km	72-½ hr

These are eleven days of rigorous walking, except for the last stretch to the sea. The further south you go, the more the rock and scree underfoot tend to be crumbly. The high villages wear a hardy and almost primitive look. The buildings, made of piled stones or slate, have a jagged, irregular appearance. This region was once the heart of the *transhumance*, when herds of sheep—twenty to thirty thousand strong— were brought up here to summer pasture, on foot, in journeys that might last several weeks. The herds are still transported here each summer, but now they come by truck or train. The only remnant of the transhumance is the faint trace of *drailles*, the tracks they once used to get here.

GR5 walks through two major parklands of France in the South Alps. Right on Day 1, the walker steps across the col des Ayes and into territory of the Parc Naturel Regional du Queyras. Created in January, 1977, the park covers some 600 square kilometers and embraces eleven communities—towns and villages and their outskirts—perched at an average altitude of 1,650 meters (5,445 feet). The park is aimed at preserving both the way of life of these high mountain places and the flora and fauna of the region. The Queyras is a flower lover's paradise, and particularly in June and July, the GR58 (Tour du Queyras) swarms with slow-moving hikers trying to take in all they can of what is said to be a unique experience—the blossoming of wildflowers in Queyrassien variety and profusion.

The other park of the South Alps is the Parc National du Mercantour. This park was established in 1979 to protect the area's flora and fauna, in particular some forty plant species and one hundred insect species said to be found nowhere else in the world. The park's incredibly odd shape, accommodating both the naturalists' demands and local objections to this nationalization of turf, causes the GR5 to pass into and out of the Mercantour on two separate occasions.

There are many firsts as you come to the end of this eleven-day section of walking. The first view of an olive tree. The first pink Mediterranean villa. The first awareness of the white Mediterranean sunlight.

Along with the firsts there are also some lasts. The last chalets. The last Alpine meadows. The last climb.

Our itinerary saves the last climb for the last day's walk—a short three hours that take the walker to Nice in time for lunch. The last climb is not much of an ascent; it is more important for the sentiment the walker brings to it and the achievement it represents. But it may serve as a reminder that, as the walker arrives at the end of his journey, the Alps are just beginning theirs.

Day 1: Briançon to La Chalp
(ca. 25 km, 6-¼ hr)

Eschew GR5 in leaving Briançon; it contrives a harsh loop to avoid city outskirts but only partially succeeds and thus is not worth the time spent in the attempt. Instead, follow the road to meet GR5 at Sachas.

The high-meadow village of Chalets des Ayes, once home to shepherds, now housing summer vacationers. Photo by Susanna Margolis.

It moves along the road to Soubeyran, then starts uphill along the torrent of Ayes, which runs hard down a dishevelled gorge between fiercely rocky narrow walls.

Chalets des Ayes is an agglomeration of stone-and-timber chalets that have been turned into summer vacation homes. We asked to refill our water bottles at one and were taken to the place where the vacationers fill theirs: a pipe in a side stream.

From here, ça grimpe! GR5 leads up through woods delicious with a minty smell, then debouches onto rock-strewn alpage to cross the Ayes on a wooden bridge and take up a dirt road—once a *draille*—to the Chalets de Vers le Col. On the far hillside of Pic des Chalanches, cows graze, while behind you is the long, grand view of the gorge tumbling down to the plain below.

The trail climbs relentlessly to the col des Ayes, which marks the passage from the Briançonnais region to that of Queyras and into the Parc Naturel Régional du Queyras. A trail forks right from here, but GR5 forks left, descending along the spongy well of meadow to Chalets d'Eychaillon.

The route turns left along road and trail into Brunissard, where the ski lift station may offer refreshment, and on into La Chalp.

This town has made itself into something of a center of Queyras crafts, mostly woodworking, a skill the inhabitants of the region have had plenty of opportunity to perfect. The Queyras has historically been one of the most isolated regions of France, so much so that it became well known as a refuge and hiding place for people on the lam: the chances of a particular oppressor or tax collector or cop bothering to come in here after a fugitive were slim.

The Queyras is the basin of the Guil River and the torrents that sweep down to it, all mingling to flow into the Durance. The western portion of the Queyras, where La Chalp is, is rich in dolomite; the eastern portion sits on schist. Links to Italy on the east and to the rest of France on the west are across high, difficult passes, most of which are barred by snow and ice for all but a few months of the year. The climate of Queyras is described by locals as "seven months of winter, five months of hell."

But within this isolated region are beautiful mountains, numerous waterways, forests of pine and larch, and wild flowers that in spring bring botanists and flower fanciers here from all over the world.

The effect of the geographical isolation, however, has been to create an independent people who have concentrated on rural self-sufficiency. At least until the Revolution, the Queyrassins gave little attention to whatever government was in charge, rarely paid taxes, and did not comply with demands for military recruits. Numbers of Queyrassins emigrated, at least seasonally, although the most famous émigrés were those who went to South America and returned home rich to build large villas. These prodigal sons are called "les Américains."

The houses here are distinctive: humans and beasts live together on the ground floor, walled by stone; above are wooden haylofts, often with balconies. Huddled within these houses, warmed by the high snow without, the beasts within, and the hay insulation above, the Queyrassins work on the wood carvings and other montagnard crafts now for sale in the shops of La Chalp.

Day 2: La Chalp to Ceillac
(ca. 30 km, 7-½ hr)

Start the day with a detour along the D902 to Arvieux, simply because it is a charming village, with a delightful store full of hiking provisions, and with a sixteenth century church whose façade includes fragments from even earlier eras. The church's dunce-cap steeple, typical of the region, is distinguished by two courses of elegant arched openings instead of the usual single hole.

To rejoin GR5, follow the D502 just opposite the church for a kilometer and a half, and for a climb of some 100 meters. Shortly after you attain the GR5, it passes through the hamlet of Les Maisons, then climbs eastward to the trail junction with GR58, Tour du Queyras. On through forest, past the artificial lake of Roue, GR5 begins its descent toward Château-Queyras, the extraordinary fortress town restored by Vauban in 1700. The homes and shops of Château-Queyras spill down from the fort, but it is the site above all that is the splendor of the place.

Heading south from the town, GR5 crosses the Guil and starts uphill along the right bank of the Bramousse torrent. It is a long climb up to the height of land—nearly 950 meters—through woods and wide meadows that offer views of the surrounding rock crests. At what seems the wide summit, GR5 crosses to the left bank of the Bramousse, debouches into spongy meadow, then heads uphill over the lip of the ridge. Once over the lip, GR5 snakes along the flank—a badly eroded side of mountain—onto a slope swarming with marmots. If you sneak along quietly, you may surprise a few before they scurry up the rocky hill, squeaking madly the whole way. Across the Bramousse gully is the thin, dusty line that is GR58, snaking along *its* flank of ridge. GR5 and GR58 meet at col Fromage, from the top of which you look down into the cramped well where the chalets of Villard sit.

The two trails move together down the slope to Villard, where a variant of GR58 comes in from Saint-Véran. GR5 now goes swiftly downhill into Ceillac, at the confluence of the Cristillan and the torrent of the Mélezet. The town is intriguing with its buildings of reddish-brown, rough-cut timber, and the church belfry is particularly notable. Ceillac is mostly a winter ski resort and summer tourist provisioning point; indeed, it is essential to stock up here as there is no further provisioning until Larche, two days away.

There is a gîte in the center of town, hotels above the town (back toward where you came in), and more lodgings 2 kilometers further along GR5—and the D60—at Pied du Mélezet, which is, as its name implies, the foot of the Mélezet torrent.

Day 3: Ceillac to Fouillouse
(ca. 27 km, 6-¾ hr)

This day's stage is marked by a fair amount of steep climbing, including the ascent to col Girardin, second highest on GR5. At the col, the walker passes from the department of Hautes-Alpes into the department of Alpes-de-Haute-Provence and enters the valley of the Ubaye.

After leaving Ceillac, GR5 crosses the Mélezet torrent and starts uphill along the Cascade de la Pisse. (Yes, that's exactly what it means.) It is a sharp, steep climb, composed of very short switchbacks, some of which are bolstered by railings, others of which should be. The trail itself is a water course and has eroded badly. It first moves away from the cascade, then toward it; suddenly, the sound of falling water is very loud, and you are there, climbing alongside the torrent to debouch into the meadow that holds the lake of Prés-Sébeyrand (or Lac Miroir).

Above the lake are the Pointe de la Saume and the jagged gray barrier of the Crête des Veyres. The meadow is majestic, isolated; the sound of high, rushing torrents surrounds the silence.

The route edges the lake and passes the bergeries of the Preynasses; there were no sheep in the sheep pens the day we passed through, but there certainly was evidence of sheep. GR5 pops up over a lip of ridge to overlook a deep well below and the Crête de la Cube opposite. It tracks a ski piste briefly, then follows the slope above the valley of the Adoux before arriving at the lake and chapel of Sainte-Anne. Every

Lac des Prés-Sébeyrand (Lac Miroir) at 2287 meters, near Col Girardin.
Photo by Ginger Harmon.

year, on July 26, the inhabitants of Ceillac and Maurin make a pilgrimage to the chapel, wearing traditional costume. Building the chapel was something of a journey of penance as well; the local people hauled sacks of building materials up to the site on their backs.

The turquoise lake the chapel adorns lies beneath the snow-limned cirque comprising Pic Heuvières, Pics de la Font Sancte, and Tête de la Petite Part. GR5 now strides along at the foot of each of these heights in turn, making for col Girardin. The walker can see the col, rising in the distance, throughout the approach. Then it's up a scree slope

Pont du Châtelet, one of the most famous sights of the Ubaye region. Photo by Ginger Harmon.

streaked by trails. Which one of these might be the *real* GR5 is anybody's guess, but as usual, the general direction is up.

Col Girardin was another candidate for Hannibal's crossing. Its 2,700-meter (8,910-foot) top is actually a wide notch between the Tête de Girardin to the east and the Tête de la Petite Part and Pics de la Font Sancte to the west—with views northwest to the massif of Pelvoux and northeast to the needle of Chambeyron.

The trail cuts downhill southeasterly, finding and following the torrent of the Séchoirs to turn southwest and emerge on the road. This valley, called Maurin, is the source of the Ubaye; the rocks that have been swept downstream from here are said to have given the river its distinctive green color.

GR5 turns right on the road and follows it, through the hamlet of La Barge, past the place called Pont Voûté (it means "arched bridge," but in fact it is a natural formation, not to be confused with the Pont du Châtelet coming up). The route goes on past the chapel of Saint-Antoine, across the valley of Châtelet and around the Châtelet rock which bars the valley, to the road junction.

Here GR5 turns left to cross the Pont du Châtelet, an arched stone bridge extending nearly 100 meters across the gorge. The bridge is one of the most famous sites in the region, a signature landmark of the Ubaye.

Once across the bridge, it is a walk of less than an hour uphill to Fouillouse. This beautifully situated village is something of a hiking center, for it gives rise to both the GR6, Alpes-Océan, and the GR56, Tour de l'Ubaye. The town sits at the gateway to a high, desolate cirque over which the Brec de Chambeyron seems to hold sway.

Day 4: Fouillouse to Larche
(ca. 21 km, 5-¼ hr)

A short day; there won't be a shorter one in the South Alps till the last day of all. The route is so beautiful, you will be glad to be able to enjoy it at your leisure.

From Fouillouse's landmark chapel, GR5 climbs the valley in a southeasterly direction. On a sparkling morning in late August, our valley walk had about it the aura of creation, so fresh and new did everything seem. We saw no other hikers, just sheep and a shepherd. The sunlight, breaking over the Brec Chambeyron's long ridge, illuminated shafts of motes and turned the ripples on the stream of Fouillouse into diamondlike facets.

Up this valley, then through larch forest with soft *sous-bois* underfoot, until the trail debouches into rocky open meadow to hug the torrent, following the curves and rises of rocky slopes—the ridge of Rocher de Saint-Ours to the west, Tête de Plate Lombarde to the east. Past the ruins of the fort of Plate Lombarde, GR5 crosses two small brooks before moving out of larch onto open plain at the foot of the slope.

The route climbs to the col du Vallonnet, at 2,524 meters (8,329 feet). The col is in the shadow of the massive Rocca Blanca to the northwest; a small col in the ridge to the southwest is just called *col sans nom*—nameless col.

From the col du Vallonet, GR5 starts south, then winds southwest across rocky, messy trail as it contours the majestic impediment of the Meyna massif to the ruined fortifications just below the col de Mallormet. The debris of telephone poles and rusted curls of wire meets the walker as he achieves the col.

GR5 winds steeply down into Larche, on the confluence of the Ubayette River and the torrent of Rouchouse.

The town, destroyed by the German forces in 1944, was entirely rebuilt after the war. Bunkers on the hill nearby attest to the former fighting here. Larche is now a customs control station for Italy, which is just down the road. Trucks piled with hay come to a grinding halt and line up for hours while the customs officers—and everybody else in Larche—go to lunch.

Day 5: Larche to Bouziéyas
(ca. 25 km, 6-¼ hr)

The third highest col of the GR5 is achieved today—Pas de la Cavale, at 2,671 meters (8,814 feet). Step across it and you pass from the department of Alpes-de-Haute-Provence into the department of Alpes-Maritimes. From here, except for the intervening mountains, it's downhill to Nice.

GR5 leaves Larche along a narrow country road that follows the Ubayette, crossing to its left bank before turning off south to Pont Rouge. This is the entrance to the Parc National Mercantour and the gateway to the beautiful valley of Lauzanier which, with the valley of Parassac to the west, is a réserve naturelle. The trail passes between the Montagne du Prayer to the east and the Crête de l'Alpette and Crête des Eyssalps to the west. Numerous sheep huts are passed—they are called *cabanes* in this region—and numerous sheep as well. The day we passed through, there were donkeys at Cabane Donadieu, nearly at the top of the valley. We were suddenly aware that we hadn't seen a cow for days. But there were plenty of marmots, and their squeaking mixed pleasantly with the whoosh of the cascades tumbling down the shadowed slopes eastward across the valley.

The trail climbs gently, although the torrent grows more furious, until the walker finds a sudden silence at the Lac du Lauzanier. The day we were there, the sudden silence was just as suddenly broken by the bell of a goat among the sheep of a distant herd.

GR5 climbs on, deeper into the glacial leavings of rocks and folded and bent boulder-hills to the Lac de Derrière la Croix. The lake sits in what seems a walled basin cut off from the world, but the walker can see the winding trail—looking steeper than it will prove to be—leading to the notch of Pas de la Cavale between the sheer têtes up ahead.

The trail climbs. Zigging and zagging upward, the walker will see more small lakes below—that is, if he takes his eyes from the scree underfoot, the negotiating of which requires a good deal of attention. We were delighted to meet two Dutch hikers coming down as we ascended, particularly when we learned they were from Maastricht. With compliments flying—us to them on their home town, them to us on what people were now beginning to call our "achievement"—we pushed on to the col.

The col notches a ridge called the Crête de la Tour and is framed by rugged-looking crags—the rock of Trois-Évêques (the three bishops) to the east, and the rock called Trois-Évêchés (the three bishops' sees) to the west. Around the corner of Trois-Évêques lies Italy, while straight ahead to the south, only 60 kilometers along the shortest-distance straight line, is Nice.

Head for it, but do so slowly; the descent down the southern slope of Pas de la Cavale is extremely steep, eroded, and slippery underfoot. The difficult downward progress lets up at a plateau-like meadow just above Lacs d'Agnel, then leads gently downward to the Combe de la Gypière. In the dead center of this flat bowl stands a trail sign marking a four-way intersection; turn right. On the ground near the sign we saw a greeting spelled out in stones: "Bienvenu à Robert." We followed the trail to the granges of Salse Morène where Susanna knocked on a cabin door. An old man opened, and Susanna asked two questions: was there drinking water nearby, and what was the meaning of the welcome sign? The answers were that there was water just ahead and that some people from Nice had come over col des Fourches, just ahead on GR5, to meet some friend of theirs named Robert. We were pretty certain it was our Robert.

GR5 crosses the gully of the Tour stream—the *eau potable*, according to our informant—then climbs the col des Fourches, at 2,262 meters (7,464 feet). Then downward, cutting the meanders of the CD64, to Bouziéyas. The gîte d'étape here is bring-and-cook-your-own as far as meals are concerned; there is also a hotel with a restaurant in the town.

Day 6: Bouziéyas to Auron (ca. 26 km, 6-½ hr)

This is a day of mountain villages; of lizards, lavender, and brittle, pumicelike stone; of the first real forest in a long time. In short, it is a day that gives the walker the true feel of southern latitudes.

Bouziéyas clings to one side of a V-shaped valley; leaving the town, GR5 crosses the stream and climbs gradually along the opposite side up to the sheep-ridden col de la Columbière, at 2,237 meters (7,382 feet). A long, downhill walk along a pleasant valley leads to Saint-Dalmas-le-Selvage, an intensely picturesque mountain town on the confluence of the Sestrière and Jalorgues streams. The picturesqueness lies in the wildness of the setting, the clustering of the gray stone houses and buildings, and the Romanesque church with its handsome bell tower. The church, despite its architectural style, was built in the seventeenth century. Inside are a sixteenth-century triptych and several paintings.

At the church, GR5 crosses the Jalorgues and climbs gently up a dirt road through a lush growth of forêt domaniale trees to the little col d'Annelle; at a mere 1,739 meters (5,739 feet), this seems like nothing at all, but do not despair—there are higher cols to come in the days ahead.

As GR5 moves on from the col, the walker really drinks deeply from "a beaker full of the warm South." Here are lizards and grasshoppers vying with hiking boots for room on the trail, and hillsides of oak as well as pine, and the scent of lavender, and the dry, parched earth seeded with crumbly stone. Habitation clings to the hillside as well— not just ruined alpine chalets, but also tree-shaded houses on terraced plateaus, with gardens and vine-covered arbors for shade. For someone who has marched from Hoek van Holland, it may be difficult to use the term "villas," but surely that is what these are—suburban villas of Saint-Étienne-de-Tinée.

Saint-Étienne itself is pink and ochre. Some of its houses wear painted decorative motifs, and many have pastel painted shutters and red tile roofs. You are really in Provence now—the Côte d'Azur—and if you still do not believe it, stop for lunch in Saint-Étienne. Whatever you order, it will be soaked in olive oil.

GR5 leaves town on the CD39, and then along it before making a right turn to enter deep forest, pop up over the hill, and descend to Auron.

This is the main ski resort of the Maritime Alps, both winter and summer, and it has the hotels, restaurants, nightspots, movie theater (!), and contrived chalet architecture to prove it. Despite this, Auron has a history, or at least a legend. According to it, Saint Aurigius, bishop of Gap, was en route home from Rome when he was threatened by highwaymen. He urged his horse to a gallop, and the noble steed leaped in one bound from the Tinée River up to the height where the town now sits— a distance of some 500 meters (1,650 feet). We thought the town should have been named for the horse.

Day 7: Auron to Vacherie de Roure (ca. 34 km, 8-½ hr)

It may seem strange, and perhaps a bit disappointing after Saint-Étienne's burst of Mediterranean color, to be plunged back into a rugged Alpine land. Rugged this day is, and very long, but it is a day on which the walker feels truly caught inside the mountains, far from town life, highways, and traffic. In fact, except for an access road to Roya on the morning's walk, and another dirt road leading to Vignols, a town GR5 skirts in the afternoon, that is the case. One implication of this is provisioning; there is none along the route, so be sure to stock up completely before leaving Auron.

There is one chance to shorten the day in the morning, and there is a way to lengthen it in the afternoon.

To shorten the day, leave Auron on the téléphérique that goes up to Las Donnas. This does not make for the earliest possible start—the first run uphill is hardly at the crack of dawn—but it saves perhaps an hour of uphill climbing. One caution: turn left and head east across the ridge to the col du Blainon as soon as you disembark from the téléphérique. (Otherwise, you will end, as we did, on the summit of Las Donnas after a grueling walk, and will then simply have to redescend.)

If you walk, the uphill trek crosses the Auron and Nabines streams before forking sharply southeast (where the téléphérique takes you southwest) and climbing steadily to the col du Blainon at 2,011 meters (6,636 feet).

From the col, which connects the Auron and Roya valleys, the walker has fine views back to Pas de la Cavale and forward to Mont Mounier. The walk down to Roya is splendid, passing bergeries, some in ruins, crossing the Lugière stream, passing granges, some in ruins, curving down slopes with the sound of the Roya in your ears until you land in the center of the minute town. There is refreshment here in the form of water from the public fountain; it's a good idea to make sure all water bottles are filled to the brim.

Down from Roya, GR5 crosses the river valley and enters Parc National du Mercantour again. GR5 now starts upward, first through cool woods, then—more dramatically—hugging the rocky right shore of the Mairis, down the opposite bank of which a sensational cascade falls.

Through the Roya cliffs, the route enters the valley of Sellevieille—denuded, exposed, rocky, without shade anywhere. But it is hardly a lifeless valley; herds of sheep roam the high meadow under *la barre* (the cliff) of Sellevieille and seem to cling to the hillsides. The trail turns east, seemingly away from its route, to zigzag up the cliff and debouch onto a tranquil *replat*. The dictionary defines this as a "flat terrace" on the shoulder of the slope of a glacial valley. That is exactly what this is—an abrupt and unsuspected plain hemmed all around by craggy heights. But a way up and through these heights brings the walker out to overlook the Sellevieille Valley he has just climbed before sending him uphill to col de Crousette.

From the col (2,480 meters; 8,184 feet), GR5 does something highly unusual: it keeps going uphill, edging diagonally up the flank of Mont Mounier toward the broken column known as the Stele Valette. From here, the trail heads back north along the crest before dropping down the slope in a southeasterly direction.

If it is a clear day, you might consider not descending just yet. Continuing along the crest for perhaps forty-five minutes, you reach the ruined CAF refuge of Mont Mounier. Another thiry minutes of easy climbing brings you to the summit of this wide-backed mountain, the last sizeable mountain on GR5. From the top, it is possible to see the Mediterranean for the first time; the view is long across the valleys of the Tinée and the Var, over the massif of l'Oisans to the sea and, in particularly good weather, Corsica. The detour up Mounier will add more than two hours, there and back, to the day; anyone attempting it might consider continuing only as far as col de Mulines on GR5, then dropping down to Beuil for a night's lodging. Even that makes the day a long one.

GR5ers not tempted by the view of the Mediterranean and those who feel the temptation but are able to resist it find themselves walking a rocky, barren, lunar-looking landscape along the Baisse du Demant. It is a smooth, easy walk, with fine views of the slopes of Mounier north, and with GR5 markers stretching brightly, like landing lights, as far as the eye can see.

At col de Mulines (1,982 meters; 6,541 feet), GR5 descends briefly to the north in fast switchbacks, then heads east again, crossing the Demant torrent, the valley of Combe Maure, and the valley of Gourgette, with the hamlet of Vignols below. The trail crosses the Gourgette stream and heads steeply up to reach, finally, the Portes de Longon, which even looks like a gateway. It opens to a high, tranquil meadow through which GR5 passes in an easterly direction, surrounded on both sides by grassy slopes and their resident cows and bleating sheep.

The trail leads to the Vacherie de Roure—part cowshed, part gîte d'étape, with very little distinction between the two. The dortoir is separated from the barn by a thin wall; the moist warmth of the sheep and cows seeps right through to where the hikers are sleeping. It reminded us of the stories we had read about bread supplies in the Alps in centuries past (indeed, until the twentieth century). In many of the small towns on the high slopes, there were communal ovens. In these, bread was baked nonstop from the end of the summer to November, when the ovens could no longer be kept hot enough. Obviously, you baked enough bread to last through the winter; just as obviously, the bread grew stale. As the months went by and the bread grew hard as a rock, the custom was to hang the loaves in the sheds, just above the animals. The warmth the cows and sheep gave off would soften the bread sufficiently that it could be hacked to pieces with a strong knife, in such a way, it is said, that pieces of loaf would shoot off into the four corners of the kitchen.

We felt a little like those loaves of stale bread in the dortoir of the Vacherie de Roure, but after this long and arduous day, the gîte's cold beer, hearty meal, and even the bovid atmosphere were just fine.

Day 8: Vacherie de Roure to Saint-Dalmas-Valdeblore (ca. 31 km, 7-¾ hr)

This stage leads the walker back into the valley of the Tinée, the river that parallels our walk to Nice and falls into the Var to flow into the sea just west of the city.

From the Vacherie, the trail continues along the Longon torrent, which tumbles downhill in several cascades. The route then descends steeply through forest to the ghost town of Rougois. From these crumbling sheds on the plateau, GR5 climbs gently halfway up the crest, offering hurtling views downward through the trees to the Tinée Valley below.

At the small col la Barre, the view opens wide, and the route begins to look inhabited as the walker marches through the hamlet of Saint-Sébastien—whose chapel is adorned with wonderful sixteenth-century gargoyles—and along the road to Roure.

Roure clings to the sheer side of the hill above the confluence of the Tinée and the Vionène stream; its houses lean against one another and are stacked on top of one another along winding streets. The town is known for its churches and chapels and for the altarpieces and frescoes they contain; but its most striking sight is perhaps the château-ruine which dominates the town and the valley below.

GR5 descends gradually, cutting the meanders of the D2205 road. Despite the proximity to automobiles, the walk is through a profusion of vegetation: wild blackberry and wild clover, sweet pea and dianthus for a burst of pink, loyal campanula as always, and, for the first time, olive and fig trees—sure signs of the Mediterranean.

The route then crosses the Tinée and enters Saint-Sauveur-sur-Tinée, the lowest elevation on GR5 since Lac Léman and the principal town of the mid-Tinée valley.

Saint-Sauveur makes a good lunch stop, unless you want to save the eating until after the next climb. Next to the town's medieval church is a Romanesque bell tower decorated with gargoyles; and don't miss the house nearby with its carving of a comb and scissors, the sign of a hairdresser's shop. Susanna also noted that some of the narrow alleyways of Saint-Sauveur were labelled "calada," not "rue"—linguistic evidence of a southern and distinctly Latinate environment.

GR5 climbs out of the town to the chapel of Saint-Roch, then follows what used to be the main road—now a dirt track—linking the high villages of the Valdeblore region as far as Rimplas. This remarkably situated town teeters on a needlelike shoulder of rock topped by a fort. From the chapel in particular are spectacular wide views of the Valdeblore towns and all the Tinée Valley.

Continuing more or less uphill and distinctly eastward, GR5 crosses the meandering highway to skirt La Bolline. The walker may want to enter the town, however, either to see its Romanesque church or to find refreshment or water. On a sunny day, after trekking this dry, shadeless landscape, something wet and cold will be very welcome indeed. The route continues to cut the road and avoid private property as it wends its way into Saint-Dalmas-Valdeblore.

Saint-Dalmas has a striking Romanesque church of the eleventh century, and the crypt of the foundation has been dated to the ninth century. In the summer of 1984, archaeological excavations were proceeding apace beneath the crypt, and the entire church looked propped up, rigged as it was with scaffolding and surrounded by trenches.

There are several hotels in the town. The one we stayed at was run by a charming older couple and was just barely occupied: a few end-of-season holidayers and a quartet of Parisians walking GR52, which leaves Saint-Dalmas for Menton via the famed Vallée des Merveilles (Valley of Wonders). The hotelier, a real mountain man of the Maritime Alps, was delighted to find that we were Americans and began telling us stories about the last months of the war here.

The Riviera rarely brings to mind images of war, as Normandy invariably does, and in fact, the 1944 military operations in Provence are still somewhat overshadowed by the D-Day landings. But the landings here were a significant part of the strategy, leading to the recapture of Marseilles and Nice, and to an Allied pursuit of German forces as far as Alsace, where the pursuers joined with other Allied troops coming from Normandy for the push eastward.

The Allied landings on the Riviera took place on August 15, 1944, and were preceded by early-morning drops of airborne troops, mostly American and British, around Le Muy. The hotelier in Saint-Dalmas remembered those landings. Because of his knowledge of the terrain, he had been forcibly assigned, as he told it, to the staff of a German officer. He was with the officer on the morning of the fifteenth when, as he said, "the sky overhead turned black with American planes and the first paratroopers landed." The Germans had tended to regard American soldiers with derision and were eager to get a better view of the troops hitting the ground. They drove to a good vantage point and pulled out their binoculars.

The first American they saw, according to the hotelier, wore "a new overcoat, 'city' shoes, and you could see that his shirtsleeves still had fresh creases." The Germans realized it was all over, and our hotelier fled west and south to meet a group of Monégasque soldiers and lead them through his mountains.

Day 9: Saint Dalmas-Valdeblore to Utelle (ca. 33 km, 8-¼ hr)

From Saint-Dalmas, GR5 follows a last limestone ridge down to Utelle. From there on, the terrain consists of the hilly terrace wall behind Nice. But this long day to Utelle is filled with short ups and downs as the walker follows the crest of the ridge, often through forests, crossing eight cols.

The trail climbs out of Saint-Dalmas in a southeasterly direction, into forest, past a spring, to reach col de Varaire. The route stays along the crest, however, through the lovely Noir forest, to col du Caire Gros or col des Deux Cayres (there are a *gros* and a *petit* to either side), where the walker can see some vestiges of military installations.

Still southeast and still along the crest, GR5 debouches into high meadows—the last real alpages of the journey—climbing and dipping below summits to reach the top of a ravine at Le Pertus. Heading downward toward Baisse de la Combe, the walker has an extraordinary view of the chapel of Sainte-Anne, 700 meters down the hill.

The trail enters the forest of Manoynas and reaches the collet des Trous, in the shadow of Mont Tournairet. The route becomes more civilized now, crossing the D332 road at various points, even passing a vacation center (once a military camp), before climbing easily to col d'Andrion. It cuts more meanders of the road as it traverses an active forestry area—the trail markings may occasionally be obscured here—to the Bouche (or col) des Fournès. Various paths intersect and the logging is ongoing in this area, so the walker needs to pay close attention to GR5 markings. The route continues south/southeast into forest on the east side of the slope. There it levels, then climbs to col de Gratteloup.

Heading down from the col, the walker enjoys his last real look at craggy crests and high meadows and gets his first glimpses of the dramatic Brec d'Utelle, a high upward spurt of rock that dominates the area. The trail scrambles over rocks to reach the Brèche du Brec (breach of the Brec); from here, a fifteen-minute climb can land the walker on the summit of the Brec, where the views are extensive in all directions.

GR5 descends among rocks to the col du Brec, with its great views, then contours on scree to the col de la Mei before a slow, cautious, rocky descent into Utelle. Watch out for snakes here; they can be venomous.

The town, which once prospered as a way station on the Nice-to-Tinée muleteers' route, sits on an outcropping of rock, from which it offers splendid views of the Vésubie valley and the Gordolasque mountains to the north. The look is now distinctly Mediterranean, almost mythically so: the plain is spotted with pink and yellow villas, separated from one another by fecund gardens, cypress, olive trees.

The town itself has not changed much since its prosperous days. A fountain sits in the middle of the square, and many of the houses wear painted sundials on their façades. The church of Saint-Véran was built in the fourteenth century and altered in the seventeenth; its carved wooden altarpiece dates from the latter.

Day 10: Utelle to Aspremont (ca. 26 km, 6-½ hr)

Of course, you *could* get there today. You could make a very early start and push on to arrive dog tired in Nice late this evening. The megawalker who has come from the Hoek van Holland may feel dog tired already; in fact, yesterday's arduous upping and downing would leave almost anyone feeling dog tired.

But these hills and hill towns behind Nice are so lovely that it would be a shame to rush them. Better, too, to arrive in Nice in energetic triumph, at the midpoint of a Mediterranean day, in time for an ocean-side lunch.

So resist the temptation to hurry, and treat this as just another day, not the penultimate leg of a journey that began months ago and whose finish you can almost taste.

Leaving Utelle, the trail actually climbs briefly before descending, steeply at first, then more gently, to the chapel of Saint-Antoine. Continue descending, past the scattered buildings of the hamlet of Cros d'Utelle atop the Vésubie gorge, to the river itself. It crosses the D2565 road, turns right for 100 meters, then crosses the Vésubie on the Pont du Cros.

The trail ascends gradually through pine forests to offer another spectacular Mediterranean scene: the ancient hilltop town of Levens, with modern villas ranged around the base of the hill.

GR5 would spurn Levens, turning left on D19. Turn right instead, and head uphill to the old town to wander its streets, dominated by the medieval stone church with tower, until you find a likely place for lunch. If, during your wanderings, you find yourself in the Rue Masséna, be sure to note the house, dated 1722, which belonged to the Masséna family. The great *maréchal* himself, called by Napoleon "l'enfant chéri de la victoire," was born in Nice in 1756.

Back to D19, which GR5 takes for just a little over a kilometer before turning sharply right on CD14; a sign points the way to Saint-Blaise. The route makes the first left turn, taking the walker between what looks like a playing field on the left and what definitely are houses on the right. The houses give way to the remains of land-terracing retaining walls (the houses have undoubtedly replaced the terraces: suburban sprawl), and GR5 enters scrubby woods and heads up the hill.

Uphill, then downhill, then up again. Little spurting ascents and descents along terrace edges, with villas always evident now, to come down to the road at Sainte-Claire. GR5 follows the road toward La Lausière, where the road ends; the route then ascends under huge sedimentary cliffs to follow along the flank of Mont Cima. Look back from here to a grand view of the Alpes-Maritimes, and downward to pink villages with azure swimming pools, and ahead at last to the sea.

GR5 crosses a ridge between Mont Cima and Mont Chauve d'Aspremont, then drops down to Aspremont, whose hilltop old quarter it would avoid, as usual. Another prettily perched village, with streets arranged in concentric circles, Aspremont, high above the Var, offers a wonderful panorama. From here, the walker can see across such famous hill villages as Vence and Cagnes-sur-Mer to the storied headland of Cap d'Antibes, while closer is Mont Chauve, Aspremont's summit ridge and, tomorrow, the very last climb of GR5.

Day 11: Aspremont to Nice
(ca. 12 km, 3 hr)

Breakfast in leisurely fashion, but not too heartily lest you ruin your appetite for *bouillabaisse* or *aioli* or *pissaladière* or *ravioli* or *salade Niçoise* or any of the other great specialties of Provençal cooking for which Nice is famous.

GR5 leaves Aspremont on the D14 road, then climbs. It is truly the last climb, and it doesn't even reach a summit, just rises to the shoulder of Chauve d'Aspremont, from which there are splendid views of the city of Nice.

The trail proceeds along the shoulder at length, then begins to head down on red earth and crumbly rock to land in a public park.

We saw a group of picnickers lolling on a blanket: a bunch of women and their bunches of children, from babies at the breast to ten-year-olds. One of the latter, a boy, was dispatched toward us. He approached shyly and asked, "Est-ce que vous venez d'Hollande?"

"Oui."

He turned and shouted it to the group on the blanket. "Elle dit 'oui!'" The blanket erupted, and we were waved over.

On his arrival in Nice the week before, Robert had been greeted by, among others, the local press and TV. In the midst of his triumph, he had not neglected to mention the other GR5ers, "les deux Américaines," whom he met and passed. So we had achieved a certain celebrity—in the eyes of these picnickers, a certain legendary quality—even before our arrival into Nice.

The women on the blanket couldn't stop oohing and ahing. One wanted desperately to give us something. "May I offer you some . . . "—she looked around the blanket littered with baby bottles and rattles, then held up a plastic bottle of water—" . . . some water," she finally said. She looked wistful and added, "It's all we have."

"Water would be perfect," we told her, and drank some.

Down from the park, GR5 comes to the D114 intersection at l'Aire Saint-Michel. It follows down the Vieux Chemin de Gairant, cutting meanders of Nice streets, till it crosses a bridge over the busy A8 autoroute, then continues straight south, downhill to the Place Alex Médecin in the Saint-Maurice district. GR5 officially ends here, but any southbound avenue takes you where you're going. Perhaps the best route is Avenue Borriglione, which becomes Avenue Malausséna, which becomes Avenue Jean Médecin, which ends at Place Masséna, from which you cross the public gardens to reach the beach.

We had lost GR5 long before Place Alex Médecin but found it again, then wandered downhill, past shops, hotels, banks, cafés (the Megawalker's Absolute Law of Travel, the Law of the Unentered Café, ceases to apply at this point) to Place Masséna. In the Albert I Gardens, a band was playing in a gazebo. We continued intrepidly onto the Promenade des Anglais, past curious or indifferent tourists, till we found a stairway down to the rock field that passes for a beach in Nice.

No sense ruining good hiking boots by sloshing them into salt water; they had, after all, served us well. We took them off before walking into the Mediterranean.

Appendix A:
The Robert Ravaioli Seventy-nine-day Racing Version of the GR5

1. Amsterdam to Noordwijk
2. Noordwijk to Ockenburgh
3. Ockenburgh to Maasluis
4. Maasluis to Rockanje
5. Rockanje to Ouddorp
6. Ouddorp to Bergh
7. Bergh to Oosterland
8. Oosterland to Bergen-op-Zoom
9. Bergen-op-Zoom to Kalmthout
10. Kalmthout to Brug 11/Kempens Kanaal
11. Brug 11/Kempens Kanaal to Grobbendonk
12. Grobbendonk to Westerlo
13. Westerlo to Diest
14. Diest to Hasselt
15. Hasselt to Zutendaal
16. Zutendaal to Kanne
17. Kanne to Jupille (Liège)
18. Angleur (Liège) to Fraipont
19. Fraipont to Spa
20. Spa to Hockai (where he first heard about les deux Américaines)
21. Hockai to Vielsalm
22. Vielsalm to Ouren
23. Ouren to Stolzembourg
24. Stolzembourg to Eppeldorf
25. Eppeldorf to Rosport
26. Rosport to Grevenmacher
27. Grevenmacher to Remich
28. Remich to Hau
29. Hau to Ottange
30. Ottange to Rombas
31. Rombas to Ars-sur-Moselle
32. Ars-sur-Moselle to Prény
33. Prény to Liverdun
34. Liverdun to Brin-sur-Seille
35. Brin-sur-Seille to Marsal
36. Marsal to Diane-Capelle
37. Diane-Capelle to Abreschviller
38. Abreschviller to Schirmeck
39. Schirmeck to Le Hohwald
40. Le Hohwald to Andlau
41. Andlau to Châtenois
42. Châtenois to Aubure
43. Aubure to Refuge Trois Fours
44. Refuge Trois Fours to Markstein
45. Markstein to Thann
46. Thann to Ballon d'Alsace
47. Ballon d'Alsace to Brévillier
48. Brévillier to Villars-dès-Blamont
49. Villars-dès-Blamont to Fessevillers

Appendix B: Dutch/Flemish Megawalking Lexicon

The Basics

alst U blieft	please (the word to use when you want to get someone's attention)
dank U	thank you
ja	yes
ne	no
goede morgen	good morning
goed middag	good afternoon
goed nacht	good night
Waar is . . . ?	Where is . . . ?
Spreekt U Engels?	Do you speak English?
(Frans?)	(French?)

rekening	check, bill
Hoeveel?	How much? How many?
Ik heet . . .	My name is . . .
Wat?	What?
Tot ziens	Goodbye
Ik ben verdwaald.	I am lost.
Ik begrijp het niet.	I don't understand.
heren	men
dames	women
toilet	toilet
geen; verboden	forbidden; don't do it
geopend	open
gesloten	closed
ingang	entrance
uitgang	exit
verboden toegang	no entry
vrije toegang	free entry
privé	private
Let op! or Pas op! or Opgelet!	Attention! Look out!

Reading the Topo-Gid

recht	right
links	left
rechtuit	straight ahead
rechtdoor	through
oost	east
west	west
zuid	south
noorden	north
volgen	to follow
lopen	to walk
oversteken	to cross
draaien	to turn
bereiken	to reach, attain
langs	along, past
onder	under
met	with
zonder	without

rand	edge, border
aansluiting	connecting
afstand	way, distance

Words about Trails

pad	path
voetpad; voetgang	footpath
wandelpad	walking path
fietspad; fietsrote	bike path
bromfietspad	motorbike path
ruiterspad	horse path
weg	road
asfaltweg	paved road
straat	street
grote weg	highway
kruising	crossing, junction
T-kruising	T-junction
bushalte	bus stop

Things Along the Way

dijk	dike
polder	polder
duin; duinen	dune; dunes
heide	heath, moor
kanaal	canal
strand	beach
brug	bridge
meer	lake
beek	brook
boom	tree
veld	field
boerderij	farm
schuur	barn
molen	windmill
dorp	village
gehucht	hamlet
kerk	church
abdij	abbey
postkantoor	post office
stadscentrum	city center
stadhuis	town hall
markt	market
winkel	grocery; shop

frituur	fried food; fast-food snack bar (esp. fried food)	kip	chicken
		paling	eel
		biefstuk	steak
		bier; pils	beer
apotheek	pharmacy	wijn	wine
VVV	tourist information	Proost!	Cheers!
		ijs	ice cream
heuvel	hill	dame blanche	ice cream sundae (chocolate fudge)

In Restaurant, Café, and Frituur

ontbijt	breakfast	gebakken	baked
broot	bread	gekookt	boiled
sinaasappelsap	orange juice	gebraden	fried
melk	milk	gestoofd	stewed
kaas	cheese	inclusief bediening	service included
broodjes	sandwiches	rekening	bill, check
friten	fried potatoes		

Appendix C:
French
Megawalking Lexicon

The Basics

s'il vous plaît	please
oui	yes
non	no
merci	thank you
bonjour	hello
bonsoir	good evening
bonne nuit	good night
au revoir	goodbye
madame	madam
monsieur	sir
mademoiselle	miss
Où est . . . ? or Où se trouve?	Where is . . . ?

Quand?	When?
Comment?	How? (Also: Beg pardon? What did you say?)
Je ne parle pas français.	I don't speak French.
Parlez-vous anglais?	Do you speak English?
Lentement, s'il vous plaît.	Slowly, please.
Je voudrais . . .	I would like . . .
Je ne comprends pas.	I don't understand.

Attention!	Look out!	**devant**	in front, ahead
Au secours!	Help!	**derrière**	behind, in back of
le w.c. (pronounced vay-say)	toilet	**jusqu'à**	as far as, up to
la toilette	toilet	**vers**	to, towards
le bain	bath		
Combien?	How much?		

Words for and About Trails

un sentier	path, footpath
un chemin	path, road
un chemin empierré	paved road
une route	path, roadway, course
une route goudronnée	tarred road
une voie	path, road, way
une piste	track, course, ski run
un lacet	hairpin bend
une passerelle	footbridge, bridge
un virage	turning, bend

un peu	a little, a bit
une carte	map
un sac à dos	pack
une boussole	compass
une ampoule	blister
eau potable	drinkable water
syndicat d'initiative *or* **office de tourisme** *or* **bureau de tourisme**	tourist office

Directions

à droite	right
à gauche	left
tout droit	straight ahead
nord	north
sud	south
est	east
ouest	west
sur	on
le long de	along
plat	flat
la pente	slope, incline
la pente douce	gentle slope
la pente raide	steep slope
haut	high
bas	low
grand	big
petit	little
étroit	narrow
large, étendu	wide
plus loin	further
pas loin	not far
court	short
une entrée	entry
une sortie	exit

Words for and About Trail Walking

une randonnée	a ramble
un randonneur; une randonneuse	a rambler, walker, hiker
une promenade	a walk, walking
se promener	walk, go for a walk
aller	go
prendre	take (a road, path)
emprunter	take (a road, path)
continuer	proceed, keep going
suivre	follow

longer	pass, go along, skirt
allonger	lengthen, delay, prolong
gagner	gain, reach, arrive at
atteindre	reach, achieve
monter	ascend, climb (uphill, up the street)
grimper	climb
descendre	descend
bifurquer	fork, divide, branch off
s'embrancher	form a junction, branch off
virer	turn, take a corner
contourner	go around, bypass
obliquer	slant, incline, edge
tourner	turn
serpenter	wind, meander
couper	cut, intersect
traverser	cross
franchir	cross, clear
déboucher	emerge, debouch
abandonner	forsake, abandon, leave

Landmarks and Things Along the Way

une haie	hedgerow
une clôture	fence, enclosure
une passerelle	footbridge
un abri	shelter, cover
une source	spring
un barrage	dam
une rive	bank, shore, edge
une église	church

un éboulis	scree, debris
une colline	hill
une montagne	mountain
un côte	slope of a hillside
une combe	dell, coomb
un crêt (Jurassic dialect)	rocky escarpment edging a *combe*
une crête	ridge, crest
un calcaire	limestone (*also* chalky)
un rocher	rock
le grès	sandstone
un coupe-feu	firebreak
un étang	pond, pool
un pont	bridge
un ruisseau	brook, stream
une ferme	farm
un bâtiment	building
un moulin	mill
une ruine	ruin
une grange	barn
la bruyère	heather, heath
un carrefour	crossroads, intersection
un gué	ford
une falaise	cliff
une chaumière	thatched hut
un chaume	the meadow the thatch comes from
un prè	meadow
une clairière	clearing
un champs	field
un vignoble	vineyard
un hameau	hamlet
un village	village
une ville	city, town
centre ville	the center of town
la mairie	mayor's office, town hall
la vieille villle	the old town
un arbre	tree
un bois	wood, timber, forest

une forêt	forest	le ravitaille- ment	provisioning
un sapin	fir tree	un café	decaffeinated
une sapinière	fir plantation, grove	décaffeiné	coffee
un épicéa	spruce	un citron	French
le sous-bois	undergrowth	pressé	lemonade (the real thing)

Signs

chien méchant	dangerous dog
renseignements	information
interdit	forbidden
défense de . . .	don't do it
privé	private
entrée	entrance
sortie	exit
fermé	closed
ouvert	open
sauf riverains	Entry only for riverside residents (*also* Entry only for those living along the road on which the sign ap- pears)

In Restaurants, Cafés, Shops, Hotels

le casse-croûte	snack, snack- bar
une charcuterie	delicatessen, butcher shop
une épicerie	grocery
une patisserie	pastry shop
une boulan- gerie	bakery
une laiterie	dairy shop
une fromagerie	cheese shop
la *or* une ali- mentation	food, food shop

le jus	juice
le lait	milk
eau gazeuse	sparkling water
une bière	beer
bière pression	draft beer
un demi	glass of draft beer
un panaché	shandy
le vin	wine
le pain	bread
le fromage	cheese
une gaufre	Belgian waffle
une buvette	refreshment bar
une boisson	something to drink
hors sac	(eating) out of the pack
Bon appétit!	Good eating!
A votre santé! *or* Santé!	Your health! (the stan- dard toast)
l'addition	the check
service compris	service included
T.V.A.	value-added tax
complet	full; no vacancy
un dortoir	dormitory (in hostels, refuges, huts)
Avez-vous une cham- bre indivi- duelle?	Do you have a single room?

(chambre à deux lits?)	(room with two beds?)	w.c. or toilette	toilet
avec or sans	with or without	le papier d'emballage	wrapping paper
bain	bath	le corde	string
douche	shower	le ruban	tape

Appendix D:
Megawalking
Laws and Principles

Megawalker's Absolute Law of Travel: The unentered café is not worth the ground it stands on.

The First Law of the Trail: If you haven't seen a trail marker for 200 meters, even 100 meters, then no matter how pleasant the path under your feet, no matter how sure you are that you are going in the right direction, no matter that this is absolutely the only possible way the trail *could* go, go back.

The Primary Principle of the Sacrosanctity of Lunch: The walker starved for lunch will, at midday, enter a town lacking cafés or restaurants at the precise hour that the food shop is closing.

The Immutable Law of the Half-Day Closing: Any town's scheduled half-day will occur on the day the walker arrives in that town.

The Laws of Inevitable Occurrences: Sooner or later, your feet will hurt. Sooner or later, you will lose something. Sooner or later, something will break or rip. (Corollary: When it breaks, it will do so at the worst possible moment.)

The Law of the Weekly Market: If the hiker comes to a town with a weekly market, it will have been yesterday.

The Law of Evening Entertainment: The hiker will arrive in a town either the evening before or the evening after the town holds a concert or theatrical entertainment.

The Law of Financial Embarrassment (The Money Law): The hiker will run out of local currency on a Friday on which his route passes through villages too small to have banks and/or where local merchants will not cash traveler's checks.

The Principle of the Perfidious Ignorance of Locals: Absolutely certain information offered by the indigenous population is invariably wrong. Trust your instincts.

The Law of the Inverse Relation of Pleasantness and Tourism: The closer you come to an area frequented by tourists, the surlier people are. The Law of the Postlunch Topography: There is always a steep hill to climb immediately after lunch. The Law of the 1,500-Mile Balisage: Trail markings will appear everywhere when the path is straight and clear, but at junctions, in towns, and where the path is obscured or uncertain, they are nowhere to be found. The Ultimate Law of Packing: What you don't need, don't bring. What you don't bring and you do need, you can usually find. What you don't bring and you do need and you can't find, you can often improvise. What you don't bring and you do need and you can't find and you can't improvise, do without.

Index

A Note to the Reader

Readers are invited to send updated information and corrections for any title in the Sierra Club Adventure Travel Guide series to the author, c/o Travel Editor, Sierra Club Books, 730 Polk Street, San Francisco CA 94109.